Longevity Hubs

# Longevity Hubs

Regional Innovation for Global Aging

edited by Joseph F. Coughlin and Luke Yoquinto

**The MIT Press**

Cambridge, Massachusetts | London, England

The MIT Press would like to thank the anonymous peer reviewers who provided comments on drafts of this book. The generous work of academic experts is essential for establishing the authority and quality of our publications. We acknowledge with gratitude the contributions of these otherwise uncredited readers.

This book was set in ITC Stone Serif Std and ITC Stone Sans Std by New Best-set Typesetters Ltd. Printed and bound in the United States of America.

Library of Congress Cataloging-in-Publication Data

Names: Coughlin, Joseph F., editor. | Yoquinto, Luke, editor.
Title: Longevity hubs : regional innovation for global aging / edited by
    Joseph F. Coughlin and Luke Yoquinto.
Description: Cambridge, Massachusetts : The MIT Press, [2024] | Includes
    bibliographical references and index.
Identifiers: LCCN 2023057560 (print) | LCCN 2023057561 (ebook) |
    ISBN 9780262049214 (paperback) | ISBN 9780262379779 (epub) |
    ISBN 9780262379762 (pdf)
Subjects: LCSH: Aging—Economic aspects. | Aging—Social aspects. | Older people—
    Services for. | Self-help devices for older people. | Technology and older people. |
    Longevity—Economic aspects.
Classification: LCC HQ1061 .L65 2024 (print) | LCC HQ1061 (ebook) |
    DDC 305.26—dc23/eng/20231227
LC record available at https://lccn.loc.gov/2023057560
LC ebook record available at https://lccn.loc.gov/2023057561

10  9  8  7  6  5  4  3  2  1

To Renee Lohman, and all those who dedicate their working lives to building a better world for older adults and their loved ones.

# Contents

# Preface

One gloomy afternoon in the waning days of 2018, Google Alerts, a service that scours the internet for new mentions of keywords, dropped a morsel at our electronic doorstep. It was a list from *Inc.* magazine, enumerating the 50 best places in America to start a business.[1] Our metro area, Boston, was ranked number fifteen—a little lower than we'd have expected, although it was nice to see our town recognized. Boston was, and remains, a major American business hub with a healthy startup pipeline befitting the area's strengths in basic scientific research, biotech, robotics, and health care—not to mention its world-class financial sector.

But these points of local pride scarcely garnered a mention in the brief piece adorning Boston's entry. Instead, to our amazement, the author, Leigh Buchanan, focused almost entirely on entrepreneurship for—and by—older people. "Home to MIT's celebrated AgeLab"—that is, our research organization, led by this book's coeditor, Joseph Coughlin—"the area has spawned a cluster of age-tech startups launching products like wireless headphones (Eversound) and virtual reality headsets (Rendever) that are optimized for seniors. In June, Amazon bought [Boston suburb] Somerville-based PillPack, which helps those who are on several medications, for close to $1 billion."

All of this was true, and we were of course pleased to see such a positive light cast on the AgeLab, which Coughlin founded in 1999 with the goal of making life better for older people and those who care for them. But at the same time, it all seemed a little overblown. Although the lab did try to work with local startups whenever it made sense, we were still just researchers, not tech-world magicians. The lab itself had stopped churning out original gadgets in the mid-aughts, focusing instead on research into the people who might interact with such technologies—not to mention the wider world of products, services, and policies that undergird life at every age, including our later years. The funding flowing through Greater Boston's old-age-facing entrepreneurship scene, too, might have been noteworthy relative to other cities, but it was still dwarfed by the economic activity of Boston's leading industries. The local quiver of fledgling businesses participating in the "longevity economy," as Coughlin termed it in his 2017 book of the same name, certainly deserved media coverage. But as near as the business of aging was to our hearts, it still seemed a trifle rich to pass over Boston's other economic interests in its favor.

Except, as we chewed it over, we had to acknowledge that the piece was right about the outlier case of PillPack. The local company, whose recent acquisition at the hands of Amazon was still sending shockwaves around town, had genuinely come out of the aging world. As the company's founder, T. J. Parker, had described to us back in 2014,[2] PillPack's primary innovation—a system for organizing pills by time of consumption, not type of medication—had come from observations Parker had made while watching his pharmacist father at work, dispensing medications for assisted living facilities.

There were a few other local heavyweights of note, too. Care.com, for instance—perhaps the country's preeminent marketplace for caregiving labor, including elder care—was headquartered in nearby Waltham. Also fitting the description of longevity-oriented companies were many of the national and international financial services firms with headquarters or significant footprints in the region, including Bank of America, BNY Mellon, Fidelity Investments, John Hancock, MassMutual, State Street, and Wellington Management—all of whom were involved in addressing the constellation of concerns around retirement planning, savings, and investment.

On the startup side, meanwhile, beyond those mentioned in the *Inc.* piece, there were a few local examples bearing potential for an aging world. Optimus Ride, for instance, came immediately to mind: an MIT spinoff that was testing its low-speed autonomous vehicles in retirement communities.[3] Backing such efforts were a handful of venture companies, incubators, and other entrepreneurial support organizations that were nurturing businesses aimed at aging consumer markets, regardless of whether they explicitly said so. (As we explore ahead, companies often pursue older consumers by stealth, studiously avoiding words like "aging," "old," or "senior.")

Local talent had been making national waves in the field of elder employment as well. Tim Driver, a fixture in national aging work and entrepreneurship circles, had founded a series of efforts to help older people beat age discrimination and find a job, including RetirementJobs.com as well as the Age-Friendly Institute.

There was buy-in from government, too. Massachusetts's then-governor Charlie Baker, whose mother had passed away in 2016 after living with Alzheimer's disease for a decade, had established the Governor's Council on Aging the following year. This effort had brought together public and private-sector actors in a way that we hadn't seen up to that point, and shone a spotlight onto aging, a topic that sometimes has to fight to be seen.

And this was all not to minimize the substantial age-related concerns of Boston's established industries—especially health care and pharma, in addition to financial services—already playing important parts in the lives of people striving to live as independently as possible, for as long as possible.

Soon we found ourselves casually comparing Boston's chances of becoming the "Silicon Valley of the octogenarian set," as the *Inc.* piece had put it, against other cities; other regions. There were the obvious contenders: Silicon Valley itself and New York, which encompassed so much entrepreneurial activity that they couldn't help but bring along some age-oriented companies in the process. Abroad, of course, there were giants to consider, such as Singapore, Tokyo, and Seoul: high-tech capitals of countries containing some of the world's oldest populations. But there were smaller cities of note, too: part of a global constellation of regions of varying size that, by reputation, were vibrating with innovative, age-oriented energy. We could rattle off a few that had been turning heads lately (at least, the heads of people who pay attention to such things): Louisville. Newcastle, in the UK. Milan. São Paulo.

The more we discussed it, the less overstated the idea seemed—in terms of both Boston's unique prospects and, more broadly, the sense that innovation, centered on the concerns of aging populations, might develop disproportionately in a handful of select geographic regions.

In fact, this notion fit intriguingly well with the mountain of academic research, dating back to the nineteenth century, exploring the geography of innovation—specifically, the question of why tight regional clumps of economic actors tend to produce so much of it.

Innovating for older consumers is tricky—far trickier than many would-be aging-market conquerors suspect. For one thing, older consumers tend to suss out and sidestep products intended for "old people"—or worse, a young person's idea of old people. Adam Gopnik, writing in the *New Yorker*, put it well: "They are a market that cannot be marketed to."[4]

This counterintuitive angle hinted at the existence of special knowledge, useful to aging-market innovators and the institutions supporting them, that might be found in certain regions and networks but not others. Such a lumpy information landscape, assuming it did exist, would fit a historical pattern. The influence of locally bound knowledge was a leading explanation for why businesses and other economic actors tend to be found in close geographic proximity: in "clusters," to use the parlance of a large, discipline-spanning body of literature.

Setting aside the mechanisms involved, if innovation for an aging world did tend to promote (or benefit from) geographic clustering, it would have real implications for the economic prospects of the regions involved—and possibly for aging populations residing both within and far beyond their borders.

It's hard to overstate the significance of global population aging. It is the consequence of what's known as the demographic transition: the once glacial but increasingly rapid[5] decline in both mortality and fertility rates that nations tend to experience in the course of their economic development. This phenomenon proceeds predictably: with a temporary "demographic dividend" arriving in the form of an oversized working-age population, which lasts until that cohort grows older. Today, most of the world's countries are facing an aging trend without historical precedent. The majority of countries are now approaching the shores of a far older future, if they're not there already. Even those with younger populations, such as Nigeria, will find themselves with a sizable older cohort within a few decades. In quite a few cases—perhaps most notably, China, given its size and particularly top-heavy population structure—these demographic changes are of geopolitical consequence.

Against such a backdrop, the notion of a cluster of aging innovation—heretofore an unnamed, background character in the world's economic ballet—could turn out to have an important role to play.

All this was running through our heads when we approached the *Boston Globe* with an essay about geographic clusters of aging innovation—or, as we termed it in the essay, "longevity hubs." Boston, we argued in our pitch, was especially well equipped to churn out the sort of innovation for which aging nations would soon be clamoring.

The editor at the *Globe*'s Opinion section, Marjorie Pritchard, was interested, but events were conspiring against us—and everyone else. COVID's pall fell over the world, and both the *Globe* and the AgeLab turned to pandemic-specific projects. In October 2020, however, we received an email from Pritchard, proposing to resurrect our nearly forgotten essay and to turn it into a larger, yearlong project. The format we arrived at was a monthly series in the newspaper and online, gathering together thinkers and actors focused on different facets of aging innovation.

This volume collects the original 32 pieces that ran in the resulting Longevity Hub series in 2021 and 2022: a joint effort by the AgeLab and *Globe* that benefited immensely from Pritchard's time and editorial expertise. Our goal here, however, is not just to create a permanent home for this work, but to explore the larger concept of longevity hubs in a global context. To that end, this book zooms out to take in testimony from key actors in other potential hubs— perhaps even *rival* hubs to Boston—from around the world.

We've chosen these cities and regions by a simple criterion: their reputation as disproportionate hot spots of innovation for aging has reached our ears. This methodology is, of course, subjective, and doubtless leaves out plenty of hubs that could merit inclusion. What this subjective approach lacks in comprehensiveness, however, it makes up for in openness. It allows us to cast a wide net over a variety of cities and regions, and assess their different modes of aging innovation, rather than fit them into some predetermined definition of "longevity hub." To this end, in addition to the suite of articles from the *Globe* about Boston and its surroundings, this book includes new essays, written in 2022 and early 2023, by representatives of a variety of hub candidates: Dubai, Louisville, Newcastle, Milan, São Paulo, Tel Aviv, and groups of cities in Thailand and

Japan. To round out the volume—and to cut against its grain—is an essay by Stephen Johnston, cofounder of the international aging-innovation network Aging2.0, who explores the potential for distributed innovation clusters to coalesce around virtual networks.

This is a new area of inquiry, and it immediately raises a list of questions. Are there different types of longevity hubs, for instance, which develop under different conditions? What keeps hubs going? Whom exactly is each hub serving? How does new knowledge about aging markets form and flow within (or among) hubs? What are their liabilities? Perhaps most important: What are a given hub's chances of becoming a major supplier for the world's aging populations?

One way to read the book ahead is as the starting shot of a race: between regions vying to become an aging world's foremost source of cutting-edge products, services, and ideas. It is also possible, however, that this will turn out to be the kind of race where multiple runners win. The opportunity, spanning sectors, continents, and consumer subgroups, may prove too big for any one hub to claim—and in the meantime, the competitors might benefit by learning from one another.

Regardless of which sort of race it turns out to be, we hope this book will serve as the first sketches of a roadmap benefiting the runners involved, as well as a world of people who deserve to thrive as their populations age.

## Notes

1. Leigh Buchanan, "No.15 Boston," *Inc.*, 2018, https://www.inc.com/surge-cities/best-places-start-business.html.

2. Luke Yoquinto, "Firms Gear Health-Related Technology Toward Baby Boomers," *Washington Post*, October 31, 2014, https://www.washingtonpost.com/postlive/firms-gearing-health-related-technology-toward-baby-boomers/2014/10/30/10a26c82-3769-11e4-8601-97ba88884ffd_story.html.

3. Pranshu Verma, "Boston Self-Driving Car Company Optimus Ride Closes Its Doors," *Boston Globe*, January 11, 2022, https://www.bostonglobe.com/2022/01/11/business/boston-self-driving-car-company-optimus-ride-is-acquired/.

4. Adam Gopnik, "Can We Live Longer But Stay Younger?" *New Yorker*, May 13, 2019, https://www.newyorker.com/magazine/2019/05/20/can-we-live-longer-but-stay-younger.

5. Matthew J. Delventhal, Jesús Fernández-Villaverde, and Nezih Guner, "Demographic Transitions Across Time and Space," Working Paper, Working Paper Series (National Bureau of Economic Research, November 2021), https://doi.org/10.3386/w29480.

# Introduction

Joseph Coughlin and Luke Yoquinto

Along with global megatrends like climate change and technological development, population aging is one of the most significant changes confronting economies around the world. Adults aged 65 and over are growing in number and prevalence: from one in ten people worldwide as of 2021, to a projected one in six by 2050.[1] The short list of causes responsible includes declining fertility and, in many (but not all) countries, the aging of a sizable post–World War II "baby boom" cohort. Meanwhile, modern progress against diverse causes of death throughout the life span has translated into longer lives for more people. (Even if, in the United States and other countries, those developments have recently sputtered due to both the COVID pandemic and dismaying increases in midlife mortality.)[2]

People's global movements play a role, too. Specific to the United States, net migration into the country collapsed following a local high in 2016; as of this writing in 2023, it has only recently showed signs of a rebound.[3] To the extent that the United States has had an engine of reproductive growth in the past several decades, that engine has been immigrant families.[4] Should their arrival numbers continue to be depressed, it would portend fewer young people in near future, reduced total fertility in the decades ahead, and, consequently, an older population overall. By 2050, adults aged 65 and up are projected to make up 20 percent of the US population[5]—a milestone that Maine, Florida, West Virginia, Vermont, and Delaware have already crossed.[6] In 2021, for the first time ever, the country's adults aged 65 and up outnumbered children under 5. By 2035, they will outnumber not just these young children but all Americans under the age of 18: an upside-down state of affairs compared to any other historical moment.

As rapidly as the United States may be aging, globally speaking, it's not even near the front of the peloton. Sub-replacement fertility, for instance—that is, when so few babies are being born that a given population would shrink without immigration—is the rule among the wealthy nations of the OECD (with the exception of Israel, as Keren Etkin explores in her chapter in this volume). In many of these nations, low birthrates combine with great longevity as well as the aging of large baby boomer cohorts, leading to extremely old populations. As of 2021, major economies with the highest proportions of adults over the age of 85 include Japan, far ahead of the pack at 5.6 percent; followed by Italy, France, Spain, Portugal, Greece, and Germany: all above 3 percent.[7]

In certain nations, meanwhile, including several in Eastern Europe, sub-replacement fertility combines with working-age population *outflows*, once again leading to home populations containing disproportionate numbers of older adults.[8]

If your main impression of the aging trend over the past decade or two has come from glancing at the occasional headline in the business press, you might think aging is mainly an issue for wealthy countries in Europe and East Asia. That was once true, but no longer. Between 1970 and 2015, high-income countries did indeed age significantly faster than the rest of the world: Their 65-plus populations expanded by 7.3 percent, while upper-middle-income nations, including China, Russia, Mexico, Brazil, Thailand, and South Africa,[9] aged by 4.6 percent. (Lower-middle-income countries such as India, Pakistan, Indonesia, and Nigeria; and low-income countries such as Ethiopia, Tanzania, and the Democratic Republic of Congo aged by 1.5 and 0.5 percent, respectively.)[10]

Today, however, many middle-income nations (including the mammoth populations of China and India) are now well into their demographic phase change. They will drive global aging in the decades ahead. Between 2015 and 2050, the 65-plus populations of higher-income nations is projected to grow by 9.8 percent—eclipsed by upper-middle-income nations' 13.4 percent. (Lower-middle-income and low-income nations will age by 6.2 and 1.9 percent, respectively.)[11]

As with wealthy countries, much of this middle-income shift will be driven by fertility declines, which almost invariably accompany increased access to education and contraceptives, and economic growth.[12] In terms of plummeting fertility, South Korea, at well below one child per woman (remember, the "replacement rate" is around 2.1), is the world's most extreme case. China, a middle-income country whose fertility is still falling even after the end of its decades-long one-child policy, is also exceptional.[13] More representative examples of the middle-income fertility story are still remarkable compared to the historical baseline, however. Take India, where in 1964 the average woman gave birth to nearly 6 children. As of 2021, that number stands at 2.03.[14] In such countries, older adults may find themselves astounded by the number of contemporaries they can count, relative to grandchildren.[15]

In most of the world's countries, variations of these changes are already in steady, inexorable motion. Barring calamity (and indeed, in the still-dangerous aftermath of the COVID pandemic, we are reminded that such an assumption is never entirely safe), wherever population aging has begun, it will continue.

Less settled, however, are population aging's downstream effects, which will touch virtually every sphere of life. Where, how, and with whom people live; the political positions they support; the culture they consume; the places they go to find meaning: these may all be affected as populations age. And—of critical importance for economic innovation—so will the products and services they use: whether they are purchased personally by older adults, or on their behalf by loved ones, organizations, or governments.

## Money Matters

Viewed at the highest possible level, the macroeconomic effects of aging are a matter of arithmetic: $x$ number of workers being economically productive and paying taxes, versus $y$ number of non-workers who consume goods, services, and tax revenues. Whenever $y$ grows relative to $x$—when the "dependency ratio" rises, as demographers and economists have it—something must give. Burgeoning older populations will demand more in terms of pension and medical payouts, at precisely the moment fewer workers will be on hand to pay taxes. Economic growth may slow[16] as the labor force participation rate falls.[17] Although aging has historically led to increases in industrial automation, as the economists Daron Acemoglu and Pascual Restrepo have observed,[18] it remains to be seen to what extent this effect will take place in difficult-to-automate jobs—especially in "high-touch" medical and care professions. The future of the already-stressed healthcare and eldercare sectors is doubly concerning, in fact, since they will see increased demand from older populations at the same time as possible labor shortages.

Faced with such pressures, what are policymakers to do? One option is to invest in technologies that magnify the productive powers of a country's shrinking pool of workers. (And yes, "workers" in this sense includes members of countries' militaries. South Korea, for instance, is adopting technologies designed to mitigate a demographically driven shortage of conscripts.)[19] Another option involves boosting the headcount of young and middle-aged workers, via liberalized immigration and work visa policies, as well as pro-natal measures. (This last approach actually temporarily exacerbates the dependency ratio by adding children to mix, who count as non-workers until they reach employment age. Its track record is also spotty: even robust pro-natal measures tend to merely slow declining birth rates rather than reverse them.)[20]

To shrink the relative demands of non-workers on government coffers and nations' finite labor resources, meanwhile, there is always the scythe of austerity, which can arrive via some combination of tax increases, government services and spending cuts, and increases to the age of eligibility for retirement or age-related medical benefits. As demonstrated by the protests that rocked France in the spring of 2023, such efforts (in France's case, a policy that raised the retirement age) often prove deeply unpopular with those affected.[21]

Finally, there is the always-tantalizing possibility of squeezing additional formal economic output from older adults through alternate means: such as the worker and employer incentives trialed during the US Department of Labor's three-year Aging Worker Initiative, which concluded in 2012; or protections for older workers, such as Japan's 2018 legislation encouraging employers to retain their employees through age 70.[22] Japan has also experimented with quotas requiring companies to retain a percentage of older workers.[23]

These are broad, nation-sized strokes, but aging's effects on smaller regions and individual communities will vary immensely. In countries where population growth is slowing or negative and, simultaneously, young people are moving out of their hometowns for the economic opportunities available in large cities, rural pockets with extremely old populations can develop. (For more on this dynamic in Japan, see Jon Metzler's chapter in this volume.) Concerningly, in the short term, these rural regions can develop shortages of the younger workers necessary to support healthcare and eldercare industries; in the longer term, whole communities can become hollowed out.

This is the bad news. However, there is good news, too, which starts to appear when you zoom in even closer on the economic activity surrounding older adults: the longevity economy. Despite what stereotypes may say, older adults are more than mere takers, hoovering up the rest of society's resources. In fact, in terms of both productivity and spending, they are complete, complex economic players, whose already-sizable impact is poised to expand markedly in the coming years.

## Titans of Spending

Forty-six percent of the gross domestic product of the United States of America: This astounding figure is what AARP and the Economist Impact determined that, in 2020, the US 50-plus population accounted for, factoring in both their direct and indirect economic activity. Globally, the 50-plus accounted half of the world's consumer spending and 34 percent of GDP: $45 trillion in the 70 countries profiled in the report. By 2050, this number is projected to more than double.[24]

These sorts of figures—already large enough to defy meaningful comprehension—are only part of the story. There is a great deal of value to be created, and money to be earned, by serving older people: their existing wants and needs, as well as sources of demand yet to be created or discovered.

Already, it's hard to overstate the spending power of the world's older consumers. In wealthy countries especially, older cohorts tend to have higher incomes than younger age groups. (In the United States, as of 2022, Americans aged 55 and over controlled more than two-thirds of overall personal wealth[25]—most of which is confined to the top 10 percent of households.) They also tend to have significant needs—especially with regard to the housing, medical, and caregiving sectors—which equate to high nondiscretionary spending.

Worldwide, too, their influence is growing. Per the World Data Lab, the global consumer class (defined as anyone who spends at least $11 per day) will grow from 3.9 billion people as of 2020 to 5.6 billion in 2030. Driving this expansion will be consumers aged 65-plus, a group that will grow by 66 percent during this time period—faster than younger ranges.[26] Older adults' spending will not be equitably distributed, however, within or among countries. A large proportion of the world's older population growth will take place in Asia, for instance, whose older residents are less wealthy than the world's average. Their purchasing power is poised to increase, however: from a state of rough parity with Europe and North America (an annual $2.3 trillion apiece) to $5 trillion by 2030.

Still, in both 2020 and in 2030 projections, the United States remains the single country with the most older-adult spending, followed by China, Japan, Germany, and France.[27]

Perhaps what's most remarkable about the spending of the older US consumer, however, is how much more of it there *could* be. Despite a growing trend of "giving while living" rather than waiting for death to pass personal wealth to the next generation,[28] US baby boomers (who control $78.3 trillion, or half of US private wealth)[29] are still the generation least interested in leaving behind an inheritance.[30] The fact that they have so much to pass down—and indeed, have already begun doing so—despite their relative aversion to it, is suggestive. It hints at a mismatch between, on one hand, the actual universe of products and services the economy is presently churning out, and, on the other, the hypothetical universe of things that would compel older consumers to whip out their checkbooks.

## Productive Aging

If there are mysteries yet to be plumbed in the spending patterns and proclivities of older consumers, their activities as economic *producers* are even less well appreciated. Contrary to stereotype, many older adults work in the formal economy. In the United States, among other countries, the COVID pandemic revealed how important these workers are to larger labor trends. In a normal year, about 3 percent of retirees churn back into the formal workforce for various reasons; but the pandemic reduced this normally constant source of workers by nearly a third,[31] while driving others to retire early.[32] These changes reduced overall labor force participation during the pandemic,[33] driving up wages and prices.[34]

As important as older adults' contributions are to the formal economy, even more significant may be their contributions to the submerged side of the world's economic iceberg: the informal, unpaid work that goes on in households, enabling everything else.

A large proportion of the work that happens in this world happens within homes, without money changing hands. The International Labour Organization estimates that the value provided by unpaid care work is worth about 10 percent of global GDP: a subset of the larger category of unpaid domestic labor, which is reckoned to be worth as much as 39 percent of global GDP.[35]

Older adults perform much of this informal and domestic work. In 2020, a team from the Harvard T.H. Chan School of Public Health published a different kind of look at older adults' influence on GDP than in AARP's aforementioned analysis, focusing not on their spending but rather their formal and informal labor, which together accounted for 40 percent of per-capita GDP in the United States, and 29 percent in a sample of European countries. In both cases, informal work made up a substantial proportion of older adults' overall labor: equivalent to 84 percent of their formal output in Europe, and around half in the United States.[36]

Older adults don't just receive care; they also provide it—so much, in fact, that their efforts can only be described as a critical social pillar. They provide elder care: In the United States, nearly a fifth of Americans who care for older adults are themselves over the age of 65.[37] And they care for those with disabilities: In the United States, adults aged 50 and up provide 27 percent of care for adults aged 18 to 49.[38]

Of special importance to the formal economy is the childcare they perform, some of which is steady; some sporadic. The vast majority of older adults (83 percent of them in the United States[39]) are grandparents, 22 percent of whom provide regular childcare.[40] Of the quarter of US families who rely on relatives as their primary source of childcare, grandparents provide 80 percent of this care.[41]

Full-time childcare is only part of the story, however; the ability to provide occasional childcare is just as important. Responding to a 2023 Harris Poll, 72 percent of working parents in the United States reported that without the help provided by grandmothers, their ability to work would be impacted negatively. Sixty-seven percent said they might have lost their job without occasional care provided by a child's grandmother, and 20 percent said they would need to quit their job without the support of a grandmother at home.[42]

These figures are striking enough to make one wonder: How many US employers realize the extent to which their workforce is being propped up by grandparents waiting in the wings?

Many other countries rely on grandparents to an even greater extent. Compared to the 22 percent of grandparents who provide regular childcare in the United States, 39 percent do so in Italy, as do 46 percent in Germany.[43]

Part of the reason grandparent childcare is so prevalent in these countries is that their older population is less likely to be taking part in the workforce—which may be related to the fact that older Americans receive less financial support from their government than do Germans and Italians. (In fact, lamentably, the poverty rate for older Americans is nearly twice that of older Germans and Italians.)[44]

For any country tempted to bolster its labor supply and cut state welfare spending by coaxing (or forcing) retirees back to work, their likely status as childcare providers is deeply inconvenient. Take

China, whose state-owned enterprises maintain, as of 2023, a retirement age of 60 for men, and 55 and 50 for women working in office and blue-collar settings, respectively—a policy dating back to the 1950s. These retirement ages are low even by the standards of countries without China's serious demographic pressures—which are compounded by a per-capita income that is still low relative to the high-income world. As a result, in 2021, China announced plans to raise retirement ages by 2025.[45] As of this writing in 2024, it has yet to act on these plans.[46]

China's government has good reason to take its time implementing this planned retirement age increase. It's not just that the changes that would likely draw protest, albeit perhaps not of the vociferousness seen in France in 2023. (That said, authoritarian regimes, including Putin's Russia, have delayed similar planned changes to retirement, possibly due to the threat of public outcry.[47]) It's also that requiring older workers to work longer would add to the labor force with one hand while taking from it with the other, due to the childcare performed by China's grandparents. Most Chinese families with young children (88 percent of them, in Shanghai[48]) rely on grandparent childcare. Mothers who have parents or in-laws helping in this way are significantly more likely to be members of the labor force than are those without grandparents at hand.[49] The availability of grandparent childcare in China may even be a mitigating influence on the country's flagging fertility[50]—a downward trend China's government is now actively striving to reverse,[51] having ended its one-child policy in 2015.

If there is extra economic juice to be squeezed out of older populations' economic output, then, extracting it may call for more than a little prudence—assuming governments would prefer not to interfere with the background domestic activities that quietly support the functioning of their society and economy.

Something similar holds true regarding private-sector ambitions to tap the wealth of older consumers. In aggregate, especially in wealthy countries (and with huge individual variation), older consumers are remarkably affluent. The quantity of money that can potentially be summoned on their behalf via taxes and government spending is similarly very large. To the extent that companies take special note of older users and consumers, however, there is often a failure to connect. In fact, the difference between offerings that succeed and those that fail in aging markets hints at something: a type of insight into older adults' wants and needs that is helpful for success in the longevity economy, but which is far from universal.

## A Landscape of Gaps

As we age, market failures and misalignments seem to find us: sand in the gears of our ability to act as engaged members of society. One underlying culprit is older adults' employment situation—or lack thereof.

Adults over age 65 have increased their labor force participation steadily since the end of the 1980s[52] (with a slight and likely temporary downturn during the COVID pandemic).[53] This measure, distinct from the employment rate, reflects not just who's working but also who's actively seeking work. More older people are doing so for one or both of two simple reasons: because they want to, and because they need to.

Despite their demonstrable desire or need to work, however, and the fact that retirements are posing serious problems in key fields,[54] older people continue to face undue employment headwinds. In response to a 2022 AARP survey, 91 percent of respondents aged 50 and over said age discrimination was common "in the workplace today." Ten percent said they had not been hired for a job they had applied for due to their age. Eight percent said they had been passed over for a promotion or a chance to get ahead, and 5 percent said they had been fired or forced out of a job.[55]

Women take a particular hit from age discrimination, compounding the gender wage gap—a twofold harm known in gerontology and other fields as "double jeopardy." The earnings of college-educated women in the United States peak earlier and lower than men: at age 44, compared to 55 for men.[56] As a result, the average woman earns roughly $400,000 less than the average man over a 40-year career. For Black, Native American, and Latina women, who face *triple* jeopardy, this gap rises to roughly a million dollars.[57]

These numbers matter, and not only for what they imply for the personal finances of those affected. They also hint at a fundamental misalignment: between the people responsible for the bulk of product and service creation (a younger and middle-aged group, leaning male), and those responsible for the purchasing and use of said products and services (a group leaning older and female).

For older women in particular, the mismatch between their economic might and treatment at work is especially severe. Women influence the majority of consumer buying decisions, including major purchases such as cars and houses.[58] In older households their power is even stronger. Women outlive men in every country in the world,[59] which means they simply outnumber them with advancing age. It's also a fact—a deeply unfair one—that women, usually of middle age or older, provide significantly more care of all kinds than men. In heterosexual marriages where one spouse takes on a care role for the other, it's usually the woman caring for the man; when an adult child cares for an older parent, that caregiving child is usually a daughter.[60] Two-thirds of the informal caregivers in the United States are women, and they spend 50 percent more time at it than caregiving men. (Elsewhere, the divide can be even more pronounced. In Japan, for instance, women account for 80 percent of the 100,000 people who quit their jobs annually to care for aging parents.[61])

The great caregiving responsibility shouldered by women the world over has complex and cascading consequences—one of which is that adult women routinely find themselves making household spending decisions for three or even four generations. Taking into account the full scope of their consumer power, there's a strong argument to be made that, as a default, consumer-facing products and services should be developed for, and marketed to, women—especially women of middle age or older.

Standing in the way, however, are barriers of representation—not only at work in general, but more specifically in the professions that shape the objects and services that populate our lives. First, to state what might be obvious, anyone who is fully retired from work is *definitionally* not represented in these professions. But even setting aside this glaring issue, older workers (and older women in particular) are underrepresented. Women account for just 19 percent of practicing industrial designers in the United States,[62] for instance, and just 15 percent of engineers and architects.[63] Meanwhile, of 9,429 designers surveyed in the American Institute of Graphic Arts' 2019 Design Census, only 3 percent were over the age of 60.[64]

In tech fields, too, issues of gender and age representation reinforce one another. The tech workforce is younger than the general workforce, with an average age of 38, compared to 43 for non-tech industries.[65] It is also more male: women account for just 25 percent of those working in "computer occupations,"[66] Pew Research reported in 2021—down from 32 percent in 1990.[67]

Age discrimination in tech has become the stuff of infamy. As venture investor Paul Graham said in 2012, he could be "tricked by anyone who looks like Mark Zuckerberg"—and as a then-22-year-old Zuckerberg said in 2007, "young people are just smarter." Among tech workers as young as their late thirties, 43 percent said in 2018 that their age would be an issue if they tried to get a new job in the sector. Baby boomers feel even more pressure: 68 percent said they felt discouraged to apply to jobs due to their age, and a quarter of them reported having been refused a promotion for this reason.[68] These concerns may help explain anecdotal reports of a cosmetic surgery boom, starting in the 2010s, among tech workers in Silicon Valley.[69]

In tech, once again, gender bias gets layered on top of ageist bias. The vast majority of women in tech roles—86 percent—report being labeled with terms like "excessively emotional" at work, and 75 percent say they are regularly saddled with more administrative duties than their male counterparts.[70] More women than men report feeling burned out at work (57 percent to 36 percent, respectively).[71] Family caregivers, too, can find themselves facing undue challenges. In response to a 2019 survey, nearly half of startup founders surveyed said tech companies were not inclusive places for caregivers to work.[72]

These issues are not limited to the United States. For instance, tech workers over the age of 35 are considered "old" in the European tech industry, per a 2021 study from Sweden's University of Gothenburg.[73] Funding for women-led startup teams in Europe is similarly dispiriting: the European venture firm Atomico reported that the proportion of venture funding raised by women-only startup teams dropped from 3 percent, as of 2018, to 1 percent in 2022.[74]

In the United States, the startup funding gap between male and female founders is well documented. For instance, women founders in California and Massachusetts are 65 percentage points less likely than men to receive venture funding.[75] Responding to a 2018 survey, startup founders rated age, then gender, as the most significant sources of investor bias.[76] The following year, 70 percent of female founders said their gender had negatively affected their ability to raise investments.[77] According to a 2020 experimental study, US investors' biases against women, older, and Asian founders are especially pronounced within the subset of companies that funders are most interested in contacting.[78]

This thicket of bias persists despite the fact that most successful founders turn out not to be young, but middle-aged. As a group of MIT and US Census Bureau economists wrote in 2019: "Key entrepreneurial resources (such as human capital, financial capital, and social capital) accumulate with age. Mechanisms by which young people are proposed to have advantages (such as energy or originality) may still be operating, but if so they appear to be overwhelmed by other forces."[79]

## Product Development

Representation in workplaces and entrepreneurial pipelines can affect which products and services get developed—and how, and for whom. (And, for that matter, what they look and feel like, and what they say about the user.)

In the absence of such representation, failure to serve older markets unfolds in two ways: First, in worthy products and services that simply never get developed. And second, in products and services that do get the green light, only to turn out not to work properly—in the broad sense that even if they do function on a technical level, older consumers often still can't (or choose not to) operate them as their designers intended.

Nonfunctional products of this sort can get made as the result of simple thoughtlessness on the part of designers—in terms of accessibility, for instance. In response to a 2014 international Nielsen survey, 43 percent of respondents said it was difficult to find easy-to-open packaging, and half said it was hard to find easy-to-read product labels.[80]

Breakdowns can occur at higher levels as well: for instance, in terms of users' mental models of how to interact with products, or what products should say about them. An example of such a mental-model mismatch comes from the automaker BMW, which, in 2001, attempted to fold the vast array of dashboard elements found in certain models into a screen-based interface. The company's consumer base—older than the average driver—was not thrilled. BMW turned to the MIT AgeLab for insight, and the lab's researchers determined that part of the issue sprung from the new system's joystick-like control device, which felt like a computer mouse in the driver's hand but behaved nothing like it. The best intentions of BMW's designers were butting up against their drivers' existing mental models, hard won over a decade or more of interacting with computers.[81] (This type of mental-model issue comes up frequently in automotive design for older drivers. Older adults' driving behaviors are deeply ingrained, developed over the course of 50 years or more. As a result, asking them to deviate from habit and place their trust in a new safety technology, for instance, can pose a challenge for even the most well-intentioned automakers and components manufacturers.)

Breakdowns can also take place when products chafe against older adults' self-image. Historical examples of such flops include Heinz's 1955 canned food product "Senior Foods" (essentially, mashed baby food for denture-wearers) and Chrysler's 1950s-era lineup of cars (designed for ease of operation over performance). More recent examples include 2007's oversized, supposedly elder-friendly German cellphone, Katharina das Große, which came across as clunky and stigmatizing.[82] The worldview behind these and other sorts of vaguely medical-feeling products (derided as "big, beige, and boring" in the aging design field) treats older people as little more than the sum of their ailments—not complex actors with a variety of motivations and goals beyond mere subsistence and safety. In a world where only 35 percent of people over age 75 see themselves as "old,"[83] products built for the stereotypical problems of "the old" or "the aged" will always face an uphill march.

So will products inexpertly marketed at older consumers. Age 49 remains the do-not-cross line for many in marketing.[84] The Economist Intelligence Unit determined in 2011 that a mere 31 percent of companies factored aging into their marketing and sales plans.[85] In the United States, older adults are portrayed in less than a fifth of advertisements[86]—and when they are, the effect is usually to perpetuate off-putting stereotypes. A 2019 AARP study of marketing imagery revealed just 15 percent of brands' images depicted adults over age 50—despite their accounting for 46 percent of the adult population. On the rare occasions older people were depicted, they were seven times more likely than younger people to be shown in a negative light, and also more likely to be shown stereotypically: dependent and disconnected, without technology at hand, rarely at work.[87]

Older adults tend not to appreciate this kind of treatment. Nearly half of age-50-plus respondents to a 2021 AARP survey said ads featuring their contemporaries reinforced outdated stereotypes, and nearly two-thirds said they wished advertisements would reflect a more "realistic image of people my age." A fifth said they had chosen not to buy a brand based on the age stereotypes in its marketing.[88]

Why do designers and marketers swing and whiff like this? A lack of representation at work is likely a factor: In the absence of actual older people in the room to set the record straight, younger designers and marketers attempting to serve older markets must necessarily turn to what they *think* they know about old age. This hodgepodge of secondhand knowledge and stereotypes can have a pernicious effect.[89] It doesn't necessarily preclude innovation for older people altogether, but it does tend to limit innovators' view of older markets to one of two lenses. One focuses on shallow, even hedonistic wants (think palm trees, golf and pickleball, cruise ships, and other leisure products). The other includes base-level health-and-safety needs (for instance: pharmaceuticals, care work, reverse mortgages, and home security systems).

These lenses aren't *wrong*, per se; no reasonable person would deny that pharmaceutical firms, for instance, or retirement housing companies are capable of adequately serving vast numbers of older people. But the view they offer of the world is not just incomplete; it produces a false sense of comprehensiveness. With both wants and needs apparently accounted for, there is no urgent need to think harder about what else might make older people's lives better.

Missing entirely, for instance, is the notion that older people, in all their variety and complexity, might have something to produce or create, not just consume—to say nothing of the products, services, and social roles that could support those ambitions.

## A Sea Change

Many of the preceding arguments will be familiar to readers of Joseph Coughlin's book, *The Longevity Economy*. Since its 2017 publication, however, a handful of events have taken place that suggest designers and marketers may lately be waking up to the opportunity afforded by the older market, as well as the complexity of the demand involved.

For instance, two technologies Coughlin described as underperforming their potential—hearing aids and personal emergency response systems—have undergone major technological and design (and in hearing aids' case, regulatory) changes since 2017.

From a simple health-and-safety perspective, to say nothing of their impact on other aspects of a user's life, both technologies are invaluable to older adults. Safety is the overt purpose of personal emergency response systems (a category, abbreviated as "PERS," that includes the well-known brand Life Alert). These devices, which often consist of a call button worn somewhere on the body, allow users to contact local emergency authorities in the event of a crisis, such as a fall. Hearing aids, meanwhile, are associated with reduced risk of injurious falls, depression, and anxiety[90]—and may even help delay cognitive decline, since there is a relationship between hearing loss and dementia.[91]

It is a problem with significant stakes, then, that most people who might benefit from such technologies have historically refused to buy, wear, or use them. Only 20 percent of people in the United States with a hearing impairment own hearing aids.[92] To make matters worse, somewhere between 5 and 24 percent of US hearing-aid owners don't wear them.[93] This lack of uptake appears not to boil down simply to cost: In the UK, for instance, where hearing aids are provided by the NHS, just over 9 percent of people with a hearing impairment wear them.[94]

The PERS uptake story is similar. As of 2012, less than 1 in 20 Americans who could benefit from such a device had one.[95] Frail, older people who possess PERS units, meanwhile, tend not to make use of them in the event of a fall—either because they don't wear them regularly, don't want to be taken to the hospital, or have difficulty with activating the alarm. In one 2008 study of adults over age 90 in the UK, owners of PERS systems did not use them in 80 percent of falls.[96]

What's holding older people back from obtaining and using such potentially life-saving products? One factor not to be dismissed is that these products carry the stigma of being "for older people"—a category, remember, that even people over age 75 tend not to apply to themselves. Efforts to overcome this stigma—for instance, by camouflaging PERS units within chunky jewelry—have not moved the dial in a significant way. It seems that even if nobody else knows you're wearing an "old person's" device, you still know it yourself—and that's enough to make many want to shut the device in a dresser drawer and forget about it.

However, significant changes have lately come to both hearing aids and PERS units. In 2018, Apple folded fall detection and emergency alert functions into its Apple Watch, which are activated as a default for users over the age of 55. Now, for the first time in history, a highly effective PERS unit can be found on a product worn by users of all adult ages, devoid of age-related stigma. (And it is not some niche product, either—Apple is far and away the world's leading supplier of smartwatches.[97]) Something similar is happening with hearing aids. Whereas once hearing aids were the only wireless electronic devices you might see in someone's ears, today they're part of a variety of headphones that users rely on to modify their audio landscape. This fact, combined with the substantial deregulation of the hearing-aid market in the United States, has opened up new avenues of exploration for manufacturers. These include new approaches to customer experience (regarding fitting, for instance, and battery replacement),[98] as well as the creation of devices that blur the line between hearing aids and in-ear headphones[99]—an opportunity a number of companies are now exploring.[100]

If the recent spate of change surrounding hearing aids and PERS is any indication, detailed knowledge of the older market—its existence, spending power, and demand peculiarities—has percolated into major tech and medical device companies.

It also hints at a problem, however. Often, the best innovations for older people are not only not identified as such, but are deliberately hidden from view. For anyone seeking to understand the extent and patterns underlying longevity economy innovation, such often-necessary obfuscation presents a challenge.

## Toward a Geography of Longevity Economy Innovation

What is a longevity hub? For the purposes of this volume, we will define it broadly: as any hot spot characterized by a disproportionate level of innovative activity aimed at the older population and related markets.

There's a reason we are using such a loose definition. It is related to why this book is primarily a descriptive, naturalistic endeavor, rather than an attempt to quantify the markets and innovative activity involved, which would be more closely in keeping with recent research trends. A great deal of successful innovation for older people sidesteps, whether deliberately or by chance, any labeling or branding that would connect it with even a whiff of the stigma of old age. Such attempts at innovation by stealth make it possible to serve the older market without ever mentioning it by name—which is often a pragmatic necessity. Many founders and funders of nakedly age-oriented companies have told us over the years that, despite all appearances, their products are not explicitly intended for older people. This impulse is practical: They fear repelling younger and older consumers alike.

As with the PERS example, successful, stealthy innovation involves more than camouflaging a product that is obviously intended for older users. Rather, it happens when companies create products that are apparently designed for users of all ages, but which just so happen to fulfill the specific requirements of certain older people. In addition to today's increasingly age-agnostic PERS units and hearing aids, historical examples of such products include the electric garage door opener (originally an assistive device),[101] the microwave oven (convenient for all, safe for older adults living alone), and text messaging (a ubiquitous communications standard that happens to be a life-changing improvement for people who are hard of hearing). Entertainment products with cross-generational appeal, as Marc Freedman explores in chapter 2 in this volume, also fit the bill. In the cases of many products that older consumers vote for with their pocketbooks every day, it's not clear whether older people were ever explicitly in the crosshairs of innovators, designers, or marketers—but nevertheless, they have adapted these products and services to meet their specific needs. On-demand and gig-economy services such as Uber, TaskRabbit, Amazon Home Services, and Instacart, for instance, can address many of the challenges of aging in place: effectively unbundling the costly suite of services that come with senior housing.[102]

There are, to be sure, still plenty of offerings aimed directly at older markets. These include traditionally age-oriented categories such as retirement, health, and financial services; as well as new ones, such the market for virtual reality in senior housing, which Kyle Rand, the founder of the startup Rendever, explores in chapter 5. Even so, the presence of stealth products and services for older demographics makes the longevity economy a category with fuzzy boundaries. If, as Adam Gopnik writes, the older market "cannot be marketed to," then it must also be difficult to quantify and delineate.[103] It is possible to measure older adults' spending, for instance—AARP and their analytics partners do this annually—but measuring innovative output aimed at the older market is, for now, beyond the scope of this book.

Rather, is our ambition that this volume will not so much resemble the report of a forester quantifying each species in a forest, but the field notebook of a team of naturalists encountering a new ecosystem for the first time. For the most part, we and our contributors will simply describe what we see, and leave the counting of the organisms to subsequent expeditions.

However new these ecosystems may be, however, we still approach them with certain expectations, based on what others have observed in comparable places. Our chief hypothesis for why innovation for older people may disproportionately happen in geographic hot spots has to do with knowledge flows. We believe aging innovation has been held back by the fact that accurate knowledge of older demographics—specifically, the existence and size of older markets, and the peculiarities of their demand—is relatively rare. Even today, on the occasions when firms do successfully target older markets, they're still doing something out of the mainstream. They seem to be acting on an exclusive bit of knowledge.

The best frame of reference for how such market knowledge can lead to tight geographic groupings comes from the cross-disciplinary web of research into regional hubs of productive activity, better known as clusters.

## What Might a Longevity Innovation Cluster Look Like?

The concept of clusters dates back to the late-nineteenth-century work of the English economist Alfred Marshall. His insights into the local economies of English industrial districts forms the backbone of what eventually became a major subfield of economic geography, political economy, economic sociology, and management science, carrying policy implications for countries around the world. Today, there is no single unified theory describing what exactly constitutes a cluster or how they form, grow, mature, and decline,[104] despite the substantial work that has gone into addressing these questions. Traditionally, however, a cluster is often defined as interconnected group of firms located in a given geographic area, which interact with similar markets, industries, or technological fields.[105] The connections between firms in such a cluster can cause it to be greater than the sum of its parts. As Marshall explored as early as 1890, a cluster can generate greater economic returns than would a single vertically integrated firm performing the same functions.[106]

In Marshall's theory, a trio of factors is responsible for clusters' competitiveness and stability. These include the advantages firms gain by sharing a local pool of suppliers and customers; by sharing a local pool of specialized labor; and from "knowledge spillovers"— that is, when useful information sloshes through a location's organizations and workers. Marshall was primarily concerned with spillovers taking place within a given industry. As he wrote in 1890, "Great are the advantages which people following the same skilled trade get from near neighbourhood to one another. The mysteries of the trade become no mysteries; but are as it were in the air, and children learn many of them unconsciously."[107]

Later additions and elaborations on Marshall's trinity of cluster-promoting causes included the hard math of the "new economic geography," kicked off by Paul Krugman in 1991.[108] This approach relies on quantitative models: taking a cluster's forces of concentration (e.g., how economic returns within a cluster can increase with scale; or how firms can save on transportation by being close to suppliers and customers), and weighing them against forces favoring dispersal (e.g., increased local housing and physical-plant rents).[109] Other notable figures include AnnaLee Saxenian, whose *Regional Advantage* included an ethnographic study of the cultural forces shaping Silicon Valley's knowledge flows.[110] The Harvard Business School strategist Michael Porter, perhaps the most influential cluster theorist since Marshall, modified the Marshallian view by holding up the nature of competition between a location's firms as a contributor to (and beneficiary of) clustering. Porter also raised the stakes of the conversation, arguing that a region or even nation's ability to compete in the global economy rests on the competitiveness of its regional networks of firms.[111]

(Not to put too fine a point on it: This competitive lens may be of interest to policymakers considering how their countries—and their countries' rivals—will respond economically to a near-global aging trend. Will success in the longevity economy turn out to be a new source of national competitive advantage? We think so.)

There exists a raft of other explanations for clustering, too, often classified as "non-Marshallian," even if they still maintain significant overlap with Marshall's theories. Perhaps most notable is the urbanist Jane Jacobs's 1969 observation that any given industry's cluster often coexists with those of other industries in the context of cities. Such co-location creates the opportunity for unplanned collisions between representatives of different industries, leading to the formation of new useful knowledge and new types of jobs.[112] Other analyses concern positive externalities driven by education and human capital,[113] or certain cities' ability to draw in and support a "creative class."[114]

Today, the prototypical cluster—at least, for the purposes of policymakers seeking to recreate it—is California's Silicon Valley. It is such an archetype, in fact, that its many would-be emulators frequently engage in silicon-based wordplay; examples include Silicon Anchor, Basin, Desert, Forest, Hill, Heartland, Holler, Mountain,

Peach, Shire, Slopes, Spuds, and Surf.[115] Even world-class cities have bought into the trend: Manhattan has its Silicon Alley, London has the Silicon Roundabout, and a Parisian suburb's cluster project was dubbed "Silicon Valley à la Française."[116]

As archetypal as Silicon Valley has proven, it is far from the only example of a tech cluster; just as tech clusters form just a subset of the wider world of clusters. In fact, it was not a tech cluster in the Silicon Valley mode that revived academic interest in Marshall's writings in the 1970s. Marshall's death in 1924, and the interwar rise of large firms exemplified by the major American automakers, led to a temporary decline of interest in his cluster-related writing. By the end of the 1970s, however, weaknesses in the large, vertically integrated (or Fordist) model had become apparent, and Marshall reentered the conversation.[117] Critical to this reversal of fortunes were the efforts of the cadre of Italian researchers collectively known as the School of Florence. This group, and the economist Giacomo Becattini in particular, sought to explain the seemingly unlikely success of a set of midsized, family-owned manufacturing firms in northern Italian communities, which produced goods including furniture, garments, footwear, textiles, leather goods, and decorative items. These firms, their suppliers, and their local communities had all prospered in the 1970s, while more vertically integrated, capital-intensive and high-tech firms had struggled against the era's economic headwinds.

This "'strange' bloom of small manufacturing businesses," as Becattini described it, looking back from the vantage point of 2002,[118] drove local increases in jobs, income, and exports.

"What," he asked, "was the reason behind this vigorous resurgence of archaic and irrational forms of manufacturing in washed-up industries?"[119] At a baseline, the small manufacturing firms and their suppliers benefited from Marshallian effects, which meant that by working in concert they could perform manufacturing feats on par with major firms while remaining competitive on cost. This outcome was considered "scandalous," he wrote, by those "who believed in the then-dominant economic theories" that still favored large, vertically integrated firms.

Another part of what was so scandalous was that these districts existed in seemingly unattractive parts of northern Italy: not within the region's industrial cities, but rather in areas that were not especially accessible by road or rail, or equipped with a surfeit of modern infrastructure. Moreover, the industries these firms belonged to—furniture, garments, and so forth—exemplified industries economists had considered "mature" and "lacking in growth opportunities."

The small firms had an advantage, however: an ability to respond nimbly to demand, which by the 1970s had become fast-evolving, discerning, and global. Also working in the small firms' favor was the fact that their districts had maintained "a sufficient cultural complexity, made up of values, knowledge, institutions and behaviors," wrote Becattini, which elsewhere had been displaced "by a generally industrial and massifying culture." This "massifying culture," meanwhile, was made up of consumers who were eager to fill their homes and drape their persons with goods that didn't feel so mass produced. The growth of the middle class in Italy and elsewhere, he argued, created "a highly variable demand for differentiated and personalized goods."

## New Frontiers in Aging Demand

Firms realizing an edge by meeting the shifting demands of a booming consumer segment: if this story sounds uncannily familiar at this point, it should. Our working hypothesis hinges on such a dynamic, involving the underserved demand not of a growing global middle class but rather the world's aging consumers. The scarcity of useful knowledge into how to meet their needs may act as a force promoting islands of economic vitality—call them "longevity hubs"—that have the potential to prosper despite economic headwinds created by global population aging.

Moreover, longevity hubs may hold ramifications for the competitiveness of regions—and nations. Michael Porter identified parallel paths to regional cluster formation in his influential 1990 book *The Competitive Advantage of Nations*. On one hand was the model exemplified by the Italian manufacturing districts, which created value by meeting fast-changing demand conditions. "These firms can develop new products and adapt to market changes with breathtaking flexibility," he writes.[120]

On the other hand was the tech-and-performance-centric model exemplified by large, German manufacturing firms, typically involved in "industries with a high technical or engineering content (for example, optics, chemicals, complicated machinery)," Porter writes. Such cases call for a highly structured approach to management, "especially where intricate and complex products demand precision manufacturing, a careful development process, [and] after-sale service."[121]

The longevity economy offers fertile ground for companies following both paths: an underserved yet constantly shifting set of requirements for consumer goods and services, coexisting with a steady need for high-tech and precision products and services in sectors including biotech, pharma, and medical device manufacturing. In some potential growth areas, such as robotics designed to be used in the workplace by older adults or in care settings, companies may need to prove their competence in both of these lanes.

In addition to the Marshallian line of thought developed by Becattini, Porter, and others, regional success in the longevity economy may be dictated by additional, "non-Marshallian" forces. Imagine, for instance, a region where valuable, new, older-market knowledge makes its way from the local older population to industry—perhaps via workers' close ties to older family members, or the involvement of older people themselves in product design processes. In such cases, issues like local quality of life for older people, including the availability of housing, may prove critical to a region's continued ability to innovate. Other important questions concern whether chance collisions can occur between local actors within and among industries; as well as the intervening role of government, private, nonprofit, and academic institutions, which may help build up a local longevity-economy-facing labor force while providing a venue for organizations to share knowledge.

Finally, there is the matter of trade. Any community that can find ways to reach across regional or national borders and serve older consumer groups living elsewhere may be able to tap the wealth of those distant populations, without necessarily taking on the full social and welfare-state-related responsibility of caring for them. This extractive model, already discernable in some existing destination retirement communities and tourist hubs, may become more common as regions develop goods and services for distant older populations—or else import those foreign older adults themselves: for health and wellness tourism, holidaymaking, and retirement living.

## Assembling This Volume

This volume represents an attempt to explore the forces that may be promoting the development of regional, economically sustainable, innovative longevity hubs. Part I consists of the 32 essays that ran in our 2021–2022 Longevity Hub series in the *Boston Globe*, which delve into the industrial, nonprofit, academic, and entrepreneurship dynamics of the first potential longevity hub to come to our attention: our hometown of Greater Boston. Included in this collection is our own op-ed that commenced the series, as well as a handful of essays written by authors outside New England. This effort also features contributions from noted entrepreneurs and executives from relatively new startups, as well as major, long-standing organizations—including Jo Ann Jenkins, CEO of AARP; Brooks Tingle, president and CEO of John Hancock Insurance; and Jean Hynes, CEO of Wellington Management. These *Boston Globe* essays are organized into topics (the "spokes of the hub," as the *Globe* put it): Aging Well, Powering an Aging Workforce, Transportation, Innovation, Caregiving, Finances, Research and Development, Housing, Health, and Living Laboratory.

Part II consists of nine essays written in 2022 and early 2023 by representatives or observers of longevity hub candidates elsewhere in the world. In the exploratory, descriptive spirit of this effort, we asked our contributors to make a case for their region's status as a longevity hub: describing local innovative dynamics, the role played (if at all) by non-industry institutions, the potential local and global impact of regional innovation, and their hub's future viability. We asked our authors to be clear-eyed not just about their hub's strengths and opportunities, but also weaknesses and threats.

As these stories arrived in our inboxes, we conducted interviews with the authors, and began to notice certain patterns relevant to the clusters literature. Two factors with potential import for longevity hub development jumped out at us. The first had to do with market categories. A given region's aging-related economic activity may belong to either traditional markets such as retirement housing and healthcare; or new markets, typically featuring a variety of startups; or both. The second concerned the geography of knowledge inflows and product outflows. Regions may gather their critical knowledge of the aging consumer from different sources, while exhibiting different ambitions to cater to either local or global markets.

## "Old-Growth" Markets

Although several of this volume's hub candidates are concentrating their innovative energy on new products and product categories for the older market, just as many appear to be ramping up investment in more traditional aging-related industries—especially health care and retirement living. These industries, though hardly new, still have considerable growth potential due to older populations' burgeoning size and spending power—including their ability to command government spending. New investment in such "old-growth" markets, as we refer to them here, may give certain hubs the means to tap the wealth not only of local older cohorts, but also those hailing from other regions and countries.

This volume explores two such regions—Dubai, and Thailand's Eastern Economic Corridor (EEC)—whose national governments are investing in retirement and health tourism services that are intended for locals as well as growing numbers of foreign expatriates.

The author of the Dubai entry, Alyaa AlMulla, describes significant government appetite for longevity economy investment, especially in the form of large real estate projects concerned with healthcare services and related entrepreneurship. The UAE has also created dedicated programs to make it easier for older adults from other countries to live there, and for entrepreneurs to build businesses there.

In the Thailand entry (which evolved out of coursework for the MIT Sloan Fellows MBA program), Pongsak and Thanasak Hoontrakul describe a fast-growing retirement housing industry with century-old historical roots, as well as a new set of government imperatives around healthcare and health tourism, particularly in the country's Eastern Economic Corridor.

In her entry on Milan and its surroundings, meanwhile, Emanuela Notari describes a city simultaneously at the regional forefront of product innovation for an aging public—especially regarding financial services—while at the same time making a strong entry into housing for older adults.

Finally, in the United States, Louisville represents an area whose outsized longevity economy contributions have historically emanated predominantly from the insurance and healthcare sectors, with the insurance giant Humana playing a particularly important role. In the Louisville entry, Humana's CEO, Bruce Broussard, describes a hub candidate with a major anchor firm, as well as a number of co-located firms of varying size, making deliberate investments into longevity economy innovation and entrepreneurship.

Louisville's focus may be expanding beyond traditional, aging-related industries, however. As Ann Markusen, then with the University of California, Berkeley, argued in 1996, regional economic hot spots can take forms other than a single, large, integrated firm or a cluster of smaller ones. They can also emerge as hub-and-spoke models, for instance: in which one or a few major companies become surrounded by smaller suppliers. The long-term "stickiness" of such districts, she writes, "depends on the degree to which mature sectors can release local resources into new, unrelated sectors."[122] It is noteworthy, then, that in 2021, Louisville's Healthcare CEO Council, which includes Humana, acquired the aging entrepreneurship network Aging2.0 (itself the subject of chapter 20 of this book, written by its cofounder, Stephen Johnston). This maneuver appears to represent a concerted local decision to explore new markets and sources of knowledge outside the Louisville region.

### "New-Age" Markets

This volume's other chapters—representing Boston, São Paulo, Japan's urban satellites (a term we use to refer to that country's string of hub candidates), Tel Aviv, Newcastle, and the online network Aging2.0 (acquired, in effect, by Louisville in 2021)—describe regional hot spots evincing greater interest in developing new products and product categories, particularly in tech fields. One notable difference between "old-growth" and these "new-age" markets is the number of industries potentially involved. Once a region branches out from traditional age-related industries like health care and housing, the potential avenues for entrepreneurial activity appear to multiply—especially within the tech sector, which comprises a variety of demand categories potentially served by a vast swath of technological interventions.

## The Beginnings of a Typology

Using the testimony from this volume's authors in their pieces, as well as our interviews with them, we have begun to sketch our impressions of different categories of hub candidates, and criteria for classifying them. One useful such criterion concerns who's making key decisions in a hub, as well as who's providing it with resources. The candidates described in this book that are most involved in old-growth markets, for instance, seem to involve fewer industries and—with the exception of Milan—tend to have the appearance of a top-down decision-making structure, with either a national government or an anchor firm calling many of the regional shots.

Fascinatingly, however, regions seem to be pursuing this pathway with various levels of government investment to draw on—maximal, in the case of Dubai; minimal in the case of Louisville, and intermediate in the case of Thailand. Similarly, new-age markets—though more often grassroots in terms of their origins and decision-making—display levels of government investment ranging from minimal, in the case of São Paulo, to intermediate in Boston, Newcastle, Japan's urban satellites, and Tel Aviv. Crucially, this support often comes in the form of funding for academic and research institutions that may facilitate communication among disparate sectors.

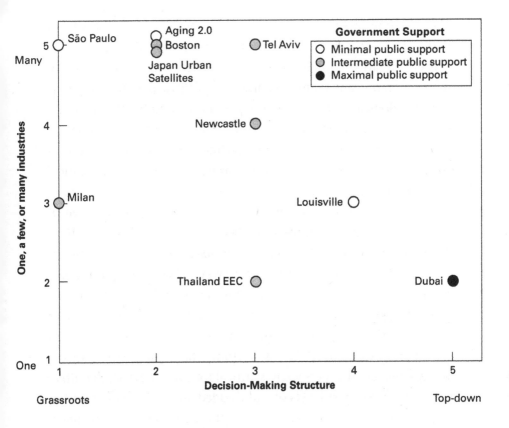

### Geographic Input/Output Dynamics

In the clusters literature, especially the subset concerned with knowledge spillovers, questions of where new, useful knowledge comes from, and how it moves through a cluster, are of great importance. In our case—in which critical knowledge may come from a deep, sometimes counterintuitive understanding of older adults' demand—such flows begin with what firms can divine about their markets.

Some of this information may be relatively portable: the sort of knowledge that travels easily through online publications, for instance, or social media, or online educational coursework. But some critical information may be more geographically constrained: hanging "in the air," as Marshall puts it, locally. For knowledge that "has a strong tacit dimension," writes Jérôme Vicente in his book *Economics of Clusters*, "transfer cost increases with distance."[123] The clusters literature contains a wealth of evidence for the existence of such geographically bounded knowledge.[124] Take patent production in technologically complex fields: the more complex the field, the more localized its patents tend to be.[125] The number of companies established near universities, meanwhile, correlates with the universities' publication output. A similar dynamic holds with spinoff firms of large companies.[126]

A variation on this theme exists regarding deep knowledge of consumer demand. As Porter described in his 1985 book *Competitive Advantage: Creating and Sustaining Superior Performance*, raw materials accrue value at every stage on their way to becoming products.[127] The greatest leaps in value occur at the very end: when automobiles are packaged with financial instruments and service agreements, for instance; or when coffee beans are assigned a desirable brand and served as an espresso.[128] Across consumer-facing industries, a keen sense of what consumers want is critical for such late, value-additive steps. "If the highest levels of value added are likely to be found in the parts of the value chain nearest the customer it is also likely that the customer will be the focus and motivation behind most innovative and entrepreneurial activity,"[129] write the Sweden-based economic geographers Anders Malmberg and Dominic Power.

But for economic producers to receive this critical knowledge of consumers and respond with agility, is it helpful for those consumers be situated nearby? Perhaps—but not always. As Malmberg and Power write, "It is not always true to say that sophisticated and participatory customers will be proximate to regional clusters. On the contrary, for many firms key customers are located far away."

What happens to longevity hubs when the aging consumer market is potentially global? Even if success is tied to deep consumer knowledge, couldn't producers still be located just about anywhere there's a ready supply of capable workers?

The outlines of answers to this question emerge in this volume. The ten cases ahead describe a variety of examples of local versus global knowledge inputs, and local versus global target markets.

Take, for instance, Tel Aviv, as described in the pages ahead by Keren Etkin. Israel is one of the youngest members of the OECD, and boasts the group's highest fertility rate. Despite a thriving tech sector, its home market in general—and especially with regard to products for older people—is relatively small. As a result, its firms frequently take aim at foreign, older markets. Etkin describes a tech-oriented aging innovation hub that is taking in market information from its local population of older people—using its home market as a "beta site"—so as to better serve larger markets in the United States and elsewhere.

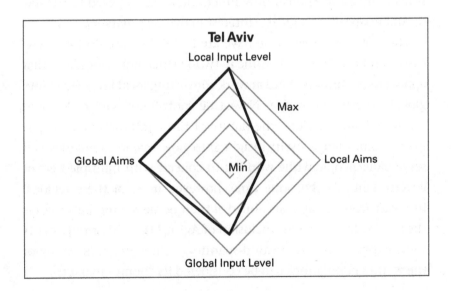

To illustrate these sorts of input-output dynamics, we used a five-point scale (one meaning minimal; five maximal) to rank our impressions of each region's knowledge inputs (that is, whether they gain insight from local populations versus global information flows), and their market ambitions (domestic versus global). We based our impressions on our authors' articles and their interviews with us. These sketches, though subjective, hint at different pathways regions may follow in their attempts to serve aging populations.

The shape formed by Tel Aviv's knowledge input and product output aims is unique among our cases. Its old-growth sectors of health care, elder care, and housing may be aimed at local populations. But in terms of new-age products, the choice of some of its firms to invest in English-only functionality, as opposed to Hebrew or Arabic, speaks to a greater interest in overseas markets.

The closest analogues we have are to Tel Aviv are Boston, Newcastle, and the Aging2.0 online network: three hub candidates that appear to be similarly hard at work converting local knowledge into global exports. (Even if, as Newcastle contributors Gregor Rae and Colin Williams explore, the nature of those international exports may be knowledge itself: insight into how major companies can serve older people while working in concert with multiple tiers of government.) At the same time, however, more of these regions' innovative energy appears aimed at their home populations than is the case in Tel Aviv. (Our inclusion of Aging2.0 in this group merits some explanation—as a world-spanning online network, many of the world's populations can be considered its "home" markets.)

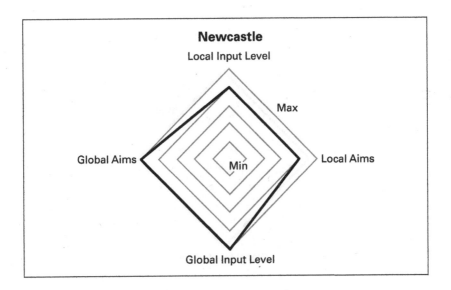

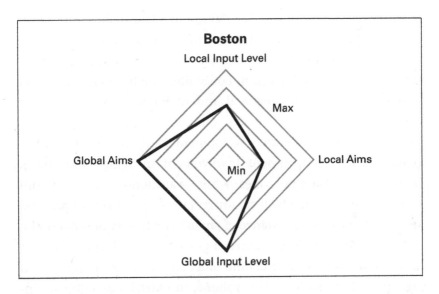

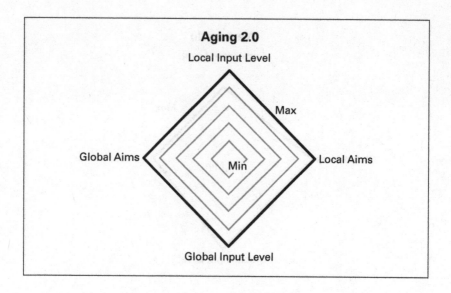

Japan's urban satellites, São Paulo, and Louisville, meanwhile, appear to be innovating with home markets squarely, if not exclusively, in mind. This group's interest ranges from old-growth markets (a major area of interest in Louisville, which develops care and insurance products for regional and national markets, both), to new-age (a major target for São Paulo, as described here by Layla Vallias, whose tech-centric development patterns coincide with a general lack of government involvement in aging innovation). Japan's urban satellites, meanwhile—vacation-friendly environments often anchored by local universities—are all within physical and electronic hailing distance of Japan's capital city or other major metropolitan areas. Tokyo exerts a gravitational effect on younger Japanese workers, leaving behind older adults in surrounding, rural regions. In his chapter in this volume, Jon Metzler describes a constellation of such areas where the disproportionately older population is exploring new modes of economic production, while retaining ties to the capital, and access to its advanced medical services.

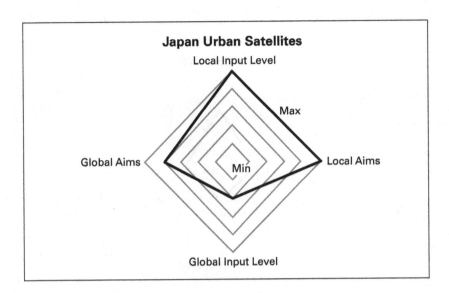

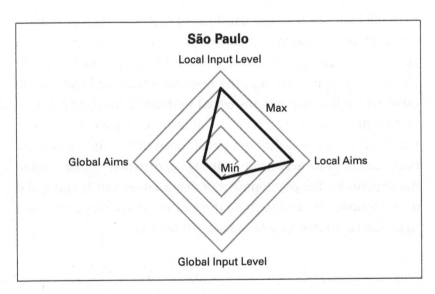

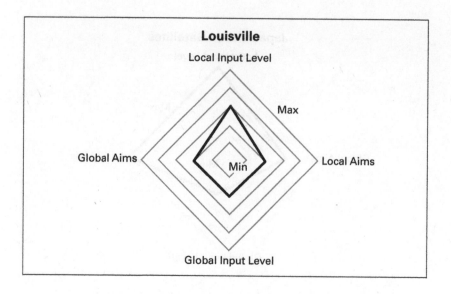

Finally, the trio of Milan, Thailand's EEC, and Dubai are notable for developing existing, old-growth product categories in order to aim them more concertedly at local and visiting populations. In Notari's telling, for instance, the first major wave of Milan's dedicated senior housing was instigated by foreign firms, which provided a model for Italian firms to emulate. In Thailand, similarly, vacationing foreign expatriates transformed slowly and organically into retiring (and healthcare-utilizing) expatriates, which created the impetus for the development of major retirement housing and health tourism industries. In all three cases, locals, too, comprise a significant customer base of old-growth services.

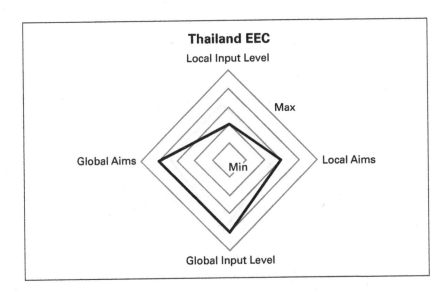

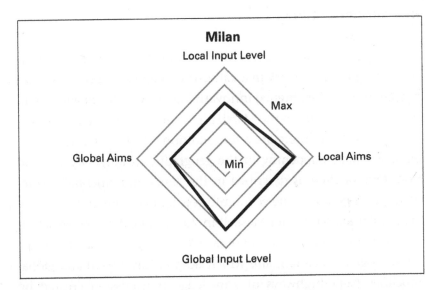

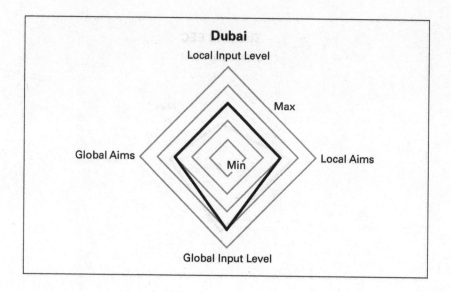

## Into Longevity Hubs

In the pages ahead, readers will encounter potentially cluster-promoting forces at work in a variety of regions, each of which has a reputation for heightened innovative activity aimed at aging populations. In addition to the Marshallian and non-Marshallian forces already discussed, there are a few additional factors that may help explain what's happening in the geography of longevity innovation. One of these is described in the "buzz-and-pipeline" framework put forward by the economic geographers Anders Malmberg, Harald Bathelt, and Peter Maskell in 2004. They draw a distinction between "local buzz" (the sort of tacit knowledge that hangs "in the air" in a given location, and which doesn't travel well) and global pipelines (superhighways of knowledge transmission created by strategic partnerships, intra-company communications, and other region-spanning social institutions and networks). Such pipelines may turn out to have an important role to play in shaping global knowledge flows in the longevity economy. Indeed, it is possible to view one of our hub candidates, Aging2.0, less as a hub in itself than a world-spanning pipeline, connecting hubs to one another.

Convening forces within regions, too—especially academic institutions—take on an outsized role in the pages ahead. This is, per the clusters literature, to be expected. Historically, some of policymakers' most successful attempts to build and create clusters have centered on government support of such "network development" institutions.[130] In addition to producing new knowledge of direct relevance to older adults via research, universities can serve as neutral ground where industry actors and government organizations can meet to share ideas and concerns. Moreover, to the extent that universities have departments and coursework devoted to aging-oriented fields including gerontology, geriatrics, and related courses of study in social work or clinical psychology, they are critical to developing the specialized labor force required by any thriving aging society. Such programs may also help put aging "on the map" for young entrepreneurs and venture capitalists, who may first encounter them in their higher education.

There's more to life than the stuff you buy and the work you do, of course. And yet, there is good reason to believe that one key to a better, longer, more sustainable old age may lie in better innovation for older people: from electronic gadgets to government policies; nutrition to transportation infrastructure; financial services to human resources directives. Such efforts, in addition to addressing specific needs, also can serve as a form of media: transmitting an urgently needed corrective about the value of older people and later life.

It is our hope that this volume's initial explorations into the geography of aging-related innovation will lead to further inquiry—including analysis of the actual benefits (or lack thereof) that longevity hubs create for the people who live within them. Hosting a successful innovation cluster is the sort of thing communities actively vie for, but it still can pose real problems for residents. As the University of Pennsylvania's Gilles Duranton has described, the net economic returns of clusters can follow an inverted "U" shape; at a certain size, a cluster's effect on local rents, wages, and congestion can impose more costs than benefits onto a community.[131] Such regions can improve their lot, however, by striving to reduce the local cost of living, especially by building housing and transportation infrastructure.

Communities are complex, and their formal economic output only represents one aspect of what transpires in them on any given day. Both within and outside the scope of economic metrics, the contributions of older adults have gone underrecognized: their productive capacity hidden in the vagaries of the informal economy; their needs, aspirations, and goals neglected due to decades of accumulated stigma; their demand as consumers at best approached reductively, at worst ignored outright.

Continuing to disregard and misunderstand older adults is a mistake that may haunt regions, and indeed countries, in the years to come. We hope these pages will help some of them avoid this fate: offering grist for the mill of innovators, funders, policymakers, and university administrators, as well as curious members of the public. We all stand to benefit from better knowledge of the large, yet poorly understood, forces poised to shape how we will live tomorrow.

## Notes

1. John Richard Wilmoth et al., *World Social Report 2023: Leaving No One Behind in an Ageing World*, ed. Gretchen Luchsinger (New York: United Nations Department of Economic and Social Affairs, 2023).

2. Anne Case and Angus Deaton, "Rising Morbidity and Mortality in Midlife among White Non-Hispanic Americans in the 21st Century," *Proceedings of the National*

*Academy of Sciences* 112, no. 49 (December 8, 2015): 15078–15083, https://doi.org /10.1073/pnas.1518393112.

3. Anthony Knapp and Tiangeng Lu, "Net Migration Between the United States and Abroad in 2022 Reaches Highest Level Since 2017," US Census Bureau, December 22, 2022, https://www.census.gov/library/stories/2022/12/net-international-migra tion-returns-to-pre-pandemic-levels.html.

4. "Modern Immigration Wave Brings 59 Million to U.S., Driving Population Growth and Change through 2065," *Pew Research Center's Hispanic Trends Project* (blog), September 28, 2015, https://www.pewresearch.org/hispanic/2015/09/28 /modern-immigration-wave-brings-59-million-to-u-s-driving-population-growth -and-change-through-2065/.

5. Sandra Johnson, *A Changing Nation: Population Projections under Alternative Immi-gration Scenarios* (US Department of Commerce, US Census Bureau, 2020).

6. Lilian Kilduff, "Which U.S. States Have the Oldest Populations?," PRB, December 22, 2021, https://www.prb.org/resources/which-us-states-are-the-oldest/.

7. *World Population Prospects 2022*, United Nations Department of Economic and Social Affairs Population Division (2022), https://population.un.org/wpp/.

8. Maria Petrakis, "Eastern Europe: The Future of Aging Populations and Economic Growth," IMF F&D, March 2020, https://www.imf.org/en/Publications/fandd/issues /2020/03/future-of-aging-populations-and-economic-growth-in-eastern-europe -petrakis.

9. UN Desa, "World Population Prospects, the 2017 Revision, Volume I: Compre-hensive Tables," *New York United Nations Department of Economic & Social Affairs*, 2017.

10. Nikkil Sudharsanan, David E. Bloom, and N. Sudharsanan, "The Demography of Aging in Low- and Middle-Income Countries: Chronological versus Functional Perspectives," 2018, 309–338.

11. Sudharsanan, Bloom, Sudharsanan, "The Demography of Aging."

12. Frank Götmark and Malte Andersson, "Human Fertility in Relation to Educa-tion, Economy, Religion, Contraception, and Family Planning Programs," *BMC Public Health* 20, no. 1 (2020): 1–17.

13. "Population Estimates and Projections | Data Catalog," World Bank, last updated May 16, 2023, https://datacatalog.worldbank.org/search/dataset/0037655 /Population-Estimates-and-Projections.

14. Max Roser, "Fertility Rate," *Our World in Data*, February 19, 2014, https://our worldindata.org/fertility-rate.

15. "World Bank Open Data," World Bank Open Data, accessed July 9, 2023, https://data.worldbank.org.

16. Michael Dotsey, Shigeru Fujita, and Leena Rudanko, "Where Is Everybody? The Shrinking Labor Force Participation Rate," 2017, https://www.philadelphiafed .org/the-economy/macroeconomics/where-is-everybody-the-shrinking-labor-force -participation-rate.

17. "The 2020 Long-Term Budget Outlook | Congressional Budget Office," September 21, 2020, https://www.cbo.gov/publication/56598.

18. Daron Acemoglu and Pascual Restrepo, "Demographics and Automation," *Review of Economic Studies* 89, no. 1 (January 1, 2022): 1–44, https://doi.org/10.1093 /restud/rdab031.

19. Chung Min Lee, "South Korea's Military Needs Bold Reforms to Overcome a Shrinking Population—Demographics and the Future of South Korea," Carnegie Endowment for International Peace, June 29, 2021, https://carnegieendowment .org/2021/06/29/south-korea-s-military-needs-bold-reforms-to-overcome-shrinking -population-pub-84822.

20. Andrew Jacobs and Francesca Paris, "Can China Reverse Its Population Decline? Just Ask Sweden," *New York Times*, February 9, 2023, https://www.nytimes.com /2023/02/09/upshot/china-population-decline.html.

21. Ellen Francis and Claire Parker, "Why French Workers Are Fighting to Retire at 62," *Washington Post*, March 30, 2023, https://www.washingtonpost.com/world /2023/03/30/why-france-protests-raise-retirement-age/.

22. Alex K. T. Martin, "Work Forever: Japan's Seniors Brace for Life without Retirement," *Japan Times*, October 17, 2022, https://www.japantimes.co.jp/news/2022/10 /17/business/senior-employment-japan/.

23. Julien Martine and Jacques Jaussaud, "Prolonging Working Life in Japan: Issues and Practices for Elderly Employment in an Aging Society," *Contemporary Japan* 30, no. 2 (July 3, 2018): 227–242, https://doi.org/10.1080/18692729.2018.1504530.

24. "Global Longevity Economy Outlook," AARP, 2022, https://www.aarp.org/content /dam/aarp/research/surveys_statistics/econ/2022/global-longevity-economy-report .doi.10.26419-2Fint.00052.001.pdf.

25. "The Fed—Distribution: Distribution of Household Wealth in the U.S. since 1989," last updated June 16, 2023, https://www.federalreserve.gov/releases/z1/data viz/dfa/distribute/chart/#quarter:133;series:Net%20worth;demographic:age;popula tion:all;units:levels.

26. "The Silver Economy Is Coming of Age: A Look at the Growing Spending Power of Seniors," Brookings, January 14, 2021, https://www.brookings.edu/articles

/the-silver-economy-is-coming-of-age-a-look-at-the-growing-spending-power-of
-seniors/.

27. "The Silver Economy Is Coming of Age."

28. "Leaving a Legacy: A Lasting Gift to Loved Ones," Merill, 2019, https://images
.em.bankofamerica.com/HOST-01-19-2701/ML_Legacy_Study.pdf.

29. Talmon Joseph Smith and Karl Russell, "The Greatest Wealth Transfer in History Is Here, with Familiar (Rich) Winners," *New York Times*, May 14, 2023, sec.
Business, https://www.nytimes.com/2023/05/14/business/economy/wealth-genera
tions.html.

30. US Trust, "2017 US Trust Insights on Wealth and Worth," 2017, http://www
.pva-advisory.com/wp-content/uploads/2017/10/2017-US-Trust-Insights-on-Wealth
-and-Worth.pdf.

31. "Even Soaring Inflation Can't Lure Many Retirees Back to Work—Bloomberg,"
August 17, 2022, https://www.bloomberg.com/news/articles/2022-08-17/-unretire
ments-fade-posing-another-hurdle-for-us-employers.

32. "Affluent Americans Rush to Retire in New 'Life-Is-Short' Mindset," *Bloomberg*, April 30, 2021, https://www.bloomberg.com/news/articles/2021-04-30/more
-americans-are-considering-retirement-because-of-covid.

33. Joshua Montes, Christopher Smith, and Juliana Dajon, "'The Great Retirement
Boom': The Pandemic-Era Surge in Retirements and Implications for Future Labor
Force Participation," 2022.

34. Harry J. Holzer, "Tight Labor Markets and Wage Growth in the Current Economy," report (Washington, DC: The Brookings Institution, 2022).

35. UN Secretary-General, "Women's Economic Empowerment in the Changing World of Work: Report of the Secretary-General," December 30, 2016, https://
digitallibrary.un.org/record/856760.

36. David E. Bloom et al., "Valuing Productive Non-Market Activities of Older
Adults in Europe and the US," *De Economist* 168, no. 2 (June 1, 2020): 153–181,
https://doi.org/10.1007/s10645-020-09362-1.

37. "Table 1. Number and Percent of the U.S. Population Who Were Eldercare Providers by Sex and Selected Characteristics, Averages for the Combined Years 2017–
2018," US Bureau of Labor Statistics, accessed July 9, 2023, https://www.bls.gov
/news.release/elcare.t01.htm.

38. Lisa Weber-Raley and Erin Smith, "Caregiving in the US 2015," *National Alliance
for Caregiving and the AARP Public Policy Institute*, 2015.

39. Jens Manuel Krogstad, "5 Facts about American Grandparents," *Pew Research Center* (blog), September 13, 2015, https://www.pewresearch.org/short-reads/2015/09/13/5-facts-about-american-grandparents/.

40. Krogstad, "5 Facts about American Grandparents."

41. "Untangling Family, Friend, and Neighbor Care | Bipartisan Policy Center," September 20, 2022, https://bipartisanpolicy.org/blog/informal-child-care/.

42. "The Unsung Heroes of the American Economy: Grandmothers," *Fortune*, accessed July 9, 2023, https://fortune.com/2023/03/08/the-unsung-heroes-of-the-american-economy-grandmothers/.

43. Krogstad, "5 Facts about American Grandparents."

44. "1. Demographic and Financial Profiles of People in the U.S., Germany and Italy," *Pew Research Center's Social & Demographic Trends Project* (blog), May 21, 2015, https://www.pewresearch.org/social-trends/2015/05/21/1-demographic-and-financial-profiles-of-people-in-the-u-s-germany-and-italy/.

45. Iori Kawate, "China's Young and Old Rail against Raising Retirement Age," Nikkei Asia, April 4, 2021, https://asia.nikkei.com/Spotlight/Society/China-s-young-and-old-rail-against-raising-retirement-age.

46. Luna Sun, "China Population: With 20 Million Fewer People Projected by 2035, Will the Retirement Age Have to Be Raised?," *South China Morning Post*, February 7, 2024, https://www.scmp.com/economy/economic-indicators/article/3251159/china-population-20-million-fewer-people-projected-2035-will-retirement-age-have-be-raised.

47. Liyan Qi, "China Is Facing a Moment of Truth about Its Low Retirement Age," *Wall Street Journal*, April 11, 2023, sec. World, https://www.wsj.com/articles/china-is-facing-a-moment-of-truth-about-its-low-retirement-age-5ed9b57f.

48. Kawate, "China's Young and Old Rail against Raising Retirement Age."

49. Du, Fenglian, Xiao-yuan Dong, and Yinyu Zhang. "Grandparent-Provided Childcare and Labor Force Participation of Mothers with Preschool Children in Urban China." *China Population and Development Studies* 2, no. 4 (2019): 347–368.

50. Ye Wang and Xindong Zhao, "Grandparental Childcare and Second Birth in China: Evidence from a Dynamic Model and Empirical Study." *Complexity* 2021 (2021): 1–15; Yongai Jin, Menghan Zhao, and Jian Song, "Parents' Influence on Women's Second Birth Intention in the Era of China's Two-Child Policy," in *PAA 2018 Annual Meeting*, PAA, 2018.

51. Nicole Hong and Zixu Wang, "Desperate for Babies, China Races to Undo an Era of Birth Limits. Is It Too Late?," *New York Times*, February 26, 2023, sec. World, https://www.nytimes.com/2023/02/26/world/asia/china-birth-rate.html.

52. Monique Morrissey, Siavash Radpour, and Barbara Schuster, "Chapter 1. Older Workers," Economic Policy Institute, November 16, 2022, https://www.epi.org /publication/chapter-1-older-workers/.

53. Mitra Toossi and Elka Torpey, "Older Workers: Labor Force Trends and Career Options," *Career Outlook*, Bureau of Labor Statistics, May 2017.

54. Joseph Coughlin and Luke Yoquinto, "When Retirement Becomes a Crisis," *Slate*, February 2, 2016, https://slate.com/business/2016/02/baby-boomers-retirements -could-cripple-professions-like-air-traffic-controller-farmer-and-geriatrician.html.

55. Lona Choi-Allum, "Older Workers Experience Age Discrimination at Work and in Hiring," AARP, 2022, https://doi.org/10.26419/res.00545.001.

56. Teresa Perez, "Earnings Peak at Different Ages for Different Demographic Groups," Payscale, June 4, 2019, https://www.payscale.com/research-and-insights/peak -earnings/.

57. Jasmine Tucker, "The Wage Gap Has Robbed Women of Their Ability to Weather COVID-19," March 2021, https://nwlc.org/wp-content/uploads/2021/03 /EPD-2021-v1.pdf.

58. M. J. Silverstein, K. Sayre, and J. Butman, *Women Want More: How to Capture Your Share of the World's Largest, Fastest-Growing Market* (New York: HarperCollins, 2009).

59. Esteban Ortiz-Ospina and Diana Beltekian, "Why Do Women Live Longer than Men?," Our World in Data, August 14, 2018, https://ourworldindata.org/why -do-women-live-longer-than-men.

60. "Caregivers of Older Adults: A Focused Look at Those Caring for Someone Age 50+," *AARP Public Policy Institute and the National Alliance for Caregiving*, June 2015, p. 51, fig. 64, http://www.aarp.org/content/dam/aarp/ppi/2015/caregivers-of-older -adults-focused-look.pdf.

61. "Women and Caregiving: Facts and Figures," *Family Caregiver Alliance*, accessed June 23, 2016, https://www.caregiver.org/women-and-caregiving-facts-and-figures.

62. Kellie Kay Walters, "Hegemony in Industrial Design: A Study of Gendered Communication Styles," in *DS 93: Proceedings of the 20th International Conference on Engineering and Product Design Education (E&PDE 2018), Dyson School of Engineering, Imperial College, London. 6th-7th September 2018*, 2018.

63. Richard Fry, Brian Kennedy, and Cary Funk, "STEM Jobs See Uneven Progress in Increasing Gender, Racial and Ethnic Diversity," *Pew Research Center Science & Society* (blog), April 1, 2021, https://www.pewresearch.org/science/2021/04/01/stem -jobs-see-uneven-progress-in-increasing-gender-racial-and-ethnic-diversity/.

64. Eliza Martin, "Does Design Have an Ageism Problem?," *Ceros Inspire* (blog), February 21, 2020, https://www.ceros.com/inspire/originals/ageism-in-design/.

65. "Four Common Tech Ageism Myths Debunked with Data," Visier, accessed July 9, 2023, https://www.visier.com/blog/four-common-tech-ageism-myths-debunked/.

66. Fry, Kennedy, and Funk, "STEM Jobs."

67. Cary Funk and Kim Parker, "Women and Men in STEM Often at Odds Over Workplace Equity," *Pew Research Center's Social & Demographic Trends Project* (blog), January 9, 2018, https://www.pewresearch.org/social-trends/2018/01/09/women -and-men-in-stem-often-at-odds-over-workplace-equity/.

68. "Dice Diversity and Inclusion Report 2018," Dice, 2018, https://marketing.dice .com/pdf/2018-06_DiceDiversity_InclusionReport_FINAL.pdf.

69. Peter Holley, "In Silicon Valley, Some Men Say Cosmetic Procedures Are Essential to a Career," *Washington Post*, January 10, 2020, https://www.washingtonpost .com/technology/2020/01/09/silicon-valley-some-men-say-cosmetic-procedures-are -essential-career/.

70. "The Gender Divide in Tech," Navisite, April 2022, https://www.navisite.com /wp-content/uploads/2022/04/Gender-Divide-in-Tech-Infographic.pdf.

71. "2021 Women in Tech Report," TrustRadius, March 8, 2021, https://www .trustradius.com/buyer-blog/women-in-tech-report.

72. "First Round State of Startups 2019," First Round, 2019, https://stateofstartups 2019.firstround.com/.

73. "Ageism Common in the Tech Industry," University of Gothenburg, March 16, 2021, https://www.gu.se/en/news/ageism-common-in-the-tech-industry.

74. "State of DEI," State of European Tech 22, 2022, https://stateofeuropeantech .com/reading-tracks/state-of-dei.

75. Jorge Guzman and Aleksandra Olenka Kacperczyk, "Gender Gap in Entrepreneurship," *Research Policy* 48, no. 7 (2019): 1666–1680.

76. "First Round State of Startups 2018," First Round, 2018, http://stateofstartups .firstround.com/2018/#introduction.

77. First Round, "First Round State of Startups 2019."

78. Ye Zhang, "Discrimination in the Venture Capital Industry: Evidence from Field Experiments," *ArXiv Preprint ArXiv:2010.16084*, 2020.

79. Pierre Azoulay et al., "Age and High-Growth Entrepreneurship," *American Economic Review: Insights* 2, no. 1 (2020): 65–82.

80. "The Age Gap: As Global Population Skews Older, Its Needs Are Not Being Met," *Nielsen*, February 2014.

81. Pierre Azoulay et al., "Age and High-Growth Entrepreneurship," *American Economic Review: Insights* 2, no. 1 (2020): 65–82.

82. Joseph F. Coughlin, *The Longevity Economy: Unlocking the World's Fastest-Growing, Most Misunderstood Market* (New York: PublicAffairs, 2017), 75.

83. "Growing Old in America: Expectations vs. Reality," *Pew Research Center*, June 29, 2009, http://www.pewsocialtrends.org/2009/06/29/growing-old-in-america-expectations-vs-reality/.

84. David Wallis, "Selling Older Consumers Short," *AARP Bulletin*, October 2014, http://www.aarp.org/money/budgeting-saving/info-2014/advertising-to-baby-boomers.html.

85. Economist Intelligence Unit, "A Silver Opportunity? Rising Longevity and Its Implications for Business," *The Economist Intelligence Unit*, 2011.

86. Martin Eisend, "Older People in Advertising," *Journal of Advertising* 51, no. 3 (2022): 308–322.

87. Colette Thayer and Laura Skufca, "Media Image Landscape: Age Representation in Online Images" (AARP Research, September 23, 2019), https://doi.org/10.26419/res.00339.001.

88. Colette Thayer and Brittne Kakulla, "Language of Aging" (Washington, DC: AARP Research, September 1, 2021), https://doi.org/10.26419/res.00466.001.

89. Coughlin, *The Longevity Economy*, 14.

90. Elham Mahmoudi et al., "Can Hearing Aids Delay Time to Diagnosis of Dementia, Depression, or Falls in Older Adults?," *Journal of the American Geriatrics Society* 67, no. 11 (2019): 2362–2369.

91. Fan Jiang et al., "Association between Hearing Aid Use and All-Cause and Cause-Specific Dementia: An Analysis of the UK Biobank Cohort," *Lancet Public Health* 8, no. 5 (2023): e329–38.

92. Wade Chien and Frank R. Lin, "Prevalence of Hearing Aid Use among Older Adults in the United States," *Archives of Internal Medicine* 172, no. 3 (2012): 292–293.

93. Abby McCormack and Heather Fortnum, "Why Do People Fitted with Hearing Aids Not Wear Them?," *International Journal of Audiology* 52, no. 5 (2013): 360–368.

94. Chelsea S. Sawyer et al., "Correlates of Hearing Aid Use in UK Adults: Self-Reported Hearing Difficulties, Social Participation, Living Situation, Health, and Demographics," *Ear and Hearing* 40, no. 5 (2019): 1061–1068.

95. Henry Edmonds, Doug Schultz, and Barbara Bosch, "Personal Emergency Response Systems (PERS). State of the Industry Sector," The Edmonds Group, 2012.

96. Jane Fleming and Carol Brayne, "Inability to Get up after Falling, Subsequent Time on Floor, and Summoning Help: Prospective Cohort Study in People over 90," *BMJ* 337 (2008).

97. William Gallagher, "Apple Watch Dominated Smartwatch Market Sales and Profits in 2022," AppleInsider, February 22, 2023, https://appleinsider.com/articles /23/02/22/apple-watch-dominated-smartwatch-market-sales-and-profits-in-2022.

98. For example, the Swiss hearing care company Sonova.

99. Nicole Wetsman, "The Line between Headphones and Hearing Aids Is about to Get Way Blurrier," The Verge, August 16, 2022, https://www.theverge.com/2022/8 /16/23307974/hearing-aids-over-counter-fda-apple-bose.

100. For instance, see Daniel Griffin, "Signia Introduces World's First Augmented Hearing Technology That Delivers an Immersive, Intelligent Hearing Experience With Exceptional Speech Clarity," PR Newswire, May 18, 2021, https://www .prnewswire.com/news-releases/signia-introduces-worlds-first-augmented-hearing -technology-that-delivers-an-immersive-intelligent-hearing-experience-with-excep tional-speech-clarity-301293933.html.

101. Coughlin, *The Longevity Economy*, 190.

102. Julie Miller et al., "Sharing Is Caring: The Potential of the Sharing Economy to Support Aging in Place," *Gerontology & Geriatrics Education* 41, no. 4 (2020): 407–429.

103. Coughlin, *The Longevity Economy*, 70.

104. Jérôme Vicente, *Economics of Clusters: A Brief History of Cluster Theories and Policy* (New York: Springer, 2018), 5.

105. Vicente, *Economics of Clusters*, 2.

106. Alfred Marshall, *Principles of Economics* (New York: Macmillan, 1890); Alfred Marshall, *Industry and Trade* (New York: Macmillan, 1919).

107. Marshall, *Principles of Economics*.

108. Paul Krugman, "What's New About the New Economic Geography?," *Oxford Review of Economic Policy* 14, no. 2 (1998): 7–17.

109. Armin Schmutzler, "The New Economic Geography," *Journal of Economic Surveys* 13, no. 4 (1999): 355–379.

110. AnnaLee Saxenian, *Regional Advantage: Culture and Competition in Silicon Valley and Route 128, with a New Preface by the Author* (Cambridge, MA: Harvard University Press, 1996).

111. Michael E Porter, *Competitive Advantage of Nations: Creating and Sustaining Superior Performance* (Simon and Schuster, 2011); Michael E Porter, "Location, Competition, and Economic Development: Local Clusters in a Global Economy," *Economic Development Quarterly* 14, no. 1 (2000): 15–34.

112. Jane Jacobs, *The Economy of Cities* (New York: Vintage, 2016); Enrico Moretti, *The New Geography of Jobs* (Boston: Houghton Mifflin Harcourt, 2012), 100.

113. Enrico Moretti, "Human Capital Externalities in Cities," in *Handbook of Regional and Urban Economics*, vol. 4 (Elsevier, 2004), 2243–91.

114. Richard Florida, *The Rise of the Creative Class, Updated Edition* (New York: Basic Books, 2019).

115. William R. Kerr and Frederic Robert-Nicoud, "Tech Clusters," *Journal of Economic Perspectives* 34, no. 3 (2020): 50–76.

116. Vicente, *Economics of Clusters*, 8.

117. Vicente, 9.

118. Giacomo Becattini, "From Marshall's to the Italian 'Industrial Districts': A Brief Critical Reconstruction," in Complexity and Industrial Clusters: Dynamics and Models in Theory and Practice (New York: Springer, 2002), 83–106.

119. Becattini, "From Marshall's to the Italian 'Industrial Districts.'"

120. Porter, *Competitive Advantage of Nations*, 108.

121. Porter, 108.

122. Ann Markusen, "Sticky Places in Slippery Space: A Typology of Industrial Districts," *Economic Geography* 72, no. 3 (July 1996): 293.

123. Vicente, *Economics of Clusters*, 39–40.

124. David B. Audretsch and Maryann P. Feldman, "R&D Spillovers and the Geography of Innovation and Production," *American Economic Review* 86, no. 3 (1996): 630–640.

125. Pierre-Alexandre Balland and David Rigby, "The Geography of Complex Knowledge," *Economic Geography* 93, no. 1 (2017): 1–23.

126. David B. Audretsch, Max Keilbach, and Erik Lehmann, "The Knowledge Spillover Theory of Entrepreneurship and Technological Diffusion," in *University Entrepreneurship and Technology Transfer* (Leeds: Emerald Group Publishing, 2005), 69–91.

127. Michael E. Porter, *Competitive Advantage: Creating and Sustaining Superior Performance* (New York: Free Press, 1985).

128. Pine Joseph and James H. Gilmore, *The Experience Economy: Work Is Theater and Every Business a Stage* (Boston: Harvard Business School Press, 1999).

129. Anders Malmberg and Dominic Power, "On the Role of Global Demand in Local Innovation Processes," in *Rethinking Regional Innovation and Change: Path Dependency or Regional Breakthrough?* (New York: Springer, 2005), 273–290.

130. Junichi Nishimura and Hiroyuki Okamuro, "Subsidy and Networking: The Effects of Direct and Indirect Support Programs of the Cluster Policy," *Research Policy* 40, no. 5 (June 1, 2011): 714–727, https://doi.org/10.1016/j.respol.2011.01.011.

131. Gilles Duranton et al., *The Economics of Clusters: Evidence from France* (Oxford: Oxford University Press, 2009).

# I

# The Boston Longevity Hub

# 1

# Boston: The Silicon Valley of Longevity?

An older population can serve as the hub for a new kind of innovation cluster.

**Joseph Coughlin and Luke Yoquinto**

In the 1980s, Boston fumbled an opportunity that would haunt it for generations. If, at the dawn of that decade, you were asked to predict where America's technological epicenter would soon develop, you might have pointed to the area defined by Route 128. There, a leading group of computer developers had set up shop, supported by a web of academic, business, government, and financial interests. The country's high-tech future was being written and, as in revolutions past, it seemed Boston would be holding the quill.

Instead, however, the future headed west. Silicon Valley, not Boston, was the site of the personal computer revolution—and several subsequent ones as well.

Today, Greater Boston has that rarest of opportunities: a shot at a do-over. More than any other region, it is showing the early signs of a new sort of innovation cluster. Boston's fledgling Longevity Hub, as we at the MIT AgeLab have begun calling it, has become a major source of creativity in response to population aging: perhaps the most significant-yet-inevitable trend coming to global economies. *Inc.* magazine has called Boston—somewhat prematurely—the "Silicon Valley for the octogenarian set." As populations in the United States and around the world grow older, individuals, regions, and nations alike will have every incentive to adopt new attitudes about what's possible in later life. Greater Boston is uniquely poised to build the tools necessary for this transformation.

Most countries around the world are home to aging populations: the consequence of longevity gains, plummeting fertility rates, and, in many cases, a postwar baby boom generation now entering its seventies and eighties. Wealthy countries such as Japan[1] and Italy,[2] home to some of today's oldest populations, are already facing the triple threat of diminished economic growth, deflation, and high taxes—all of which can result when a country's nonworking older population rises relative to its labor force. Many countries, the United States included, are poised to follow in their demographic footsteps. The country reckoning with perhaps the starkest set of demographic challenges, however, is China, whose population is aging faster[3] than that of any medium- or low-income country. China's one-child policy and improvements in life expectancy have created a sharp demographic cutoff, which will soon necessitate enormous spending increases on such social programs as pensions and health care. The price tag may turn out to be so large that it could affect the country's military ambitions.[4]

With facts like these, it's easy to see why the knee-jerk economic response to global aging is to treat it primarily as a liability. From this point of view, the only thing a country can do about its aging population is try to mitigate its impact: by expanding working-age immigration (thereby increasing the ratio of workers to nonworkers), investing in automation (making the workforce, especially in health care, more efficient), and raising the retirement age (forcing older people back to work—cruelly, in many cases).

But the real opportunity—for both Boston and the world's aging populations—comes not from fighting old age, but by embracing it. The truth is that older people don't act solely as a drain on the economy. Rather, in their roles as both consumers and producers, they constitute a vital part of it. The more integrated they are with the rest of the economy, the more everyone involved stands to benefit.

In the United States, the economic impact of older adults is already remarkable. Americans aged 50 and up account for just 35 percent of the US population, but, according to the AARP,[5] they controlled 83 percent of all household wealth as of 2018, and were responsible for 56 cents of every dollar of consumer spending—a figure expected to rise to 61 cents by 2050. Their unpaid activities, including elder care, child care, and volunteerism, add another $745 billion worth of production to the US economy. Their labor force participation, too, continues to rise, part of a long-term trend that started in the 1980s.[6]

But older people's potential economic activity only begins with what they're up to now. Tools to address their future needs, wants, goals, aspirations, and overall quality of life are either lacking or haven't been imagined.

In terms of pure consumerism, the demand of tomorrow's older adults would be gargantuan. For a hint, look past what they're spending now to what they're not. Cerulli Associates estimates[7] that the US baby boomer generation will bequeath some $48 trillion to its heirs and charities in the next 25 years. To be sure, this sum is far from equitably distributed. But even if you ask only the wealthiest boomers, barely more than half will tell you that leaving behind an inheritance is important to them. That means there is money waiting to be spent on better living in old age, except traditional sources of consumer-facing innovation have fallen down on the job of earning those dollars. Where they have failed, clever entrepreneurs, attuned to the future wants and needs of older people, will sense opportunity.

But older people are not purely consumers. The story of older employees, as well as older adults' unpaid contributions to society, is one of catastrophic missed opportunity. Many industries are hemorrhaging intellectual capital as a result of waves of retirement,[8] while in other industries, older workers have to fight both outright and implicit ageism for the right to contribute meaningful work. Traditional unemployment metrics, which don't categorize retirees as unemployed, paper over the reality: many would keep working if given the right opportunity.[9]

Nature abhors a vacuum, and yet these gaps persist: between older consumers and those who might service their demand; between older workers and those who would benefit from their labor. There's a simple reason: the mythical narrative we've inherited about aging.[10] In the mid-to-late 1800s, prevailing medical theories suggested rest was the only natural activity for older people. This recumbent attitude, which made its way into the many aging-related institutions that sprang up during this time, persists to this day. Products for older people are limited mainly to medical and leisure goods, while opportunities for them to join in economic production remain all too scarce.

Older adults know better. What aging is "supposed" to mean is necessarily different from their lived experience, if only because the diversity on display in later life is indescribably broad, encompassing every conceivable level of health and wealth, every type of personality, every background. Perhaps that's part of why, in response to a 2009 Pew poll, only 35 percent of people aged 75 and up reported feeling "old"[11]—our inherited definition of the term is too specific to describe such a teeming variety. Meanwhile, older people are out there, living, pursuing what's meaningful to them, chasing their goals and aspirations, and striving, like everyone else, for a high quality of life—ideally one on par with, if not better than, their middle age.

To deliver such a quality of life, products, policies, and services for older adults must adapt to meet their true needs, not outdated, stereotypical ideas of what's good for them.

*

That's where Greater Boston comes in.

Even if the opportunities presented by aging populations were limited just to automation and health care, Boston's unique strengths in robotics, artificial intelligence, and the life sciences augur well for a world that's about to become obsessed with automation and the extension of "healthy life expectancy": that is, how long the average person can expect to remain in good health. Local drug companies like Moderna may justly claim an outsized share of the spotlight in this regard, but health care comprises far more than pharmaceuticals. Care.com, for instance, one of the leading technological lights in the vitally important eldercare sector, is headquartered in Waltham. For another remarkable local success story, see Amazon's $1 billion acquisition of the Somerville online pharmacy PillPack, an idea that began in a nursing home.[12]

Speaking purely in terms of entrepreneurship, meanwhile, the region is already home to one of the country's leading startup ecosystems. Thanks in no small part to its renowned colleges and universities, the local supply of technological prowess is off the charts. And New England's financial sector is proving itself capable of pulling double duty: funding local startups while offering the financial products and services people need to plan for a stable retirement.

But to imagine what old age might be like in the future, Boston's current strengths are just the beginning. What's needed now—and what could really set Boston apart—is new, a shared narrative around aging.

In fact, back in the early 1980s, a shared narrative may have been part of why Route 128 lost its technological crown to Silicon Valley.

The Boston area's then-hidebound corporate structures may have prevented the cross-pollination of ideas[13]—a situation exacerbated by corporate noncompete clauses, legal at the time in Massachusetts but banned in California. (In 2018, Governor Baker signed a noncompete reform bill into law.)[14] Out West, meanwhile, where ideas and personnel flowed relatively freely within and among companies, a new understanding of the computer market was brewing. Silicon Valley's desktop-sized "microcomputers," though initially less powerful than Boston's refrigerator-sized offerings, were far more user-friendly and affordable, making them a good fit for individuals, not just the institutional customers served by the Boston firms. Soon, they had taken over the market—for individual and institutional buyers alike.

*

The challenge for Greater Boston is to nurture this same sort of unspoken, shared understanding attuned to older people and aging societies.

In this regard, too, Greater Boston maintains an advantage, which may have begun as early as 1999. That year, the Beacon Hill Village, the first-ever "virtual retirement community," began operating under a radical premise: Older people could help each other thrive while remaining in their own homes, not an age-segregated community. Today, the rapidly growing Village-to-Village Network, founded to evangelize the Beacon Hill concept, has taken root in 230 US locations, and the concept has spread abroad as well.

For Boston to transform into the Longevity Hub, this sort of iconoclastic thinking must become commonplace—no mean feat. It will require the simultaneous alignment of several moving parts: what we call the "spokes" of the Hub.

Consider: For companies to truly understand older consumers, they must hire older workers and eldercare-givers. But for informal family caregivers to be able to go to work, they will need a hand to ease their responsibilities at home. Meanwhile, for researchers to turn basic science breakthroughs into useful products for older adults and caregivers, there must be a startup ecosystem attuned to those consumers. And so on. No single spoke acting alone will be sufficient to change how we think about aging, but acting together, they can bring the Longevity Hub into being.

To that end, the MIT AgeLab and Globe Opinion are taking on a yearlong project devoted to setting up Boston's Longevity Hub. Over the course of 2021, we will bring you monthly op-eds, online Op-Talks, and later in the year, hopefully, in-person events, all designed to help coax the Hub's spokes into alignment.[15] These spokes, meanwhile, will include inventing transportation strategies for a nondriving population; breaking new ground in age-friendly housing, empowering the longevity workforce; expanding the finance sector's role in funding both later life and longevity innovation; sparking research and development for an older society; augmenting the powers of caregivers; updating the startup pipeline for the longevity economy; rethinking health care; and imagining a new, shared, later-life culture.

Perhaps the most important spoke of all concerns life on the ground in New England—home, in Maine, New Hampshire, and Vermont, to the country's three oldest states by median age. The region itself can serve as a living laboratory: a way to make sure that the Longevity Hub's offerings benefit the people who live here first and truly improve quality of life across the generations.

Boston has already developed connective tissue capable of convening the disparate forces involved in such an ambitious undertaking, including not just the MIT AgeLab and Globe Opinion but also elder-oriented startup incubators like AGENCY and Aging2.0 as well as the Governor's Council on Aging, which Charlie Baker established in 2017 with the goal of making Massachusetts the most age-friendly state in the nation.

Writing a new narrative of later life is a bootstrap problem: It's hard to create without believing in it, but it can be hard to believe until you've seen it in the world around you. By making ground-breaking creativity and inventiveness for older adults both seen and felt, Greater Boston and New England will be able to offer the world a new vision of old age. We need to change how we think about aging: not as a liability to be solved so much as a world-historical opportunity to be seized—and a real chance to live better as we live longer.

## Notes

1. "Old Age Is the Next Global Economic Threat," *Bloomberg*, October 20, 2020, https://www.bloomberg.com/view/articles/2020-10-20/old-age-is-the-next-global-economic-threat.

2. Simone Tagliapietra and Francesco Chiacchio, "Italy's Pension Spending: Implications of an Ageing Population," Bruegel, April 26, 2018, https://www.bruegel.org/blog-post/italys-pension-spending-implications-ageing-population.

3. Jie Feng et al., "Aging in China: An International and Domestic Comparative Study," *Sustainability* 12, no. 12 (2020): 5086.

4. Keith Crane et al., "Forecasting China's Military Spending Through 2025," RAND Corporation, November 25, 2005, https://www.rand.org/pubs/research_briefs/RB162.html.

5. "The Longevity Economy Outlook," AARP, 2019, https://www.aarp.org/content/dam/aarp/research/surveys_statistics/econ/2019/longevity-economy-outlook.doi.10.26419-2Fint.00042.001.pdf.

6. "Labor Force Participation of Seniors, 1948–2007: The Economics Daily: U.S. Bureau of Labor Statistics," July 29, 2008, https://www.bls.gov/opub/ted/2008/jul/wk4/art02.htm?view_full.

7. Andrew Osterland, "What the Coming $68 Trillion Great Wealth Transfer Means for Financial Advisors," CNBC, October 21, 2019, https://www.cnbc.com/2019/10/21/what-the-68-trillion-great-wealth-transfer-means-for-advisors.html.

8. Joseph Coughlin and Luke Yoquinto, "When Retirement Becomes a Crisis," *Slate*, February 2, 2016, https://slate.com/business/2016/02/baby-boomers-retirements-could-cripple-professions-like-air-traffic-controller-farmer-and-geriatrician.html.

9. Nick Montgomery, "31% of Retirees Say Continued Inflation Would Motivate Them to Rejoin the Workforce," *American Staffing Association* (blog), August 17,

2022, https://americanstaffing.net/posts/2022/08/17/retirees-say-continued-inflation-would-motivate/.

10. Joseph Coughlin and Luke Yoquinto, "Why Do People Get Old? History Offers Up Some Very Weird Theories," *Washington Post*, April 9, 2023, https://www.washingtonpost.com/national/health-science/why-do-people-get-old-history-offers-up-some-very-weird-theories/2017/12/08/418367c4-ca3d-11e7-b0cf-7689a9f2d84e_story.html.

11. "Growing Old in America: Expectations vs. Reality," *Pew Research Center*, June 29, 2009, http://www.pewsocialtrends.org/2009/06/29/growing-old-in-america-expectations-vs-reality/.

12. Luke Yoquinto "Firms Gear Health-Related Technology toward Baby Boomers," *Washington Post*, April 16, 2023, https://www.washingtonpost.com/postlive/firms-gearing-health-related-technology-toward-baby-boomers/2014/10/30/10a26c82-3769-11e4-8601-97ba88884ffd_story.html.

13. AnnaLee Saxenian, *Regional Advantage: Culture and Competition in Silicon Valley and Route 128, with a New Preface by the Author* (Cambridge, MA: Harvard University Press, 1996).

14. Laura Franks, Mark W. Batten, and Samantha Regenbogen Manelin, "Massachusetts Passes Non-Compete Reform Law," Law and the Workplace, August 13, 2018, https://www.lawandtheworkplace.com/2018/08/massachusetts-passes-non-compete-reform-law/.

15. This piece, the first in the Boston Globe's Longevity Hub series, was published on February 15, 2021.

# 2

# Aging Well

## Lady Gaga, Tony Bennett, and the Power of Bringing Generations Together

A new crop of creative collaborations is leading the way with aspirational illustrations of the value and contributions of generations joining forces for mutual benefit and the greater good.

Marc Freedman

When the 2022 Grammy Awards were held, Lady Gaga performed a moving tribute to her duet partner Tony Bennett. Their record *Love for Sale* won the Grammy for best traditional pop vocal album and engineered (nonclassical) album, and was up for album of the year. Bennett and Gaga were born 59 years apart, but together they swing. Their latest debuted in the top 10 of the Billboard 200 album chart, an unprecedented 59 years after Bennett achieved the same success with "I Left My Heart in San Francisco," and nearly a decade after the artists came together for their first hit project, "Cheek to Cheek."

As a pair, Bennett and Gaga accomplish something neither individual—or generation—could do alone. In addition to lending new life to a set of Cole Porter standards, they give new hope to those suffering, as Bennett is now, from Alzheimer's. Just as important, Bennett and Gaga offer a shining illustration of an emerging cultural shift. In the face of long-standing ageist stereotypes and zero-sum characterizations of generations at each other's throats, they illuminate the power of cross-generational connection and collaboration.

Bennett and Gaga's duet flips the script on a long-standing pattern at the border of culture and aging. For much of the past half-century, scholars and observers have called out depictions of older adults in cultural products—TV, music, ads, movies—as overly stereotypical, a poor representation of the complexity of the actual lives and capacities of older people. *Love for Sale*, however, together with a whole new crop of creative collaborations, does just the opposite, leading the way with aspirational illustrations of the value and contributions not just of older people but of generations joining forces for mutual benefit and the greater good.

In short, something is in the air—and on the air, nowhere more noticeably than on television.

Consider *Hacks*, an HBO show about bridging the generational divide that has been both a commercial and critical hit. It won three Emmys and the Golden Globe for best comedy series, beating out Apple TV's *Ted Lasso*. Described as a "love story" in the guise of a "hate story,"[1] the show unites a 25-year-old comedy writer (played by Hannah Einbinder) and a 70-something standup comedian (Jean Smart) facing career-ending crises.

Forced together by their agent and with nowhere else to turn, the pair eventually overcome their own prickly personalities and generational hostility to find mutual affection and professional salvation. It's another tale of old and young doing together what neither could do alone.

*Hacks* is not the only award-nominated show this year to highlight the best of older and younger generations working together.

Hulu's *Only Murders in the Building* and the French series *Lupin*, on Netflix, brought in both large audiences and critical recognition while connecting older and younger characters—across age and race—to solve crimes and pursue justice.

The recent Oscars, meanwhile, have been awash in films about intergenerational connection. Kenneth Branagh's *Belfast* was nominated for seven Academy Awards this year, including best supporting actress for Judi Dench and best supporting actor for Ciaran Hinds, who play wise and loving grandparents in the drama.[2] Their roles recall last year's best supporting actress winner: Yuh-Jung Youn, the quirky grandmother in *Minari*.

This year's best documentary Oscar went to *Summer of Soul*. One of that film's most indelible moments features a cross-generational duet between a young Mavis Staples and her mentor Mahalia Jackson, a musical pairing every bit as inspired and inspiring as the Bennett-Gaga collaboration.

The high-profile pattern extends beyond today's music, TV, and movies. One of the past year's breakthrough podcasts, *70 Over 70*, features the 41-year-old host Max Linsky interviewing older people, including the 99-year-old Norman Lear and 91-year-old labor leader and social activist Dolores Huerta. A theme throughout a number of the podcast's conversations: the promise of generations coming together.

Generational collaboration is in the air in dance, art, and theater, too, and it's worth celebrating. Even more important, these collaborations come just in time. New research from the Stanford Center on Longevity shows that America in 2022 is arguably one of the most age-diverse societies we've ever known.[3] A quarter of the population today is under 20, a quarter is over 60, and the remaining half are in between. For the first time, there are roughly the same number of people at every age, from birth to 70.

But this timely shift in the zeitgeist brings with it a challenge: Can we realize on the ground what's taking shape in the air?

For much of the past century, our limiting cultural tropes about aging and generational relations have been mirrored by the abject age segregation of society: arrangements that cluster young people in schools, middle-aged people in workplaces, and older people in retirement communities, senior centers, and nursing homes.[4]

But here, too, there's reason for optimism. A rising generation of social innovators has started to forge groundbreaking new models—such as the MIT-incubated intergenerational home-sharing platform Nesterly[5]—that are as creative in bringing the generations together as older models, like age-restricted retirement communities, were in splitting them apart.

What's needed now are communities willing to cultivate a critical mass of age-integrating innovations so people all across the life course can find proximity and shared purpose in the course of daily life. Communities that can realize abundant opportunities to live together, work together, learn together, and come together to tackle pressing problems that everyone has a stake in solving.

It's not culture or demography that are holding back a better experience of aging right now; it's the organization of everyday life. The stakes involved in rectifying this situation are profound: We have a chance to make the most of the age and cultural diversity that's already an indelible feature of contemporary life and is destined to be a hallmark of the twenty-first century.

For a sense of what the payoff could be, look no further than Lady Gaga and Tony Bennett's deeply moving rendition of "I Get a Kick Out of You," nominated for a best music video Grammy. They make the promise of the song's title palpable, revealing cross-generational connection to be so much more than a strategy to avoid strife between old and young, or even a new route to productivity.

They show us a vast potential source of love and joy.

Marc Freedman, founder and co-CEO of CoGenerate, is the author of *How to Live Forever: The Enduring Power of Connecting the Generations*.

## The Joy of Intergenerational Learning

In some of the most vibrant older populations around the world, healthy living tends to coincide with continuous learning, as well as regular interactions among older and younger generations.

**Anne Doyle**

Can you imagine starting a business at age 60? Teaching a college class for the first time at 70? Playing a daily table tennis game at 80? Rekindling a love of making art at age 90—with a goal of selling a painting by the time you reach 100?

The increase in the average American lifespan over the last century is an unexpected gift of an extra 20 to 30 years full of possibilities. How we use this extra time can have a profound impact on our communities, as well as on our own individual physical and mental health. There are a few elements to a healthy, empowered longer life, including connecting with others across generations, focusing on what matters most, and seeking moments of joy every day. One of the most important of these is learning. As Stanford psychologist Carol Dweck's research has demonstrated, a "growth mindset"[6]— the belief that talents can be developed with practice—positively impacts health and well-being. This mindset, of great importance for the development of schoolchildren, also pays dividends across our lifespan.

Too often, the narrative Americans encounter around aging suggests that it is natural to step back from education upon leaving the workforce due to a lack of compelling economic reasons to gain or update skills. But outside that narrative, there are many examples that tell a different story. In some of the most vibrant older populations around the world, healthy living tends to coincide with continuous learning, as well as regular interactions among older and younger generations.

In Sweden, for instance, older adults—in addition to their flexible housing and health care options—routinely meet in study
circles in after-school classrooms, and join community folk dances
with people of all ages. In Ikaria, Greece,[7] one of the world's "Blue
Zones,"[8] known for residents' extreme longevity, older adults participate in music-filled, multigenerational community events, such
as outdoor dance festivals and religious gatherings. In Singapore,
home to yet another long-lived population,[9] partnerships between
young and old are fostered in purposefully designed intergenerational recreational and community centers.

Closer to home, in Newton, Lasell Village, an intergenerational
senior living and learning community located on the campus
of Lasell University, has introduced new ways to integrate older
and younger adults over its 22-year history. The village requires
residents to commit to 450 hours of education each year, including classes, physical and cultural engagement, volunteering, and
professional work. Why 450 hours? It meets similar educational
requirements for its nontraditional older students as for the university's undergraduates.

In classes on subjects as varied as fashion history communication, forensics, and exercise science, younger and older students
and faculty learn from one another. In a popular course on social
movements, for instance, classmates swapped personal stories of
the women's movement of the 1970s and the Black Lives Matter
movement of today. Older adults returning to campus decades after
finishing their formal education often report renewing old interests as well as pursuing new ones, and approaching life with fresh
curiosity. The result, as one enthusiastic resident described it, is an
"explorer's" mindset.

Importantly, the knowledge flows both ways; Lasell residents frequently offer their wealth of knowledge and experience for the benefit of younger students. For example, residents and undergraduates
partnered to develop a career panel where young people pursuing

careers in medicine, business, or education shared conversations with residents who had a lifetime of experience in those fields. A retired physician paired up with an undergraduate student and a graphic design professor to redesign duplicate bridge playing cards for those with low vision, selling the cards at the Carroll Center for the Blind. When COVID-19 disrupted in-person classes, over 50 residents volunteered to teach. There were a dazzling variety of topics drawn from lifelong experiences, ranging from literature to military history and cultural experiences. Several residents even joined a group of PhD researchers at the MIT Media Lab to codesign personal robots to help solve daily needs, such as medication and appointment reminders, or remembering to take their keys.

This shared commitment to continuous learning is a key component of what makes a living and learning model successful. Just as we continue to draw knowledge from communities around the globe, including Sweden, Greece, and Singapore, others are now learning about the Age-Friendly University movement,[10] now endorsed by institutions of higher education on five continents. One of the ten key principles for Age-Friendly Universities is "to promote intergenerational learning to facilitate the reciprocal sharing of expertise between learners of all ages."

Aging well means rejecting stereotypes about what it means to grow old. It means looking locally as well as globally for new models. It means integrating intergenerational living and learning models into senior living design to spark innovation and create a sense of purpose. It means looking forward with a sense of possibility.

Recently, a friend in her seventies told me her watchword is "onward." "We keep going," she told me. "We embrace opportunities to redefine, reinvent, reimagine . . . to make every new transition rewarding." That's advice to live by, at any age.

Anne Doyle, CEO of Spark Living and Learning, served as president of Lasell Village from 2015 to 2022.

## Notes

1. James Poniewozik, Mike Hale, and Margaret Lyons, "Best TV Shows of 2021," *New York Times*, December 7, 2021, https://www.nytimes.com/2021/12/03/arts/television/best-tv-shows.html.

2. "Belfast," IMDb, https://www.imdb.com/title/tt12789558/.

3. Sasha Shen Johfre, "Report on Intergenerational Relationships," Stanford Center on Longevity's New Map of Life Program, August 2021, https://longevity.stanford.edu/wp-content/uploads/2021/11/Johfre_NML_IntergenerationalRelationships.pdf; "Century-Long Lives Are Here. We're Not Ready," Stanford Center on Longevity, https://longevity.stanford.edu.

4. Leon Neyfakh, "What 'Age Segregation' Does to America," *Boston Globe*, August 31, 2014, https://www.bostonglobe.com/ideas/2014/08/30/what-age-segregation-does-america/o568E8xoAQ7VG6F4grjLxH/story.html.

5. Dugan Arnett, "Empty-Nester + Young Adult = Perfect Roommates?," *Boston Globe*, October 20, 2018, https://www.bostonglobe.com/metro/2018/10/20/gets-cheap-rent-she-gets-companionship-and-help-around-house-could-this-curious-roommate-pairing-solution-housing-crisis/sS87tL8fqB5QH8LewzpmZJ/story.html.

6. Carol S. Dweck, *Mindset: The New Psychology of Success* (New York: Random House, 2006).

7. Max Fisher, "A Greek Island's Secrets to Long Life, in 11 Bullet Points," *Washington Post*, October 25, 2012, https://www.washingtonpost.com/news/worldviews/wp/2012/10/25/a-greek-islands-secrets-to-long-life-in-11-bullet-points/.

8. Dan Buettner, *The Blue Zones: 9 Lessons for Living Longer from the People Who've Lived the Longest* (Washington, DC: National Geographic Books, 2012).

9. "Life Expectancy at Birth, Total (Years)—Singapore," World Bank, accessed July 9, 2019, https://data.worldbank.org/indicator/SP.DYN.LE00.IN?locations=SG.

10. "Age Friendly University," Dublin City University, June 2022, https://www.dcu.ie/agefriendly/principles-age-friendly-university.

# 3
# Powering an Aging Workforce

## Why Employers Should Recruit and Retain Older Adults

When it comes to aging, working longer solves (almost) everything—for employers and all of their employees.

**Tim Driver, Jody Shue, and Alice Bonner**

Too many of us know someone with a story like this one shared with us from a person in Fitchburg: "I was let go one month shy of my 60th birthday. Worked at my company for 28 years. Some of my colleagues retired early, in their late fifties. They couldn't take the harassment, pressure, and exhortations to work many overtime hours and wanted to leave on their own terms rather than waiting to be thrown out."

This gentleman's employer viewed age as a liability. Smarter organizations view their employees' longevity as an asset: Their experience, lower turnover rates, ability to foster higher customer satisfaction, and diverse perspectives are among the crucial contributions older workers offer.

It's more urgent than ever that more organizations recognize these contributions. As the world's population ages, legacy approaches to aging and the workforce are no longer viable. Expectations of retirement between 60 and 65 were appropriate when life expectancy was shorter, but with the gift of longevity, the way we think about aging and employment must shift.

By working longer, older adults are more likely to remain physically and mentally active, are better able to support themselves financially, and (our research shows) stay four times more socially engaged. With studies showing that social isolation is a health determinant equal to smoking 15 cigarettes per day,[1] social engagement alone must be viewed as vital to good health.

Postponed retirements are similarly beneficial to the economy as a whole: increasing GDP, providing skilled (e.g., the life sciences[2]) and less-skilled (e.g., retail[3]) labor in a tight labor market, and reducing public health costs because people are active and engaged.

When it comes to aging, working longer solves (almost) everything—for employers and *all* their employees.

In our roles with the Age-Friendly Institute and RetirementJobs. com, we've found that there are three main reasons why employers choose to recruit and retain older adults: to reduce turnover, to improve customer satisfaction, and to augment diversity initiatives.

**Reduce turnover.**    The average length of service of a worker over 50 is 10 years, according to government data. That's three times higher than those under 50.

**Improve customer satisfaction.**    Experts tie lower turnover to higher customer satisfaction. They've observed, for example, that a longer-tenured employee is better able to show a customer where an item is located in a store because the employee has more in-store experience. Satisfied customers are then more likely to be return customers and even build rapport with store staff. Businesses appreciate that even the slightest increases in customer satisfaction impact store profitability.

**Augment diversity initiatives.** Employers recognize the benefit of having a workforce that mirrors their communities and customers. This recognition has spurred the growth of diversity, equity, and inclusion (DEI) programs that now include a focus on age.

The sectors where there are the greatest employer demand and associated employment opportunity for older adults include health care (particularly in-home elder care), transportation, security, government, and credible work-at-home companies. There are employers, for example, hiring thousands of online tutors to teach English as a second language.

In order to help older workers connect with employers who value what they bring to the table, we launched the Certified Age Friendly Employer program 15 years ago.[4] To earn the "age-friendly" designation, organizations must meet our criteria across a dozen categories related to compensation, benefits, and workplace culture. We conduct quantitative reviews of these categories and others and review qualitative evidence about C-suite commitment to hiring and retaining employees as well as creating an environment that is respectful of workers 50-plus. CAFE program participants now also include tech and creative firms, where age bias was once believed to be the most entrenched.

Of the more than one hundred employers on the institute's national CAFE list, many are from Massachusetts. They include 2Life Communities, Benchmark, Fidelity Investments, Lasell Village, Mass General Brigham, and Point32Health (formerly Tufts Health Plan). These companies benefit from improved brand value and also learn where they stand compared with peer groups by industry sector, region, and organizational size.

Policymakers are also championing the cause by shining a light on employers deemed age-friendly. The US Senate Special Committee on Aging has recognized the CAFE Program. One of the top recommendations from Governor Charlie Baker's Council to Address Aging was the further promotion and encouragement of age-friendly employers. The Baker administration should put even more meat on this bone. To bolster the state's position as a longevity hub, Massachusetts should lead the nation in creating policies that motivate employers to keep older people like the person from Fitchburg on staff.

In our roles, we are fortunate to hear stories about age-friendly employers every day. We met a Needham man whose employer kept him on staff in a phased-retirement role when he turned 65. The arrangement was good for him, his employer, and younger staff coming up through the ranks behind him who were able to benefit from his experience, mentorship, and institutional knowledge.

Despite the persistence of antiquated and sometimes discriminatory ways of thinking about aging and retirement, many stories like these exist. We need more of them.

Tim Driver is president of the Age-Friendly Institute. He also founded RetirementJobs.com. Jody Shue served as executive director of the Age-Friendly Institute. Alice Bonner is a past director with the Age-Friendly Institute and the former Massachusetts secretary of the Executive Office of Elder Affairs.

## Massachusetts Lays a Solid Foundation for Engaging Older Workers

With a solid foundation in place, there is much that can be done to fully integrate the "longevity dividend" of older workers and volunteers into the economy and society.

Doug Dickson

People over 50 want to contribute to the economy and to society. Exceeding 37 percent of the Massachusetts population, people over 50 now encompass four generations—the Greatest, Silent, Boomer, and a growing share of Gen X. They are an expanding resource and eager to contribute, yet older adults are too frequently shut out of opportunities to use their experience and live financially secure lives.

Because of outdated thinking about the life course—education and career, followed by an increasingly long retirement—and a mistaken belief that older people can't measure up, businesses are shunting to the sidelines the segment of our population with the most experience. Ironically, this occurs just as people reach their peak of productivity, problem-solving, relationship management, and other skills. As a result, we sacrifice the investment we have made in their development, we lose the value of their economic contribution, and worse, we turn a performing economic asset into a potential liability. We also deny individuals the chance to remain active, learn and grow, feel valued, pay their way, and contribute to their communities.

Makes no sense, right? If Massachusetts and New England are to become the Longevity Hub, as proposed in this Globe Opinion series, the region can begin by changing the way we think about, value, and engage the talent of people over 50. A quarter are currently working, but many more want to work and can't find open doors. Half of all new businesses are started by people over 50, and they are twice as likely to succeed,[5] yet more aren't encouraged to open their own business. Nearly half of all volunteer hours are contributed by people over 50,[6] but that number could grow much larger—nearly three-quarters of those over 50 don't volunteer at all, a huge untapped opportunity. And about 40 percent are caregivers for grandchildren and other family members, enabling others to work, yet these contributions go unrecognized.

Massachusetts is fortunate to have an ecosystem in which a cross section of players from all sectors innovate and work collaboratively to assist people over 50. A distinctive twist on this collaboration is its focus on alternatives to traditional jobs. These include freelance, contract, remote, gig, and entrepreneurial roles. These forms of independent work are new to many people over 50, but they offer flexibility and autonomy, which many at this stage of life seek, while leveraging skills, experience, and connections. More than a third of all work now falls into this category, and this is an area of unrealized opportunity for older adults.

This Massachusetts ecosystem, and the broad array of initiatives it generates, lays a solid foundation for change. Here are some examples.

- Encore Boston Network brings together individuals, organizations, advocates, policymakers, researchers, and others around an explicit mission to leverage the assets of people over 50, a collaboration unique to the region.
- The 50+ Job Seekers Networking Groups, sponsored by Massachusetts Councils on Aging and funded by the Executive Office of Elder Affairs, tailors its programs to the specific needs of older workers statewide, a one-of-a-kind initiative.
- The Age-Friendly Institute, affiliated with Age-Friendly Ventures and RetirementJobs.com, based in Waltham, has pioneered Certified Age-Friendly Employers, enabling businesses that qualify to demonstrate their commitment to older workers. The AARP Employer Pledge, a related program, also invites employers to affirm the value of experience.
- Operation ABLE offers employment and training opportunities for job seekers from economically, racially, and occupationally diverse backgrounds, including older workers and the underemployed.
- Founders Over 55, a Massachusetts-based collective that has tripled in the past year, draws together resources like AGENCY, Cambridge Innovation Center, Encore Boston Network, and SCORE to provide support for older entrepreneurs.
- Discovery Centers for Civic Engagement, an innovative pilot program sponsored by the Massachusetts Councils on Aging, is

designed to connect older adults to nonprofit, municipal government, and other service opportunities in local communities.

- MSA Connects for Good, the most advanced volunteer engagement platform anywhere, enabling connection to age-appropriate service opportunities, was recently launched statewide by the Massachusetts Service Alliance.

- Fellowship programs offered by Conservation Law Foundation, Empower Success Corps, Lawyers Clearinghouse, and others connect senior-level professionals to a range of causes that benefit from their experience.

- Literations, a Massachusetts-based affiliate of AARP Foundation Experience Corps, brings the mentoring skills of older adults to bear on the literacy achievement gap in Boston public schools. This is one of several regional social action groups, and with support, more are possible.

With this solid foundation in place, there is much that can be done to fully integrate the "longevity dividend" of older workers and volunteers into the economy and society.

For example, employers should include age in their diversity, equity, and inclusion policies, demonstrating their intent to welcome older workers. We can help employers understand the benefits of hiring people over 50, but also the myths that too often stand in the way.

Protections against age discrimination have been weakened over time. They should be strengthened to give older workers a fair chance to challenge adverse employment decisions. Employers should drop age identifiers from job applications and change hiring practices that work against older job seekers. Employers must also understand the need for flexibility and other policy changes that address older-worker interests.

Covering transportation and other expenses, and investing in stipends and incentives, can make a difference for many who cannot otherwise afford to volunteer their talent. Commonwealth Corps and

AmeriCorps, intended to provide service opportunities for people of all ages, can be reshaped and grown to more effectively encourage intergenerational learning, connection, and contribution.

The state needs to explore ways, perhaps through tax credits, to recognize the work of family caregivers when it enables economic activity that would otherwise not be possible. Finally, there needs to be investment in the ecosystem to build an infrastructure through which people over 50 can learn about and take advantage of opportunities to contribute. With clear-eyed commitment, the state and region can make economic engagement of older adults a centerpiece of the Longevity Hub and a model for other states to follow.

Doug Dickson cofounded and served as board chair of Encore Boston Network.

## Notes

1. "What to Know about Emotional Health," WebMD, 2021, https://www.webmd.com/balance/what-to-know-about-emotional-health.

2. Colin A. Young, "Vaccine Makers Are Struggling with a Labor Shortage in Mass.," *Boston Globe*, July 28, 2021, https://www.bostonglobe.com/2021/07/28/business/vaccine-makers-are-struggling-with-labor-shortage-mass.

3. Abha Bhattarai, "Retail Workers in Their 60s, 70s and 80s Say They're Worried about Their Health—But Need the Money," *Washington Post*, October 25, 2012, https://www.washingtonpost.com/business/2020/03/30/retail-workers-their-60s-70s-80s-say-theyre-worried-about-their-health-need-money/.

4. "Certified Age Friendly Employer Program," Age-Friendly Institute, https://institute.agefriendly.org/initiatives/certified-age-friendly-employer-program/.

5. "2019 Small Business Trends Infographic," Guidant Financial, 2019, https://www.guidantfinancial.com/learning-center/infographics/2019-small-business-trends/.

6. "Giving in Retirement: America's Longevity Bonus," Merrill Lynch and Age Wave, 2015, https://agewave.com/what-we-do/landmark-research-and-consulting/research-studies/giving-in-retirement-americas-longevity-bonus/.

# 4
# Transportation

## Getting from Here to There

There is no single, technological silver bullet to transport elders, but that doesn't mean a more scattershot strategy couldn't work.

Joseph Coughlin

As spring gives way to summer and the country emerges from the coronavirus pandemic, with nearly two-thirds of adults having received at least one dose of a COVID-19 vaccine, Americans are eager for safe interactions beyond the confines of their households. To those who study how we live as we grow older, this drive for in-person connection offers a hint to a long-standing question: Can elder loneliness be solved with screens and virtual reality headsets alone? The answer is no. Video calls are a good social stopgap, but sooner or later most people need the real thing.

And that raises another question: If screens alone can't bring us together, what in the realm of mobility and transportation can do the job?

The United States is not prepared for a future when nearly 20 percent of the population is age 65 or over, and nearly a quarter of that group will not be able to drive. To make matters worse, older Americans live disproportionately[1] in rural and suburban locales where mass transit is scarce. The stakes involved are huge: nothing less than the physical and cognitive well-being of the fastest-growing segment of the population. Older adults' levels of isolation, depression, and general life satisfaction—and even the age at which they enter long-term care facilities—are all connected[2] to how easily they can get from point A to B.

Meanwhile, the seeming silver bullet offered by fully autonomous vehicles has turned out to be something of a dud. Massive technical challenges must be overcome before vehicles can operate at high speeds safely in all environments and weather conditions without someone in the driver's seat ready to take over at a moment's notice. That reality has proved so forbidding that a wave of consolidation[3] has recently washed over the autonomous vehicle industry.

It's not clear that the robo-taxi approach would have made that much of a dent in the elder transportation problem anyway. Older drivers often make the fraught decision to give up the keys not just out of the sense that it's the right time but also because a specific health issue forces their hand. Frequently, such issues necessitate more help than just the occasional ride—such as assistance with getting into and out of a vehicle and accompaniment during appointments or errands. In such cases, the hands-off nature of even the most flawless robo-taxi would not help vast swaths of the older, nondriving population.

But the lack of a single technological silver bullet doesn't mean a more scattershot strategy couldn't work. There is a quiver full of possible approaches—a number of which hail from New England. Investment in such strategies could meet the needs of different subpopulations of older adults, extending mobility across the age span.

Two new approaches that are viable now, with little change to physical or economic infrastructure, are the subject of other articles in today's Longevity Hub entry. Ryan Chin, cofounder of Boston's Optimus Ride, describes the company's autonomous vehicles, which, by limiting their operation to small, self-contained areas such as retirement communities, create the conditions for safe autonomous travel. Another promising idea, put forward by Independent Transportation Network America's founder Katherine Freund, involves an innovative approach for setting up a nationwide tech-supported network of volunteer drivers.

Beyond these approaches exist strategies that are technologically proven but call for renewed public investment. A reinvigorated approach to mass transit, for instance, with a strong commitment to accessibility, could increase the reach of transit into suburban locales while making it not just usable but inviting to those with disabilities. Consider, for instance, calls to adapt the MBTA's commuter lines to more resemble Munich's S-Bahn,[4] a rail system that operates with remarkable frequency thanks to its streamlined accessible station architecture and boarding procedures.

Another transportation option that many (albeit far from all) older adults rely on is the oldest mode of all: walking. A strong commitment to safe walkability—at all times of year, but especially during winter—when combined with mass transit and paratransit services would aid older residents.

Yet another approach would involve creating physical and regulatory infrastructure for small, low-speed electric vehicles. In several Sun Belt retirement communities, residents who feel uncomfortable operating a car have adopted golf carts as their primary mode of transportation. In such areas, every main road is flanked by cart paths. Meanwhile, environmentalists extol the low-emission, medium-distance travel made possible by electric bicycles.[5] Cities and towns around the nation could undergo an infrastructure push to make electric golf carts and e-bikes both a viable, safe way to get around, at least when the weather permits.

When considering the possibilities for elder transportation, it's important to keep in mind that the needs of older adults are diverse. One might find one innovation helpful but not another. The answer to such a variety of needs may be to think more broadly about what constitutes travel. Instead of approaching a given journey as a car or train trip, it may make sense to consider the merits of all conceivable transportation possibilities at once.

One promising approach involves combining different modes of transportation in one mobile app so that travelers can summon them or link them together as needed. This approach, known as Mobility as a Service, is still in its early days in the United States but has the potential to help people take advantage of new and even hidden transportation resources, from faith-based networks of volunteer drivers and area agencies on aging to idle school buses and airport vans. The ability to bring all assets to the table for older adults' transportation could prove transformational for how we live as we age.

Countries around the world are discovering how crucial it will be to keep their older adults physically connected with the rest of society. Answers to that need may prove to be among the most important outputs that our regional longevity hub can offer in the coming decades.

Joseph Coughlin is director of the AgeLab at the Center for Transportation and Logistics at MIT and author of *The Longevity Economy: Unlocking the World's Fastest-Growing, Most Misunderstood Market.*

## When It Comes to Autonomous Vehicles, Seniors Can Lead the Way

Retirement communities are relatively sheltered, low-speed environments that are ideal for autonomous vehicle transportation systems.

**Ryan Chin**

Senior citizens and new technologies haven't always mixed well. Setting up a mobile device or unboxing a new computer can be challenging for even those who have bridged the digital divide. While much of today's technology often feels out of reach for America's senior citizens, autonomous vehicles might be the breakthrough technology that enables seniors to easily and independently get from point A to point B without the worries of safety, security, and traffic.

Senior citizens operating their own vehicles can be dangerous to themselves and to others. Men ages 80 to 84 have one of the highest car crash death rates, according to the Insurance Institute for Highway Safety.[6] Elderly female drivers don't fare much better, experiencing only slightly lower fatality rates than male teenagers. Couple these alarming fatality rates with the knowledge that 94 percent[7] of these accidents are caused by human error and it becomes clear that seniors need better transportation options. Enter autonomous vehicles as the safer alternative to reduce crashes and fatalities. AVs are not programmed to drive over the speed limit, operate under the influence of alcohol or drugs, become distracted, get lost, fall asleep, or engage in road rage.

Independent living neighborhoods and retirement communities are well-suited for autonomous vehicle fleets to become a safe and easy-to-use mode of transportation. Boston-based Optimus Ride was founded with this application in mind. We are focused on delivering the fastest path to fully autonomous driving, and early on we identified campuses and similar localized communities as the optimal way to create safe, efficient, and equitable mobility for all. The path to widespread AV adoption is not without its technical, regulatory, and societal challenges such as equitable access; however, small communities, like retirement communities, present relatively sheltered, low-speed environments that are ideal for autonomous vehicle transportation systems to have a real impact. A community-based approach offers both safety benefits and the ability to customize the autonomous experience for the needs of the passengers. Optimus Ride has deployed fleets of autonomous multipassenger shuttles designed to be flexibly routed for individuals or small groups, providing mobility within the community. In many deployments, we provide "first- and last-mile" mobility, enabling riders to connect to transit systems to travel outside the community.

For example, when a fleet of AVs was deployed at Fairing Way, a 55-plus life-plan community at Union Point in South Weymouth, the senior community members were actively engaged and eager to ride. The key to rider engagement and adoption is developing an AV ride experience that is safe, simple, and easy for anyone to use. A typical senior-friendly rider experience entails booking a ride using a mobile phone app and having a range of times for any trip[8] as well as a convenient pickup/drop-off location within the community. In this case, the AV fleet then serves as a community shuttle, waiting as passengers enter and exit the vehicle.

Shortly after the fleet was deployed at Fairing Way, Optimus Ride found that the majority of the senior residents behaved as if they were being chauffeured by a professional limousine driver while in the AV. They either started using their cell phones, talked to other riders, or simply enjoyed being a passenger. Many senior riders became champions of the technology by advocating its use with other community members, friends, and family. Despite the perception that older Americans, and Americans in general, are hesitant to ride in AVs, early deployments of Optimus Ride in senior living communities have shown that demonstrations, education, and advocacy of AVs lead to acceptance and increased use by seniors.

The potential impact of AVs for anyone over the age of 65 is significant. The Census Bureau has projected that by 2035 approximately 78 million people in the United States will be 65 years or older,[9] and this population will exceed the total number of those under the age of 18. Additionally, the number of seniors living in 50-plus majority concentrations has tripled since 2000. By taking a thoughtful approach to how we as a society use autonomous vehicles, we can unlock the industry's advancement for senior citizens in their backyards.

The transformation of mobility systems will not happen over-night through some magical AV silver bullet for the silver genera-tion—there will be a period when human and robotic drivers will coexist. But this transition can be accelerated here in Boston—the hub of innovation for America.

Ryan Chin, who cofounded Optimus Ride, is the Cofounder and COO of TRAM.Global, a decarbonization technology company that measures and reduces carbon emissions for individuals and companies.

## Look to the Nonprofit Sector to Give Older Adults a Lift

The nonprofit sector may be ideally poised to take on the challenge of older-adult transportation, but the best solutions occur when all three sectors of the economy come together—government, industry, and nonprofit.

**Katherine Freund**

Transportation is the lifeblood of everyone's day-to-day activity. But if the blood supply for the nation's hospitals were provided the way transportation for the nation's aging population is organized, there would soon be lethal shortages. Both systems rely heavily on citizen volunteers, but there is a world of difference between them. Volun-teer blood donation is organized at the national level by a single nonprofit organization, the Red Cross, while volunteer efforts to drive older adults are organized one community at a time. Across America, older adults are struggling to find rides for health care, shopping, and basic socialization.

People who stop driving tend to outlive their decision by about a decade,[10] and when they do stop driving, their lives change. The majority of older Americans live in rural or suburban communities[11] that lack the density for traditional mass transportation. When public transit is available, the same functional changes that make driving difficult make public transit equally challenging. What family in America has not worried about a loved one who treasures the independence afforded by driving but is in danger of hurting themselves, or others, and needs to let go of the keys? For many older drivers, it is a Hobson's choice, deciding between driving unsafely or becoming dependent on favors from family and friends.

The problem is neither small nor inexpensive. By 2030, there will be 61 million baby boomers ages 68 to 84, for whom transportation costs, accounting for 17 percent of household expenditures,[12] will be second only to housing. Will the federal government pay for the rides of older adults who stop driving? According to the Congressional Budget Office,[13] mandatory public spending for people ages 65 or older grew from 5.8 percent of Gross Domestic Product in 2005 to 7.5 percent in 2018, to a projected 9.8 percent in 2029. Mandatory spending for older adults amounted to roughly $1.5 trillion in fiscal 2018, about 85 percent of which was for Social Security and Medicare. Will the public accept adding the cost of transportation to this total?

What about a private-sector solution? Can older adults rely on for-profit services like taxis, Uber, and Lyft? A recent environmental scan of senior ride-hailing services available for older Americans,[14] funded by the Centers for Disease Control and Prevention, found that 70 percent of rides performed by Uber and Lyft were limited to just nine densely populated cities,[15] including New York and San Francisco, and only 4 percent of riders were age 65 and older. Moreover, the independent-contractor labor model used by for-profit ride-hailing companies prohibits them from directing drivers to provide any of the assistance so many older adults require, whether it is an arm to lean on for balance, help carrying packages, or folding a walker.

The nonprofit sector, however, has advantages the for-profit sector lacks. Nonprofits can operate where it's not profitable for an Uber or Lyft to serve. Nonprofits are not constrained by market forces to serve only densely populated areas, and they succeed in rural and suburban areas in great part because labor is the largest expense in transit, and nonprofits can leverage the invaluable efforts of volunteer drivers.

What's missing is a unifying nonprofit organization at the national level. Just as the US Armed Forces asked the Red Cross to create and operate a national blood donor program in World War II,[16] our country should create a national volunteer driver program to mobilize Americans to give an older person a ride. With current pent-up demand for access to health care and services as we emerge from the confines of the coronavirus pandemic, now is the time.

The nonprofit sector may be ideally poised to take on the challenge of older-adult transportation, but the best solutions to unmet needs occur when all three sectors of the economy come together— government, industry, and nonprofit. New England is already home to one such convening force: the organization I founded more than 25 years ago, ITNAmerica, which provides technology, research, and operational support to help local nonprofits meet the mobility needs of older adults. Cars and volunteer miles may be traded for credits to pay for future rides. With its specialized software, ITN was specifically designed and built for older adults and people with visual impairments, but it can serve any adult with special needs, with volunteer drivers stowing folding wheelchairs and rolling walkers into trucks and backseats. As a volunteer driver in Portland, Maine, I earned credits, which I transferred to my mother's ITN account in Connecticut, where another volunteer drove her. In 2005, we rolled out nationally as ITNAmerica, and by 2018, we had delivered a million rides.

Developed through research support from the Federal Transit Administration, technology support from two of the world's largest technology companies, Esri and Salesforce, and philanthropic support from dozens of foundations, ITNAmerica's cloud-based platform is now poised to scale to meet the growing need for affordable rides. All that is needed is a national effort to recruit safe, trained volunteers. It can work.

Americans numbering in the millions volunteer to lie down and give their blood away each year. Surely they can also be inspired to give someone's mother a ride.

Katherine Freund is founder and president of ITNAmerica.

## Notes

1. John Cromartie, "Rural Aging Occurs in Different Places for Very Different Reasons," U.S. Department of Agriculture, December 20, 2018, https://www.usda.gov /media/blog/2018/12/20/rural-aging-occurs-different-places-very-different-reasons.

2. Laura Fraade-Blanar, et al, "Older Adults, New Mobility, and Automated Vehicles," AARP, February 2021, https://www.aarp.org/content/dam/aarp/ppi/2021/02 /older-adults-new-mobility-automated-vehicles.doi.10.26419-2Fppi.00132.001 .pdf.

3. Andrew J. Hawkins, "The Autonomous Vehicle World is Shrinking—It's Overdue," *The Verge*, May 7, 2021, https://www.theverge.com/22423489/autonomous -vehicle-consolidation-acquisition-lyft-uber.

4. Christof Spieler, "Ideas, Not Just Infrastructure: What the US Could Learn from the Munich S-Bahn," *Trains Buses People*, August 5, 2018, https://www.trainsbuses people.org/blog/2018/8/5/ideas-not-just-infrastructure-what-the-us-could-learn -from-the-munich-s-bahn.

5. David Zipper, "E-Bikes for Everyone!," *Slate*, February 25, 2021, https://slate.com /technology/2021/02/e-bikes-act-electric-bicycles-subsidy.html.

6. "Fatality Facts 2021: Older People," IIHS HLDI, May 2023, https://www.iihs.org /topics/fatality-statistics/detail/older-people.

7. "Traffic Safety Facts," U.S. Department of Transportation, February 2015, https:// crashstats.nhtsa.dot.gov/Api/Public/ViewPublication/812115.

8. Joseph Coughlin and Luke Yoquinto, "Boston: The Silicon Valley of Longevity?," *Boston Globe*, February 15, 2021, https://www.bostonglobe.com/2021/02/15 /opinion/boston-can-become-longevity-hub.

9. William E. Gibson, "Age 65+ Adults Are Projected to Outnumber Children by 2030," AARP, March 14, 2018, https://www.aarp.org/home-family/friends-family /info-2018/census-baby-boomers-fd.html.

10. Daniel J. Foley, Harley K. Heimovitz, Jack M. Guralnik, and Dwight B. Brock, "Driving Life Expectancy of Persons Aged 70 Years and Older in the United States," NIH, August 2002, https://www.ncbi.nlm.nih.gov/pmc/articles/PMC1447231/.

11. Alexander Hermann, "More Older Adults Are Living in Lower-Density Neighborhoods," JCHS, January 7, 2019, https://www.jchs.harvard.edu/blog/more-older -adults-are-living-in-lower-density-neighborhoods.

12. "Consumer Expenditures—2021," U.S. Bureau of Labor Statistics, September 8, 2022, https://www.bls.gov/news.release/cesan.nr0.htm.

13. Government Publications Office, *Budget and Economic Outlook 2019 to 2029.* "The Budget and Economic Outlook: 2019 to 2029," U.S. Congressional Budget Office (Government Printing Office, 2019).

14. "Environmental Scan of Ride Share Services Available for Older Adults," NORC, December 5, 2019, https://cdn-west-prod-chhs-01.dsh.ca.gov/chhs/uploads/2020 /02/NORC_ITN_OlderAdultRideshareEnvironmental-Scan_Final_12.2.19-c.pdf.

15. "The New Automobility: Lyft, Uber and the Future of American Cities," Schaller Consulting, July 25, 2018, http://www.schallerconsult.com/rideservices/automo bility.pdf.

16. "From WWII to Today: Blood Services Helps Patients across the U.S.," American Red Cross, March 19, 2018, https://www.redcross.org/about-us/news-and-events /news/2018/From-WWII-to-Today-Blood-Services-Helps-Patients-Across-the-US.html.

# 5
# Innovation

## Collaboration Should Focus on Health, Wealth, and Self

All three are inextricably interconnected and factor fully into how people think about their futures.

Jo Ann Jenkins

Since 2020, the world has been turned upside down by the COVID-19 pandemic. But 2020 also marked another milestone that will change our world: The number of people 65 and older outnumbered children under age 5 for the first time in history.[1] And this is just the beginning.

Over the next two decades, the number of people aged 65 and older will nearly double to more than 72 million[2]—or one in five Americans. And most 65-year-olds today will live into their nineties. Some researchers believe that the first person who will ever live to 150 is alive today.[3]

Aging is about much more than demographics. More and more, people are embracing age as a period of continued growth.

Instead of seeing only retirees, we're beginning to see a new type of experienced, accomplished workforce. Instead of seeing older people as a drain on society, we're witnessing an exploding consumer market that is bolstering the economy. And instead of seeing a growing pool of dependents, we're seeing the growth of intergenerational communities with new and different strengths.

However, many of the products and services and systems that support us as we age (e.g., those pertaining to living independently, health care, retirement planning, and caregiving) were designed for a twentieth-century lifestyle and don't adequately support the way we live today, nor do they reflect the advances in technology that allow us to live better as we grow older.

What can business and social organizations do not only to help people achieve and afford enriching lives but also to help them thrive as they age? How can they create solutions that help people live better throughout their lives? The answer, as with so many of the profound challenges our society faces, is innovation. But unless businesses and organizations overcome outdated attitudes and stereotypes about aging, they may miss out on a multitude of opportunities to create innovative products and services for a growing and influential market segment.

They can focus on three areas—health, wealth, and self. Health refers to innovating solutions that empower us to take better care of ourselves and our loved ones and to have access to affordable, high-quality care that enables longer, healthier lives. Wealth is about creating solutions that empower us to earn, save, manage, and protect financial resources to support longer lifespans. And self is about empowering people to enjoy their longer lifespans and live fulfilling and satisfying lives, by creating opportunities for them to build and maintain social connections and engage with their communities and the broader world.

Crucially, although a given product or company might fit into just one of these categories, all three are inextricably interconnected.

They factor fully into how people think about their futures—where they're going to live, how they're going to get around, how they're going to stay connected to their friends and family, how they're going to get health care and long-term care when they need it, how they're going to make their money last.

That's why collaboration among people and organizations who look beyond the stereotypes and apply an interdisciplinary approach to solutions is so important. This type of communication across sectors can lead to solutions that one organization or company may not create on its own. For example, it leads to technological advances that bring smart technologies into the home to assist individuals in living independently longer in those homes, monitoring and managing their daily activities, and keeping them connected to family and friends to avoid becoming isolated. It leads to more imaginative uses of digital technology for self-care—wearables for monitoring and tracking vital signs, online support communities, health care navigators or care coordinators to help manage older adults' health care and facilitate long-distance caregiving. And it leads communities to develop comprehensive strategies to change their physical infrastructure and the way they deliver services, including housing and transportation services, to make communities more livable and age-friendly.

At AARP, we created AARP Innovation Labs to help shape the future of aging, promote healthy aging, support family caregivers, and help older Americans build financial resilience and combat social isolation. Through our own research and collaborations with technology companies, startups, and entrepreneurs, we created products such as Alcove VR and HomeFit AR to foster virtual reality family connections and enable age-ready home improvements, respectively, to help people live better as they age.

Innovation will be the key to helping people take advantage of generally longer and healthier lives in the coming years and decades. Empowering innovators and, just as crucially, establishing a medium where they can communicate with one another and their consumers, is critical to ensuring that this inventive energy truly makes a difference in helping people live better as they age.

We also match them with testbeds—businesses and organizations that want to provide an environment to help startups test solutions—where they have the opportunity to translate data into actionable insights in order to determine product efficacy, usability, or market fit for fostering solutions to aging issues including caregiving, chronic illness management, social isolation, housing, and more. For example, the Massachusetts eHealth Institute supports pilots and clinical trials at its Digital Health Sandbox Network sites, allowing companies focused on digital health to test-validate their solutions in the real world and develop the evidence they need to accelerate growth.

Innovation will be the key to helping people take advantage of generally longer and healthier lives in the coming years and decades. Empowering innovators, and, just as crucially, establishing a medium where they can communicate with one another, and their consumers, is critical to ensuring that this inventive energy truly makes a difference in helping people live better as they age.

Jo Ann Jenkins is CEO of AARP.

## What We Need as Entrepreneurs

We are only at the beginning of an agetech boom here in Boston. As we continue, there are a few critical gaps that must be filled.

**Kyle Rand**

With 56 percent of total American spending coming from those over the age of 50, the growth of older adults' sphere of economic influence, known as the Longevity Economy,[4] is so substantial that forecasters refer to it as a megatrend.[5] It is set to fundamentally overhaul the way we think about and plan for the future, both as individuals and as a society, and Boston is poised to become the epicenter of the longevity-focused innovation that the modern world needs.

As an entrepreneur in this space, I've never been more excited about the future. Within Greater Boston, industries are aligning and talking about the future of aging. Government officials are speaking and acting on behalf of this demographic, building infrastructure and policy approaches that will empower a healthier aging population. Startups and cutting-edge technology firms are building purpose-driven technology that includes robotics, artificial intelligence, and virtual reality (my area of expertise, through the work we do at my company, Rendever). Crucially, Boston boasts one of the most forward-thinking healthcare hubs in the world, which has adopted a proactive approach to working with these startups and industry partners to create a better future for all.

That dedication is starting to come to fruition. Five years ago, it was almost impossible for a longevity entrepreneur to have a conversation with a venture capitalist and walk away feeling they had a strong grasp of the profound opportunities posed by aging, as opposed to just the challenges. And one couldn't even fault them; the longevity industry was still in its early days, and people everywhere had poor societal appreciation for the aging demographic (an issue that still desperately needs to be overcome). There were, however, plenty of investors casually interested in the longevity space, if only because the financial projections were clear: There would be too many older people, bearing too much wealth for the longevity economy not to be worth a bet or two.

But those early bets were limited by the fact that there were few success cases to point to. Worse, the best-known products aimed at older people were boring: designed for ease of use, not beauty or elegance. Complicating matters, many players involved in the medical side of things were relying on Medicare funding, which made it harder to take a startup to "exit"—that is, to an acquisition or IPO. Few large players were interested in purchasing scrappy startups building the new industries powering the longevity economy. And so the question remained: What would it take to demonstrate how truly powerful—and profitable—it could be to innovate for this burgeoning consumer demographic?

The good news is that, as more innovators look to join in, Boston boasts a strong backbone capable of supporting them. There is a growing community of entrepreneurs with a deep understanding of the intricacies of needs of different groups of aging individuals.

We are only at the beginning of an agetech boom here in Boston. As we continue, there are a few critical gaps that must be filled. A new sort of startup incubator is necessary—one that goes beyond the industry-standard support for early stage growth and brings the aging (or caregiving) end-user to the forefront. It would be a community space that nurtures agetech startups while offering community services to the local aging population: an open, physical location for idea flow, product feedback, and organic community building. Founders would benefit from the chance to engage with and learn from the demographic they're designing for, and older adults would get the opportunity to air their desires for products, which would help eager innovators navigate around outdated stereotypes about what older adults want and need. A modern, open space for multiple generations to come together around technology and community life would permit people across age groups to share space, interact, and enjoy life.

Finally, we can't talk about fueling the fire of aging innovation without mentioning the most standard form of economic fuel: financing. The number of active, aging-specific venture firms is still dismally low, and that needs to change. There's a big opportunity for a major venture firm to land in Boston and take ownership of this unique opportunity. We ultimately need to create a collective understanding where "longevity" takes hold as a modern buzz-word—a conceptual lodestar keeping innovators focused on building a better old age. The next step in this process comes down to providing dedicated structural support. We need the dedicated space and the dedicated investors. These gaps are waiting to be filled by individuals and firms aligned with the mission of making the world a better place to age. If that's you, I invite you to pay our community a visit. What you find here may amaze you.

Kyle Rand is cofounder and CEO of Rendever.

## For Insight, Look to Older Entrepreneurs

They have profound insights into the unmet needs of the aging population.

**Danielle D. Duplin**

A growing number of late-career adults are opting for a new path: entrepreneurship.[6] The appeal is twofold: to build something meaningful—and just as important, to design a work life that works for them.

To help companies improve the aging journey, a cross-sector group of Boston business leaders formed AGENCY: Worldwide Innovation for Living Longer and Aging Better. We launched AGENCY at the Cambridge Innovation Center with a seed grant from the Baker-Polito administration to help forge a larger longevity-centered innovation hub in New England.[7] We knew the trillion-dollar global agetech market opportunity would pique the interest of entrepreneurs. What we didn't know was just how strongly older adults themselves would be drawn to the work.

Many are leveraging Boston's robust startup resources to help lift their new ventures. Peter Nash, an expert in team-building, and Susanne Greelish, an experienced food-industry rep, met at an AGENCY event and cofounded Ginger Gems, a healthy snack company they are incubating at Commonwealth Kitchen in Dorchester.

Some founders retired from their first careers only to plunge back into action, itching to fix a problem or turn their passion projects into income-producing businesses. Daria Myers and Robin Albin, for example, left their senior executive roles in the cosmetics industry to launch Everlusting, a brand that reframes beauty with a line of desirable sensorial products for "unstoppable women of a certain age."

To support and amplify this powerhouse of untapped potential, AGENCY convened the Founders Over 55 Collective (F55+). The group quickly bloomed to 400-and-growing members who tune in for virtual panel discussions, skill-building, and networking. F55+ members are unabashedly reinventing themselves as entrepreneurs despite the prevailing ageist stereotypes that startups are the purview of the young.

Older founders are breaking the mold of the idolized tech-founder persona—one who is so obsessed with their venture that they miss out on life. Instead, they are maintaining balanced lifestyles while doing what they've always wanted to do—and getting paid to do it.

For example, Ross Ozer's early retirement package gave him the runway to launch RJOStudiosCo to sell his own handcrafted home décor and men's fashions on Etsy. This financial services senior executive turned maker now has the scheduling freedom to also pursue his other passions for travel and theater.

Another advantage that older entrepreneurs enjoy is a lifetime of business relationships. Dianne Austin endured chemo treatment while working full-time at a hospital. Dismayed that no wigs matched her "beautiful Afro kinky curly hair," she and her sister launched Coils to Locs to offer diverse wigs via Dianne's connections with hospital gift shops and address a healthcare disparity for women of color.

That said, ageism challenges still exist. Older entrepreneurs who are uncomfortable in risking their own nest eggs and finding venture capital unwilling to bet on them, do spend considerable time seeking alternate sources of funding. Cash prizes from incubators and early wins from special interest groups have otherwise helped some jumpstart their businesses.

Julie Lineberger and her architect husband designed an accessible home addition after her godson became paralyzed. Veterans groups took note, and Julie launched WheelPad L3C to make her ADA-compliant Personal Accessible Dwellings that allow people with mobility challenges to live at home in comfort and dignity. Julie earned the top prize at AGENCY's Pitchfest for Vitality with AARP Innovation Labs and now, at 64, she is ramping up production to meet WheelPad's pandemic-fueled growth as an alternative to nursing homes.

Other seasoned founders parlay Small Business Innovation Research grants and collaborations with larger partners to increase their visibility for add-on funding. Jayanthi Narasimham, a tech expert in Boston, was concerned about her mother's declining health in India, 8,000 miles away. At 60, she is working with geriatricians to pilot WatchRx, her agetech wristband that allows eldercare teams to remotely manage medication reminders, monitor geofence wandering, and track vital signs.

Regardless of their motivation, company size, or business model, people who start a business later in life consider their age to be an asset and when mixed with a powerful cocktail of ambition, restlessness, savvy, networks, and life experiences, it can lead to entrepreneurial success and personal satisfaction.

The wellspring of talent in this cohort cannot be ignored. The economic impact of their contributions cannot be discounted. The mental health benefits that come from sustaining a growth mindset, social connections, and meaningful work at their own discretion cannot be underestimated.

Let's not marginalize the value of older founders or block their path with outdated ageist mindsets. Instead, let's ensure our business ecosystem welcomes age diversity as a bedrock of innovation and belonging. Hire them, buy from them, partner with them, fund them, be them. You just might catch a glimpse of your own future of running a business—and a life—you love.

Danielle D. Duplin is a cofounder of AGENCY: Worldwide Innovation for Living Longer and Aging Better and cofounder of the Founders Over 55 Collective.

## The Barriers to Innovation

Successful aging-market solutions require an interdisciplinary approach, drawing on expertise in software, medicine, biology, finance, policy, and beyond.

**Joseph Chung**

The innovation economy has produced countless disruptions and revolutions in how we consume everything from news to noodles, while creating unprecedented returns along the way for entrepreneurs and investors. Yet relatively little of this energy and capital has focused on the senior care and longevity markets. We're starting to see that change, however—and Boston can become the critical hub where the world's longevity innovation ecosystem will develop.

Boston, with its undisputed position as the life sciences capital of the world, owes a large part of its reigning biological status to the computer startup ecosystem that came first. Long before Kendall Square began measuring lab space by the millions of square feet (and measuring lives saved by the millions as well, thanks to Moderna's COVID-19 vaccine), Boston had already nurtured a virtuous cycle spanning three essential components: a multitude of world-class research universities developing new breakthroughs, a spectrum of innovative companies driving commercialization and acquisitions, and venture capital willing to take significant risks to achieve outsized rewards. These elements continue to attract and retain the most valuable resource of all: a vibrant community of talented innovators.

However, successful innovation in longevity requires an extra ingredient, owing not only to the complexities of the human body and mind as they age, but also the byzantine and counterintuitive nature of almost every aspect of the care delivery and payment systems. Successful aging-market solutions require an interdisciplinary approach, drawing on expertise in software, medicine, biology, finance, policy, and beyond.

There are still barriers to cementing Boston's role as the world's longevity innovation hub. First, awareness of the magnitude of the opportunity is still low. For example, the United States spends over $1 trillion annually—nearly 5 percent of GDP—to care for seniors through a system that has existed largely unchanged for decades.[8] Furthermore, the senior population is the wealthiest in history, with a total net worth of over $40 trillion. Longevity is perhaps the last and largest undisrupted market on the planet.

Second, because so much of the longevity market is administered by federal and state governments, the longevity industry needs to include innovators in administration, regulation, and legislation in our entrepreneurial and investment ecosystem. Many fortunes have been made by using technology to outpace regulation—bypassing taxi rules, for example, while enabling strangers to drive each other around for money, or sidestepping hostelry laws while permitting strangers to rent out rooms to each other. Aging, however, is so complex, and the role of government in ensuring safe products and services so all-permeating (and so necessary), that reengineering aging will require a more cooperative, regulation-sensitive approach—for example, integrating the informal, family-delivered home care system with the formal system of hospitals, clinicians, and insurance companies by developing data sharing pathways so that a senior's doctor can see exactly how their patient has been eating, sleeping, moving, and managing in between visits.

I recently encountered an example of such cooperation through the state-run MassVentures Start Program. Kinto, the agetech startup where I am CEO, was awarded major grants from the National Institutes of Health through the Small Business Innovation Research program to develop a digital therapy for families coping with Alzheimer's. However, these funds could not be used for sales or marketing expenses, which presented a challenge for us in finding the money to bring our innovations to market. Fortunately, MassVentures developed a grant program specifically for SBIR winners to address this specific gap, while also providing its grantees access to mentorship and advice. As intended, we've been successfully applying those dollars to develop relationships with our local powerhouse health systems and senior care agencies.

The final missing ingredient is a commodity that is paradoxically both plentiful and scarce: money. Despite the recent record levels of venture investment in Boston, disrupting a new market such as longevity requires taking new risks and embracing long timeframes of uncertainty. For all of Boston's many advantages, we still carry the vestiges of our risk-averse puritanical past, and we tend toward conservatism in our investing even when we are bold at everything else.

The longevity market can change that. The pumps are primed and the engine is running. We still need buy-in from innovators in sectors, particularly local and federal government, which have not traditionally participated in early venture creation. But the talent we need is readily, locally available. So is insight into the complexities of later life. The last, critical accelerant for Boston's longevity innovation hub is a Silicon Valley level of visionary capital.

Major investors must put their money where their future is. Only that will enable longevity innovators to address the challenges, and opportunities, of what is literally the market of a lifetime.

Joseph Chung is a cofounder and CEO of Kinto and cofounder and managing director of Redstar Ventures.

## Notes

1. Kelsey Nowakowski, "There Are Now More People over Age 65 than under Five—What That Means," National Geographic, July 14, 2019, https://www.nationalgeo graphic.co.uk/history-and-civilisation/2019/07/there-are-now-more-people-over -age-65-than-under-five-what-that-means.

2. Barbara Gabriel, "By 2040, One in Five Americans Will Be over Age 65," AARP, May 7, 2018, https://www.aarp.org/politics-society/history/info-2018/older-popula tion-increase-new-report.html.

3. John Nosta, "The First Person to Live to 150 Has Already Been Born—Revisited!," Forbes, February 3, 2013, https://www.forbes.com/sites/johnnosta/2013/02/03/the -first-person-to-live-to-150-has-already-been-born-revisited/?sh=5b8bb48059b9.

4. Joseph F. Coughlin, *The Longevity Economy: Unlocking the World's Fastest-Growing, Most Misunderstood Market* (New York: PublicAffairs, 2017).

5. Lan Ha, "How Ageing Populations and Rising Longevity Drive Megatrends," Euromonitor International, September 11, 2019, https://www.euromonitor.com /article/how-ageing-populations-and-rising-longevity-drive-megatrends.

6. Matthew Pozel, "The New Adventures of Older Entrepreneurs," Ewing Marion Kauffman Foundation, August 15, 2019, https://www.kauffman.org/currents/the -new-adventures-of-older-entrepreneurs/.

7. Robert Weisman, "In with the Old, and in with the New," *Boston Globe*, March 3, 2019, https://www.bostonglobe.com/business/2019/03/03/startups-focusing-aging -have-home-new-kendall-square-incubator/a5mwgtbAM67nfXwQicjqwM/story.html.

8. "NHE Fact Sheet," Centers for Medicare & Medicaid Services, 2021, https:// www.cms.gov/Research-Statistics-Data-and-Systems/Statistics-Trends-and-Reports /NationalHealthExpendData/NHE-Fact-Sheet.

# 6
# Caregiving

## I Became a Caregiver in My Late Twenties—and Found Little Support to Guide Me

My employer offered no voluntary benefits for family caregivers and less than half of the paid leave it offered to new parents. The best professional advice I found was helpful, but expensive.

**Libby Brittain**

I became a family caregiver the way Ernest Hemingway described how you go bankrupt: gradually, then suddenly.

My mother—a reliably energetic and independent person who had for years run a thriving legal practice—had changed. She sounded agitated and overwhelmed. She stopped wearing makeup or seeing friends. She was suddenly disorganized, asking me the same questions over and over and writing my answers down on sticky notes.

I moved home from New York City to San Francisco to support her—being careful to protect my job in the high-growth technology industry, nervous about the impact that I knew family caregiving roles can have on women's careers. Right away, I discovered that her daily life was much more chaotic than it seemed from afar: There were errands that needed to be run, clothes that needed to be organized, and bills that needed to be paid. These tasks—and dozens of others that I'd soon learn were called "activities of daily living"—became my responsibilities.

Eventually, I realized that what I had suspected was a mild depression was actually dementia. I added "care coordination" tasks to my list of responsibilities, including researching diagnosis and treatment options, organizing her insurance information, and securing a spot on new-patient waiting lists at several neurology clinics. My mother was finally diagnosed with early onset Alzheimer's disease a few months after she turned 65.

I became a caregiver in my late twenties—around the same age many women become mothers. And so I expected to receive at least some of the support that many of my friends and colleagues did when they took on their new role as a parent. I expected family and friends to rush in, eager to pitch in however they could. I expected my employer to offer voluntary benefits like care navigation services and several months of paid time off. I expected to find dozens of books, podcasts, and experts who could answer my complex medical, legal, financial, and emotional questions. Most of all, I expected insurance—either my mother's or mine—to cover most of the cost of her care.

Instead, I learned that family caregivers suffer from many of the same gaps in our caregiving infrastructure that parents do—and get even less support.

Friends and family felt uncomfortable talking about caregiving and its taboo themes of death and money. My employer offered no voluntary benefits for family caregivers and less than half of the paid leave it offered to new parents. The best professional advice I found from estate-law attorneys and care managers was helpful, but it was also expensive—and Google searches turned up few expert voices I could rely on in the way my parent-friends relied on Emily Oster or Taking Cara Babies. Last, Medicare hasn't covered even $1 of the cost of my mother's four years at a memory care senior living facility in Phoenix, which costs over $80,000 per year.

Most importantly, I learned that even though I felt lonely, I wasn't alone. I'm only one of more than 40 million Americans— over a quarter of whom are millennials like me—who spend an average of $7,000 per year out of pocket providing unpaid care for an adult like their aging parent or spouse.[1]

Over time, I've shared my caregiving story with hundreds of others in person and over the internet. Many of them have confided that they, too, are surprised by how little support they've been offered by their communities, their employers, and their governments. The same questions come up among family caregivers: Where are the trusted products and services that offer holistic support for our caregiving responsibilities? Where are the modern brands that show up with humility and authenticity, treating us like capable caregivers and smart consumers? And why didn't anyone prepare us for this?

These conversations showed me that I had an opportunity to combine my professional background as a technologist with my personal experience as a caregiver to build a new piece of caregiving infrastructure.

Now I'm the founder of a venture-backed company called Quilt. We are creating a new source of trusted information and support that will accompany family caregivers throughout their caregiving journey. Our first product—a library of expert-led videos taught by physicians, attorneys, and other professionals—will be available to caregivers later this year.

Every caregiver knows they aren't *just* a caregiver. Caregivers are also spouses, parents, siblings, friends, and colleagues. I would add another important identity to that list: Caregivers are consumers. Millennials start to turn 40 this year, a new decade that will bring new caregiving responsibilities for my generation along with it. I believe we will look to the marketplace to deliver long-term services and supports that are thoughtful, proactive, and community led—the kind of products and services we can increasingly find in other consumer categories.

My generation's expectations are clear. Now it's up to us to build the modern caregiving infrastructure we are looking for—and that we all deserve.

Libby Brittain founded and served as CEO of Carol, a technology company whose goal was to build a modern support system for America's 40-plus-million family caregivers.

## In the Face of an Eldercare Crisis

The number of people needing care is far outpacing the number of available care workers.

**Sheila Lirio Marcelo and Wayne Ysaguirre**

Care for the elderly in Massachusetts is in crisis. Recent research by the Care Institute—a national nonprofit focused on improving the nation's care infrastructure—reinforced what we already knew: Increasing longevity, a fragmented approach to the way elder care is provided across the nation, and a complex and confusing payment system are accelerating the care gap. Addressing these complex issues is key to rebuilding the economy after the coronavirus pandemic.

By 2050, 26 million people—one in twelve Americans—will need paid elderly care, according to the Family Caregiver Alliance.[2] The pandemic has acted as an accelerant, driving a spike in unmet needs. As demand for home and community-based services increases, the supply of care is inadequate. Many care workers have left their jobs due to home demands, safety concerns, health issues, increased unemployment benefits, and alternative employment. In a May 2021 survey of their member organizations, Mass Home Care found that 3,600 people were waiting to be matched with a home care worker.

All states face workforce challenges providing direct elder care, but Massachusetts' high cost of living makes its need pronounced. Its median direct care worker annual earnings of $21,550 are just $1,350 above the national average. This leaves 54 percent of caregivers reliant on public assistance—12 percent higher than nationally. Despite the focus on diversity, the care workforce remains 84 percent female (86 percent nationally) and 57 percent people of color (59 percent nationwide).[3]

Structural issues cloud the picture. Medicaid's focus on those living in poverty has produced adverse implications for the wider population's access to long-term services. People living longer while managing chronic health conditions and limited resources puts increasing strain on the system, while the wider long-term care support system is overcomplicated and inadequate. Multiple programs within Medicaid vary in system design and eligibility, and the Department of Veterans Affairs, Older Americans Act, non-Medicaid state programs, and the Medicare Advantage Plan form a complex matrix. Traditional Medicaid doesn't cover long-term care, while a lack of alignment has led to a complex network of payment, eligibility, supply, and demand.

Challenges remain in scaling elderly home care as a full-time profession. While care may be available in two-hour increments three times a week, it's virtually impossible for an aide to craft a 40-hour week. The work is hugely fragmented in different locations; travel expenses are usually not reimbursed; and making a career across the various systems is challenging. While an estimated 4.6 million people nationally provide services through government-funded programs, another 800,000 serve the private care market, which has little regulation and few certification requirements or integrity-of-service provision measures.

Addressing this crisis is imperative. Massachusetts is investing in innovative ways to create advancement opportunities, address critical needs, and improve the viability and image of elderly care occupations. It has pioneered free online training for entry-level occupations under its Personal and Home Care Aide State Training program and offers enhanced training for home care aides working with Alzheimer's patients or those patients with mental health or social isolation issues. However, several crucial gaps need to be addressed.

## Standards-Setting and Alignment

At present, a certified home health aide with years of experience is unable to provide that same level of care in a nursing home without completing nurse aide certification. Revising this system could provide tremendous benefits to workers, employers, and patients, at significant cost savings.

## National Certification

The concept of a "universal aide," or standardized American elder-care worker, has gained limited traction due to the siloed nature of America's long-term care system, but it could be a start to professionalizing the occupation and providing better workforce opportunities. While Massachusetts stakeholders have expressed interest in developing a certification, few are getting into the details of making it happen.

## Pipeline Development Strategy

Too few people see direct care as a viable employment option. In Wisconsin, the WisCaregiver Careers initiative is mounting a multimedia campaign aimed at recruiting and training 3,000 new workers. Massachusetts should do the same.

## Support from Business and Citizens

Paid family leave, flexible work accommodations, and affordable and reliable childcare and eldercare services require a professionalized sector with family-sustaining wages, training, and support; advancement opportunities; and healthcare benefits. Businesses and citizens can play a key role in getting the state and federal government to overhaul the system.

One innovation could be a Care Worker Bill of Rights, similar to the one that Senator Elizabeth Warren proposed for essential workers during the pandemic. Adapted for the care workforce, it could include health-and-safety precautions, collective bargaining, financial protections against food and housing insecurity, and job security reclassification.

Massachusetts and America need a professionalized care sector. These challenging times offer a perfect opportunity to provide one.

Sheila Lirio Marcelo is the CEO and co-founder of Ohai.ai, and the founder of Care.com. Wayne Ysaguirre is chief of workforce innovation at the CAYL Institute.

## Bringing Home Care Up to Scale

Home care is a growing but fragmented industry. It needs to scale up along with the generation it serves.

Seth Sternberg

If there's one concept the baby boomer generation is intimately familiar with, it's going big. They've been doing everything big—"at scale," as folks like to say in the tech industry—their entire lives: entering school, joining the workforce, marrying, retiring, and now, aging. Per the US Census,[4] 10,000 of them have turned 65 every day since 2010. By 2030, the youngest among them will be over 65.

It's on us to serve our largest generation as they enter this final phase of their lives. And compassionate and demographically savvy small business owners are answering the call. Over 20,000 nonmedical home care businesses are currently operating independently in the United States. That's also the challenge. It's a highly fragmented market with many ways of operating. Technology can help streamline operations, standardize care, and provide better jobs to caregivers and better care to older adults.

Running a home care agency is hard. Agencies face enormous responsibility for their clients, providing assistance with activities of daily living like preparing meals, going for walks, or even getting in and out of bed. They're also responsible for creating quality employment for their caregivers in homes where they can perform at their best. The fragmented state of the industry makes this harder. If an agency could scale its business, it could provide caregivers with enough hours, working with clients whose needs best match their skill sets, schedules, and geographic locations. But they can't scale without enough caregivers. And caregivers can't stick around without stable employment. If a client cancels service, the caregiver probably will be forced to find another agency to fill the hours they need. It's a classic catch-22.

The answer is technology that can help a care agency find the right client for a caregiver's particular skills and help fill that caregiver's schedule. Do that well—care for the caregiver—and agencies will be able to better care for their clients.

That was what my cofounders and I set out to do when we started Honor. At our core, we're a service company. We develop technology to strengthen the relationships between our caregivers—we call ours care professionals—and clients. Technology helps us learn which caregivers are right for which clients, and vice versa. We ask care professionals for their preferences up front, and learn over time where they perform best and what clients respond well to. Our technology then helps us consistently present care professionals with opportunities that are a good fit. This gives them agency to choose their schedules and their clients. The goal is to make care professionals happier in their work, perform better, and stay with us longer.

In home care, we hear variations on this story all the time: "We started our agency after our parents needed care and we couldn't find the right services for them." The vast majority of people get into this business for all of the right reasons. They want to help their communities and provide a better aging experience than their parents had. The limitation is that they can't provide this great care experience to everyone, since many agencies are still operating in an analog world. Add a constantly improving technology layer to streamline operations and standardize care, and those agencies can suddenly offer their local and personal care experience at scale. And, ultimately, provide better care and better jobs.

Our society has a huge challenge before us—to care for the generation that did everything at scale. We owe our own moms and pops this kind of innovation. If we do it right, our own generation, and those after us, will reap the benefits as well.

Seth Sternberg is cofounder and CEO of Honor.


## Caregiving Is a Critical Service under Stress

Caregivers help with injections and infusion pumps. They operate ventilators, home dialysis, and feeding tubes. They manage care of post-surgical incisions and other wounds. And they need help.

**Nancy LeaMond**


You won't find family caregiving in a classic definition of infrastructure. Yet the 42 million[5] Americans who provide care for loved ones—representing all races, income levels, and generations—provide a service that is critical to society.

Like roads and bridges, family caregivers must bear up under severe stress. Financial sacrifice, medical responsibilities, and a relentless challenge to balance in-home duties with outside jobs often go with the role. A lack of guidance to navigate a confusing, disjointed system of care only adds to the stress.

In many ways, the pressures are increasing, and the coronavirus pandemic exposed our failure to value and invest in a safe and effective long-term care system. Filling the cracks in our tenuous system of providing and funding long-term care in the system will require investment and innovation in both the public and private sectors grounded in the realities that caregivers confront every day.

In recent years, people's homes have become health care's new frontier, and family caregivers are increasingly handling tasks once performed only by nurses and other trained professionals. With little fanfare, caregivers have become a new group of healthcare providers, adding to a workload that already includes household tasks, personal care, shopping, transportation, coordinating various services, and managing finances.

They help with injections, infusion pumps, and other forms of complex medication administration. They operate ventilators, home dialysis, and feeding tubes. They manage care of post-surgical incisions and other wounds. Six in ten caregivers now have such responsibilities, AARP research shows, and there may be a cost to all these pressures. The health of caregivers themselves has declined over the last several years, a trend that is especially pronounced among Hispanic and Asian populations, women, and individuals with less education.[6]

COVID-19 only made things harder as local services shut down. An AARP survey with S&P Global found that three out of four family caregivers reported rising stress in the pandemic—with more than a third citing a "strong" increase.[7]

The unpaid efforts of caregivers have real worth, and it makes sense to think of family caregiving as a large, diverse—and valuable—industry. In Massachusetts, 844,000 family caregivers provide services worth more than $11 billion a year.[8] Nationally, unpaid caregiving was worth $470 billion in 2019,[9] a figure that is probably higher today.

Caregivers reflect a cross section of the population and share many of the same needs. They spend an average of 26 percent of their income on caregiving activities, including housing, medical, and other expenses.[10]

But look closely, and differences jump out.[11] Underserved communities face particular challenges and financial strain. Hispanic/Latino caregivers report spending almost half (47 percent) of their income on caregiving activities, with Black Americans spending 34 percent, Asian Americans spending 22 percent, and white Americans spending just 18 percent.

Two-thirds of Black American and Hispanic/Latino caregivers provide help with medical and nursing tasks, yet for white caregivers the figure is barely above half. A rural-urban gap also exists, with 62 percent of rural caregivers helping with medical and nursing tasks, compared with 56 percent in more populated areas.[12]

Solutions are desperately needed, and the public and private sectors each have a role to play. The goal should be a future in which caregivers' quality of life is transformed with supportive policies and products that ease their burdens.

Financial support, guidance on home medical treatments, navigating the healthcare system, caring from a distance, monitoring loved ones' safety and personal finances, assisting individuals with dementia, and safeguarding caregivers' own health (physical, mental, and financial) are just some of the areas where people need help.

Family caregivers should not face financial sacrifice. Fortunately, policy initiatives to assist caregivers are gaining bipartisan support and have taken effect in many states, with more in the pipeline. In Massachusetts, Senators Jason M. Lewis and David M. Rogers are sponsoring legislation that would establish a tax credit of up to $1,500 for eligible caregivers.[13]

At the federal level, the recently introduced Credit for Caring Act would provide tax credits of up to $5,000 to eligible working family caregivers.[14] The Biden administration's infrastructure proposal includes $400 billion for home- and community-based services, although middle-class families generally will not be eligible for Medicaid support. Government policy reforms are only part of the answer, however. Technology and innovation can create a better future for family caregivers.

Caregivers themselves can contribute to these efforts. After all, who understands their needs better than those on the front lines? Over the past five years, venture capitalists have poured more than $2.5 billion into startups aimed at the market for elder care and home health care, according to Crunchbase News, a service that covers innovation and investment.[15]

But business remains in the early stages of creating the products and services that caregivers will embrace. They need more solutions tailored to specific needs—solutions that are culturally appropriate and user-friendly. Companies need to look to data on where caregivers spend their time, money, and emotional energy. Entrepreneurs should be sure to seek insights from consumers who have provided care.

As the nation's population ages and in-home care becomes more routine, innovations will be needed more than ever. No one was looking as family caregiving became part of the infrastructure of America's well-being. Its role is now far too big to ignore. Keeping it strong should be a national priority.

Nancy LeaMond is chief advocacy and engagement officer at AARP.

## There's an Innovation Gap in Caregiving

Providing care is not only necessary for a decent quality of life and a functioning society; it also is, and always has been, a cornerstone of the human experience.

**Lisa D'Ambrosio**

Caregiving for elders is an ancient practice, echoing back to the dawn of human history. Although the need for care may be immutable, the fundamental math involved is changing.

Longevity gains—the triumph of more than a century's worth of public health and nutritional victories—have resulted in a growing population of older adults in the United States and many other countries.[16] Meanwhile, the aging of the sizable baby boomer generation and declining fertility rates mean that the elder population is growing not only in absolute terms but also relative to the young. In 2020, there were about 56.1 million people aged 65 or older in the United States—17 percent of the population. In 2034, there will be more Americans aged 65 and older than children.[17] These shifting demographics will lead to a drop in what's known as the caregiver support ratio:[18] the number of adults ages 45 to 64 who are available to provide care to those 80 and older. Between 1990 and 2010, the caregiver support ratio hovered at around 7 caregivers per care recipient, but by 2030 the ratio is estimated to decline to 4 to 1, hitting 3 to 1 by 2050.

One major caregiving question faced by aging countries is whether technological innovation can help make up for the demographic shortfall. It's a concern not only for professional caregivers, but also for the 42-million-and-rising Americans who provide informal care to family members and loved ones.[19]

Technology has been touted as one potential, albeit partial, solution to the caregiving crunch,[20] but what hasn't been clear is which areas of life for caregivers and care recipients stand to be most affected. Experts from academia and industry expect technological advancements in caregiving in the next 10 years to be concentrated around extended applications of existing technologies, such as smart-home and wearable technologies. They project that the greatest impacts of tech innovation will be on relatively "low touch" activities, such as social engagement, medication management, and transportation. They expect technology to have little impact on more complex, "high-touch" activities, such as feeding, dressing, and bathing.

It appears that caregiving faces an innovation gap. Although there is plenty of inventive energy pouring into some caregiving needs, the core tasks of caregiving—the ones requiring the most intensive, even laborious attention—appear to be last in line for a technological helping hand.

Part of the reason tech has been applied so unevenly to caregiving is that easier technological challenges tend to get solved first. It's well beyond the current state of the technological art, for instance, for a robot to safely help a care recipient with the toilet or with getting dressed. But a subtler cause may be that the needs of caregivers are poorly understood. The vast majority of caregiving goes on in private homes, is experienced only on an individual basis, and is also in a state of constant flux, as needs evolve and the job of caregiving changes in response. As a result, despite the fact that caregiving is an extremely common activity, it's also remarkably opaque.

Perhaps the most straightforward way to shed light on such private yet nearly universal experiences is simply to ask people about them. For example, the MIT AgeLab CareHive draws on a multi-generational caregiver panel comprising more than 1,400 current and former caregivers who can speak to a variety of under-reported concerns and demands. Caregivers reported concerns about the reliability of certain technologies, such as various engagement or communications tools, for instance, which aren't designed with care recipients in mind, or lack the flexibility to accommodate varied care situations. Caregivers "are shunning technology because it doesn't seem to work," one caregiver commented. Tech providers often seem to "have a solution, but just to things that aren't the problem."

The innovation gap facing tomorrow's caregiving-intensive society has its roots in a different sort of lacuna: an information gap. Providing care is not only necessary for a decent quality of life and a functioning society; it also is, and always has been, a cornerstone of the human experience. We'll do ourselves no favors by ignoring or turning a blind eye to caregivers. Far from it: To reimagine an innovative future of care, developers, policymakers, and researchers must first understand the requirements of those who provide and receive it. It's an essential question. After all, many of us will find ourselves occupying one or both of those categories in the years ahead.

Lisa D'Ambrosio is a research scientist at the MIT AgeLab.

## Notes

1. "Family Caregivers Face High Out-of-Pocket Costs," AARP, 2019, https://www .aarp.org/caregiving/financial-legal/info-2019/out-of-pocket-costs.html.

2. "Selected Long-Term Care Statistics," Family Caregiver Alliance and California's Caregiver Resource Centers, updated February 2015, https://www.caregiver.org /resource/selected-long-term-care-statistics/.

3. "The National Direct Care Workforce Resource Center," PHI (blog), accessed July 9, 2023, https://www.phinational.org/national-resource-center/.

4. America Counts Staff, "By 2030, All Baby Boomers Will Be Age 65 or Older," U.S. Census Bureau, December 10, 2019, https://www.census.gov/library/stories/2019 /12/by-2030-all-baby-boomers-will-be-age-65-or-older.html.

5. AARP Family Caregiving, "Caregiving in the U.S.," May 2020, https://www.aarp .org/content/dam/aarp/ppi/2020/05/full-report-caregiving-in-the-united-states.doi .10.26419-2Fppi.00103.001.pdf.

6. AARP Family Caregiving, "Caregiving in the U.S."

7. Nathan Stovall, Azadeh Nematzadeh, Lindsey White, and Laura Skufca, "COVID-19 Could Rapidly Expand Family-Leave Policies; It Could Also Deal a Serious Blow to Women in the Workforce," S&P Global, https://www.spglobal.com/en/research -insights/featured/markets-in-motion/covid-19-could-rapidly-expand-family-leave -policies-it-could-also-deal-a-serious-blow-to-women-in-the-workforce.

8. Cindy Campbell, "How the Family Caregiving Tax Credit Could Support MA Caregivers in 2021," AARP, September 8, 2021, https://states.aarp.org/massachusetts /how-the-family-caregiver-tax-credit-could-support-ma-caregivers-in-2021.

9. Susan C. Reinhard et al., "Valuing the Invaluable 2023 Update: Strengthening Supports for Family Caregivers," AARP, https://www.aarp.org/ppi/info-2015/valuing -the-invaluable-2015-update.html?cmp=RDRCT-VALUN_JUN23_015.

10. Nancy Kerr, "Family Caregivers Spend More Than $7,200 a Year on Out-of-Pocket Costs," AARP, June 29, 2021, https://www.aarp.org/caregiving/financial-legal /info-2021/high-out-of-pocket-costs.html.

11. Laura Skufca and Chuck Rainville, "Caregiving Can Be Costly—Even Financially," AARP, June 2021, https://www.aarp.org/research/topics/care/info-2016/family -caregivers-cost-survey.html?CMP=RDRCT-PPI-CAREGIVING-102416

12. AARP Family Caregiving, "Caregiving in the U.S."

13. Cindy Campbell, "How the Family Caregiving Tax Credit Could Support MA Caregivers in 2021," AARP, September 8, 2021, https://states.aarp.org/massachusetts /how-the-family-caregiver-tax-credit-could-support-ma-caregivers-in-2021.

14. "Credit for Caring Act Would Provide Tax Credit to Family Caregivers," AARP, July 15, 2021, https://www.aarp.org/caregiving/financial-legal/info-2021/new-credit -for-caring-act.html.

15. Joanna Glasner, "Funding Surges for Startups Serving Older Adults," Crunchbase News, June 4, 2021, https://news.crunchbase.com/startups/eldercare-senior -home-care-startups-funding/.

16. Joseph Coughlin and Luke Yoquinto, "Boston: The Silicon Valley of Longevity?," Boston Globe, https://www.bostonglobe.com/2021/02/15/opinion/boston-can -become-longevity-hub/.

17. Lauren Medina, Shannon Sabo, and Jonathan Vespa, "Living Longer: Historical and Projected Life Expectancy in the United States, 1960 to 2060," February 2020, https://www.census.gov/content/dam/Census/library/publications/2020/demo/p25 -1145.pdf.

18. Donald Redfoot, Lynn Feinberg, and Ari Houser, "The Aging of the Baby Boom and the Growing Care Gap: A Look at Future Declines in the Availability of Family

Caregivers," AARP, https://www.aarp.org/content/dam/aarp/research/public_policy _institute/ltc/2013/baby-boom-and-the-growing-care-gap-insight-AARP-ppi-ltc.pdf.

19. "Caregiving in the U.S.," AARP Family Caregiving, May 2020, https://www .aarp.org/content/dam/aarp/ppi/2020/05/full-report-caregiving-in-the-united-states .doi.10.26419-2Fppi.00103.001.pdf; "Support for Greater Government Role in Health Care for Older Adults," The Long-Term Care Poll, September 12, 2022, https://www.longtermcarepoll.org/project/support-for-greater-government-role-in -health-care-for-older-adults/.

20. Deborah Vollmer Dahlke, David Lindeman, and Marcia G. Ory, "How Technology Could Be a Solution to Caregiver Shortage for Seniors," The Conversation, July 25, 2019, https://theconversation.com/how-technology-could-be-a-solution-to -caregiver-shortage-for-seniors-103878.

# 7
# Finances

## Health, Longevity, and the Goals of Financial Industries

Will the public's relationship with chronic disease be the same as before the pandemic or will our experience with COVID-19 change how we think about even noninfectious disease?

**Brooks Tingle**

The US population is growing older, and one reason for this trend is that we simply live longer than we used to. Although the COVID-19 pandemic has depressed life expectancy to its lowest point in two decades, Americans still enjoy lifespans far longer, on average, than in the more distant past. Since 1900, US life expectancy at birth has risen from about 47 years to just above 77 today.[1]

Much of those gains reflect what public health professionals call the "epidemiological transition," a profound change not just in terms of when we die, but of what we die from. Thanks to advances in public health and medicine, the twentieth century saw chronic diseases overtake infectious diseases, a gradual trend that remained almost clad in iron—that is, until March 2020, when infectious disease reasserted itself.

Over time, as COVID-19 becomes endemic, we will eventually turn the spotlight back to the diseases that most concerned public health officials prior to 2020, including heart disease, cancer, and diabetes. When that happens, one of the most important questions yet to be addressed in the pandemic is whether the public's relationship with chronic disease will be the same as before, or if our experience passing through COVID-19's gauntlet will have changed how we think about even noninfectious disease.

That open question may turn out to be an opportunity to improve how we live as we age—not just for individuals but for organizations that serve them. World-leading financial services firms headquartered in Boston and elsewhere—life insurers, in particular—may find themselves in a prime position to influence this issue for the better.

The shift from infectious to chronic diseases that had been occurring for decades prior to COVID-19 had contributed to a growing gap between life expectancy and "healthy life expectancy": the number of years a person is likely to live in good health. According to new research from RAND and John Hancock's Vitality Program, the number of years that someone can expect to live in poor health in the United States has jumped 14 percent since 1990.[2] In theory, we could have reversed this trend with greater attention paid to healthy behaviors and baseline indicators of health, but we also know that such changes are difficult to put into practice.

The pandemic, however, may be making people more cognizant of their baseline health. In addition to important factors like age and vaccine status, one of the most consistent factors[3] affecting outcomes and recovery from COVID-19 is an individual's level of health prior to infection. The acute danger posed by COVID-19, as compared with the slow-boil nature of chronic disease, appears to be spurring some Americans to rethink long-standing health behaviors. In one major survey of US consumers, for instance, almost 70 percent of respondents claimed that one thing they would "do differently as a result of COVID-19" would be to exercise more and stay more active.

Fortunately, it is possible to make the distant, future benefits of healthy choices feel more immediate—without the threat of COVID-19. There is a natural alignment between consumers' interests in health and longevity and the goals of financial industries, which benefit the longer their customers stay with them. This is especially true of the life insurance industry. Historically, life insurers' relationship with their customers' lives was purely transactional: collecting premiums, evaluating risk, paying claims. But the time is right for life insurers to do more: develop meaningful and personal relationships with customers by shifting the focus to both the length of life and how we live it.

John Hancock's Vitality Program is one example of how financial companies can engage more fully with their customers' lives, and their well-being.[4] It is a technology-enabled program that covers a broad spectrum of activities including exercise, nutrition, sleep, preventive screenings, and mindfulness. It is designed to reward customers—wherever they are on their health journey—for the small, everyday things they do to stay healthy or improve their health.

This shared-value approach can make a difference and is expanding around the globe with such solutions now offered in over 20 countries. John Hancock Vitality Plus policyholders take nearly twice as many steps as the average American. And nearly half of members report body mass index reductions since joining the program, with 40 percent having reduced their "Vitality Age," a statistical indication of overall health relative to chronological age.

Although life insurance is perhaps the clearest example of a financial services industry whose interests align with consumer longevity, it is far from the only one. Life insurance has always been more about dying than living, and finance has always been about what money can do to make life better. Financial companies—especially those in Boston's increasingly longevity-aware business community—should dare to think big and join the effort to build a better old age.

Brooks Tingle is the president and CEO of John Hancock Insurance.

## How the Financial Services Industry Can Impact Retirement

Besides helping individuals meet their retirement savings and spending needs, they can also invest in businesses that will contribute to improved life experiences for older individuals.

**Jean Hynes**

In the coming decades, aging populations will have a profound impact on societies worldwide. How exactly this process will unfold remains an open question, however, and the financial services industry will play an important role in answering it.

Investment management firms are well positioned to influence the outlook for aging societies—and not only by helping them save and invest. Retirement investments are a form of economic energy, and that energy can be sent coursing into companies and sectors whose products and services will help meet the needs of tomorrow's burgeoning older population. As a result, in a rare confluence of interests, investment firms have the opportunity to impact aging populations in two ways: by helping individuals meet their retirement savings and spending needs, and by investing in businesses that will contribute to improved life experiences for older individuals.

The first step involves helping more people save and invest for retirement more effectively. Over $37 trillion is currently invested in US pension plans, including roughly $10 trillion in more than 600,000 employee-directed defined-contribution plans—401(k)s and the like. The investment management industry can help these numbers grow even further, ensuring more Americans enjoy a secure and productive retirement.

In the especially important case of employee-directed defined-contribution plans, there is opportunity for investment managers to improve outcomes for clients: by encouraging employers to auto-enroll employees in defined-contribution plans, for instance, and auto-escalate their contributions over time, without a cap. Similarly, by making continual enhancements to target-date strategies, which allow employees to "set and forget" a plan that gradually shifts their portfolio from higher risk to lower risk as they age, investment managers can improve retirement outcomes for participants.

There are also opportunities to develop new income and pay-out solutions for retirees. Historically, retirees often withdrew their assets from their plans in a lump sum, but today they increasingly opt to keep their savings "in plan," taking their distributions over time. To improve the so-called distribution phase, firms should strive to simplify the distribution process and create payout-like funds that in some cases could permit retirees to receive payments regardless of how long they live.

At the same time, investment management firms seek to invest client assets in businesses and sectors that they believe offer attractive, risk-adjusted long-term returns. One such area is the "longevity economy"—the expanding universe of products and services that stand to make life better for older people. Older demographics represent a remarkable growth market, with fertile conditions for innovation in many industries and businesses.

The longevity economy offers a wide array of potential investment opportunities. One of the most obvious targets is the healthcare sector. Advances in basic science, the advent of new drug discovery tools, and new treatment modalities are enabling the development of high-impact drugs with the potential to extend longevity and improve quality of life. On the timeline involved in retirement planning, however—typically a span of 30 or more years—the potential upside of cutting-edge medical research is even more enormous. This past year, for instance, saw the first use[5] of the gene-editing tool CRISPR-Cas9 to treat disease in humans. Future applications of this type of work may make a healthy old age achievable for far more older adults than is currently medically possible.

Beyond the healthcare sector, Wellington Management's recent Future Themes[6] research suggests that technology and personalization, two highly dynamic economic areas, will probably underpin future retirement. Artificial intelligence technology may prove ubiquitous in the lives of older adults by 2050, if not before, with any number of innovations supporting their physical and mental health. New technologies may help create novel forms of leisure and social activity, for instance, ranging from virtual games to augmented-reality experiences.

AI and robotics may also facilitate the development of increasingly personalized services and care, with health care and nutrition among the most tangible examples. We may see companies offering food and diets scientifically tailored to individuals' personal nutritional requirements, based on their genetics, metabolism, environment, and personal wellness goals. Older adults might benefit from AI-driven monitoring of their physical condition through easy at-home blood testing. And each older individual could be encouraged to live a healthy lifestyle through a combination of personalized health insights, nutritional interventions, and behavioral nudges. The upshot would be enormous: more years of healthy, independent life.

Investment firms have the chance to serve aging populations not only by helping them achieve a more secure retirement, but also by funding the companies whose products and services will make a better old age possible. Boston may prove an especially important hub of such activity. A number of notable investment and financial firms are headquartered in Greater Boston or operate major offices in the region. Boston's world-class stable of financial companies, combined with the growing awareness in the region of the opportunities afforded by the longevity economy, can help shape how we'll live as we age. We—as a community, and as an industry—must make the most of it.

Jean Hynes is CEO of Wellington Management Company.

## Longer Lifespans Require Secure Financial Futures

The main idea behind financial wellness is that individuals can plan for their financial future in a more comprehensive way than in decades past.

**Lorna Sabbia**

As many as half of 5-year-olds in the United States can now expect to live to 100, a population that is projected to swell in the decades ahead.[7] Longer lifespans don't guarantee a financially secure later life, however. If anything, in the absence of significant planning, extreme longevity may make financial security harder to attain.

In an effort to change that, a growing number of financial advisory and service providers are turning to a new, more holistic mode of thinking about personal economics. The trend is centered on one key concept: financial wellness.

The main idea behind financial wellness is that individuals can plan for their financial future in a more comprehensive way than in decades past, when they focused primarily on the dollar amounts in their bank or retirement accounts. An emphasis on financial wellness, by contrast, reflects a deeper understanding of where one's money is now and where it will flow in the future, ideally helping individuals meet their short-term needs while they save for their unique mid- and long-term priorities.[8] Wellness is also about establishing healthy behaviors: financially sound savings, investment, and spending practices that will benefit individuals over the course of a long life.

Bank of America's recent Workplace Benefits Report found only about half of US employees feel "financially well." [9] It is of paramount importance to our aging nation that this number increase.

One good place to start would be to help Americans plan for major expenses such as healthcare costs. Major healthcare bills can have a harmful ripple effect on finances and well-being, but there are tools individuals and institutions can leverage to help mitigate such threats. One involves knowing how and when to take advantage of such tools. Take health savings accounts, which allow an employee to set aside pre-tax money to pay for qualified medical expenses. There were 30 million HSAs at the end of 2020,[10] helping to cover an estimated 63 million Americans. However, access still needs to be expanded.

Caregiving is another major source of expense Americans must plan for. During the COVID-19 pandemic, the "sandwich generation"—middle-aged adults caring both for their parents and children—have faced unprecedented childcare and virtual-schooling responsibilities, all while simultaneously providing support to older family members at heightened risk of harm due to COVID. Every year caregivers cover an estimated $740 billion worth of their care recipients' expenses.[11] They also perform financial work for their loved ones, handling bills, taxes, insurance, and more. Making a wrong turn while executing such tasks can prove costly, necessitating a level of advice above and beyond how to merely cultivate one's wealth.

Financial services companies can also perform an invaluable service to their customers—and to an aging world—by helping them continually revisit their goals, priorities, and saving and investment strategies. Bank of America, for instance, has launched a trio of online programs designed to help customers achieve three pillars of financial wellness: education, planning, and assessment. BoA's Better Money Habits platform, launched in 2013, offers free financial education content and tools for people at all life stages. The site's Life Plan and the Financial Wellness Tracker are designed, respectively, to help Americans set and track near- and long-term goals, and assess their overall financial wellness—creating personal action plans in the process.[12]

Through such efforts, financial companies have the potential to improve their clients' financial outlook. To share the benefits of financial wellness with a broader segment of the US population, however, another set of institutions must get involved: employers. BoA research indicates that 95 percent of employers feel a sense of responsibilities for their employees' financial wellness,[13] even if they're not necessarily familiar with the term. However, fewer than half of employers communicate with employees more than twice a year about their retirement benefits plans; for healthcare plans, this statistic drops to less than a quarter of employers.

Digital innovations offered at both individual and institutional levels may help rectify such shortfalls. Artificial intelligence and machine learning, in particular, may help individuals take important financial wellness steps. Such technologies may make financial services more accessible to a wider set of clients than ever before.

As we plan for the 100-year life, the standard retirement playbook must evolve. To put more Americans on the path to financial wellness, employers and financial industry leaders must commit to better supporting employees' full financial journeys—and that starts with adopting a more holistic, realistic view of old age itself. Aging is not something that only happens in the distant future. It is a complex, lifelong process, and everyone should have the opportunity to meet it armed with a set of nuanced, personalized, lifelong financial practices and strategies.

Lorna Sabbia is the head of retirement and personal wealth solutions at Bank of America.

## Notes

1. Maureen Stanley, "1900–2000: Changes in Life Expectancy in the United States," SeniorLiving.org, March 22, 2023, https://www.seniorliving.org/history/1900-2000 -changes-life-expectancy-united-states/; Elizabeth Arias et al., "Provisional Life Expectancy Estimates for 2020," NVSS, July 2021, https://www.cdc.gov/nchs/data /vsrr/vsrr015-508.pdf.

2. "Pioneering Algorithm Calculates the Number of Years Individuals Can Expect to Live in Good Health," Vitality, October 12, 2021, https://vitality.international/our -insights/news/pioneering-algorithm-calculates-the-number-of-years-individuals-can -expect-to-live-in-good-health.html.

3. Klaus W. Lange and Yukiko Nakamura, "Lifestyle Factors in the Prevention of COVID-19," Global Health Journal, Special Issue on Global Responses to COVID-19 Pandemic: Challenges and Opportunities, 4, no. 4 (December 1, 2020): 146–152, https://doi.org/10.1016/j.glohj.2020.11.002.

4. Vitality, https://vitality.international.

5. Heidi Ledford, "Landmark CRISPR Trial Shows Promise against Deadly Disease," Nature, https://www.nature.com/articles/d41586-021-01776-4.

6. Wellington Global, https://www.wellington.com/en.

7. "The New Map of Life," The Stanford Center on Longevity, November 2021, https://longevity.stanford.edu/wp-content/uploads/2021/11/NMOL_report_FINAL -5.pdf.

8. "Life Priorities: How to Prioritize Every Stage in Your Life," Bank of America, accessed July 9, 2023, https://bettermoneyhabits.bankofamerica.com/en/life-priorities.

9. "Workplace Benefits Report," Bank of America, 2022, https://business.bofa.com /content/dam/flagship/workplace-benefits/id20_0901/documents/2022-WBR.pdf

10. "2020 Devenir & HSA Council Demographic Survey," Devenir Research, 2020, https://www.devenir.com/research/2020-devenir-hsa-council-demographic-survey/.

11. "The Hidden Financial Dimensions of Cognitive Decline and Caregiving," The Gerontological Society of America, 2021, https://www.geron.org/images/gsa/docu ments/GSA_Hidden_Financial_Dimensions.pdf.

12. "Create Your Life Plan (Track It & Achieve It) at Bank of America," Bank of America, https://promotions.bankofamerica.com/digitalbanking/mobilebanking/life plan; "Financial Wellness for Employees," Bank of America, https://business.bofa .com/en-us/content/workplace-benefits/solutions-and-services/financial-wellness -for-employees.html.

13. "Workplace Benefits Report," https://business.bofa.com/content/dam/flagship /workplace-benefits/id20_0905/documents/2021-WBR.pdf.

# 8
# Research and Development

## Needed: Federal Leadership on R&D for Our Aging Society

Adults aged 65 and over will outnumber children by 2034. By 2060, they will account for nearly a quarter of Americans.

**Joseph Coughlin and Luke Yoquinto**

The US population is in the midst of a once-in-history transformation. Adults aged 65 and over will outnumber children by 2034.[1] By 2060, they will account for nearly a quarter of Americans.[2] This new demographic reality will change life in ways both sweeping and mundane. It is imperative that we as a society do everything we can to make sure these changes are good ones, befitting the gift of longer life.

Even if the meaning of "old" changes for the better, however, the possibilities of later life will still be constrained by technological and medical reality. Happily, when it comes to science and technology, the realm of the possible can be stretched. This work, in the form of research and development, has the potential to explode limitations on what we can achieve, and even imagine, in the decades ahead. But disorganized half-measures will no longer suffice. Federal leadership elevating R&D for our aging society needs to be a top priority.

Elder care, for instance, is in dire need of a technological breakthrough. Demand for professional care is already outstripping the existing home care workforce.[3] The size of the population requiring assistance is growing so rapidly that, barring changes to the national workforce (which might be achieved by welcoming in more immigrants, already responsible for a disproportionate share of care work), it will become harder to fill these positions over time.[4] Costs will go up, and many older adults may be forced to go without the support they deserve—and require.

Technological and research breakthroughs could change this equation. More research is needed in the field of robotics, for instance, before machines can safely help families and eldercare professionals with crucial, backbreaking jobs, such as helping someone out of bed. Further work is also required to better explore how older adults and their families actually use technologies—knowledge critical to making sure new devices genuinely improve lives.

The economic case for pouring support into aging-related research grows clearer when it comes to health care. The United States spends more than its peers on health care (about 17 to 18 percent of GDP, compared to an average of 11 percent in other wealthy nations).[5] Population aging stands to magnify those costs substantially, since individual healthcare expenditures generally increase with age.[6] Based on projections made by the Centers for Medicare and Medicaid Services Office of the Actuary, the $3.8 trillion the United States spent on health care in 2019 may grow to $6.2 trillion by 2028 and $11.8 trillion by 2040.

The good news is that remedies for the older population's health problems may also heal some of its cost problems. Deloitte predicts that current rates of progress toward curing disease, combined with other cost-saving steps including placing a higher priority on preventative care, may help reduce 2040 healthcare spending from CMS's estimate by as much as $3.5 trillion.[7]

Any strides we make against the "big four" age-related diseases—Alzheimer's, cancer, cardiovascular disease, and diabetes—will have major implications. Alzheimer's (and other forms of dementia) remains an especially important economic target. Alzheimer's has not yielded to recent medical research breakthroughs in the same way that cancer and cardiovascular disease have. To make matters more economically dire, because the prevalence of dementia increases exponentially with age, any strides we make in extending the human lifespan bring along the cruel side effect of higher incidences of dementia—and with it, increased demand for high-intensity care.

This reality is sobering, but it underscores the need for ramping up age-related disease research across the board: not just in health care and robotics, but also in smart-home tech, user design, transportation, workplace technologies, education and training, and nutrition. R&D in these fields won't just improve lives; it will also strengthen tomorrow's economy.

The federal government must step up and provide not only funding but something even harder to come by: leadership. A new federal agency could serve as an agenda-setting and convening force, connecting business innovators with researchers on topics ranging from molecules to marketing, policies to financial products. Such an agency could launch a nationwide education initiative arming service professionals, from geriatricians to geriatric care managers, with technologies and strategies designed to make their lives easier and their work more effective. Leveraging the procurement power of public agencies, it could prioritize equitable tech access and affordability. And as older adults begin to rely on new technologies in unforeseen ways, it could help develop a legal framework around emerging issues of privacy, data ownership, and consent.

Innovation is always an act of optimism. Federal leadership on age-ready R&D would stand as a continuous reminder that living longer can, and must, be about living better.

## Budding Technology Should Be Adapted for Elder Care

These developments, when applied to monitoring devices, have the potential to enable precision and adaptive, data-driven interventions, granting clinicians and caregivers critical insight into the health status of patients.

**Deepak Ganesan, Niteesh Choudhry, and Benjamin Marlin**

Most older Americans would prefer to stay in their homes as long as possible. Unfortunately, biology sometimes gets in the way. More than 85 percent of older adults live with at least one chronic illness, and 10 percent live with Alzheimer's disease or Alzheimer's disease–related dementias (AD/ADRD). The development and progression of such illnesses creates significant barriers to successful aging at home. However, thanks to developments in multiple technical fields, including artificial intelligence and hardware design, it may be possible to equip tomorrow's older adults to face this challenge more effectively.

Wearable and contactless health and activity-sensing devices, including smartwatches, have been adopted over the last decade, and many have monitoring capabilities related to such wellness-related factors as physical activity, sleep, and stress. These technologies have the potential to help older adults age safely in their own homes by detecting acute adverse events like falls, as well as predict the onset and progression of chronic illness.

Simultaneously, a variety of industries have adopted artificial intelligence–based data analysis methods. These developments, when applied to monitoring devices, have the potential to enable precision and adaptive, data-driven interventions, granting clinicians and caregivers critical insight into the health status of patients. They also have the potential to monitor the home environment, enhancing residents' safety.

However, many of these technologies, starting with most wearable health-monitoring devices, have not been developed with older adults and their caregivers in mind. Specifically, many existing health technologies are burdensome for older adults to use, are not sufficiently accurate for medical purposes, and sometimes come with algorithmic biases that make them less effective for older users. For example, commercial sleep trackers can be inaccurate for older adults with disordered sleep, frequent waking, and medication-induced sleep disruptions. They can also fail to capture the day/night (circadian) rhythm sleep patterns of individuals with AD/ADRD. Similarly, wearable and mobile devices designed for general consumers can prove burdensome for older adults due to complex user interfaces, small display sizes, and the need for frequent charging.

Another critical issue is that the resulting deluge of fine-grained data generated by such devices, though theoretically full of useful information for caregivers and clinicians, are rarely actionable. For example, clinicians treating AD/ADRD patients are often asked to advise families on how to navigate "transition points," such as deciding when and whether to hire a caregiver, asking for additional family help, or moving a family member to an assisted living facility or nursing home. Data from health-monitoring devices could potentially factor into such decisions, but they are currently not presented in a way that reflects important considerations such as changes in caregiver burden, or the level of support AD/ADRD patients need to complete activities of daily living (e.g., eating, dressing, personal care).

The way to overcome these issues is to do research, and a lot of it. One new effort, which we lead, is the Massachusetts AI and

Technology Center for Connected Care in Aging and Alzheimer's Disease, a multidisciplinary research center spanning the University of Massachusetts Amherst, Brigham and Women's Hospital, Massachusetts General Hospital, Brandeis University, and Northeastern University.

An especially promising research thread involves applying artificial intelligence to shortcomings of current technologies deployed in the service of aging at home and patients with AD/ADRD. There are three broad settings where AI has the potential to make a remarkable difference in how older adults and their care providers interact with such technologies. First, AI algorithms may be trained to spot concerning patterns in data flows that correspond to beneficial, and adverse, health outcomes. Second, AI can help package data flows in such a way that they become more immediately useful to caregivers and clinicians. And finally, AI tools may help future designers create increasingly adaptive, even personalized, treatment technologies.

These research threads require not just dedicated clinicians and computer scientists, but also significant shared research resources, including homelike "living labs" that are highly instrumented with sensors to validate new technologies over prolonged periods. Also necessary are specialized lab facilities for studying technologies and assistive devices for monitoring sleep, human motion, and medical rehabilitation.

An essential part of this research practice involves circling back to key stakeholder groups, including patients, caregivers, and clinicians, who can provide feedback on the usability and utility of the technologies. What works at an institutional scale may also hold true at the level of communities experimenting with new approaches to all aspects of later life, from housing to urban planning to tech. When it comes to making improvements for a better old age, actual, real-world outcomes are the only outcomes that matter.

Deepak Ganesan, director of the Massachusetts AI and Technology Center for Connected Care in Aging and Alzheimer's Disease, is a professor in the Manning College of Information and Computer Sciences and director of the Center of Personalized Health Monitoring at UMass Amherst. Niteesh Choudhry, director of MassAITC, is a professor at Harvard Medical School, and director of the Center for Healthcare Delivery Sciences at Brigham and Women's Hospital. Benjamin Marlin, associate director of MassAITC, is an associate professor at the Manning College of Information and Computer Sciences at UMass Amherst.

## How Science, Technology, and Industry Can Work Together to Cure Alzheimer's

The Alzheimer's research community must acknowledge the gaps in the current approach to curing the disease and make significant changes.

**Li-Huei Tsai**

Alzheimer's disease, the sixth leading cause of death in the United States,[8] has defied our best efforts to find a cure or even a treatment that can substantially slow its devastating degradation of the brain. The now decades-long sequence of high-profile setbacks in Alzheimer's drug discovery and development underscores the unique challenge this disease presents.[9]

For the sake not only of tens of millions of patients and families worldwide, but also the sustainability of the US healthcare system and economy,[10] the Alzheimer's research community must acknowledge the gaps in the current approach to curing the disease and make significant changes in how science, technology, and industry work together to meet this challenge.

The brain's complexity is evident not only when its processes are humming along smoothly but also when problems crop up. Alzheimer's is the epitome of such a profoundly complex problem. Confounding early hopes for a straightforward solution, it has not turned out to be a disease attributable to just one runaway protein or just one gene. In fact, although Alzheimer's is referred to as a single name, we in the Alzheimer's research community don't yet know how many different types of Alzheimer's there may be and, therefore, how many different treatments might ultimately prove necessary across the population.

Over the past several years, we have continued to identify more genes (and lifestyle factors such as healthy diet and exercise) that convey some degree of protection against Alzheimer's or, conversely, risk—both individually and, more vexingly, in combination. Often they affect multiple cellular and molecular processes, or pathways. For instance, some risk genes affect how certain cells handle fat molecules like cholesterol. Others seem to warp the brain's immune response. Understanding how these pathways go awry, and whether these dysfunctions are distinct or derive from common underlying mechanisms, is a largely unexplored question for determining which therapies need to be developed and whom they will help.

Traditionally we've pursued small-molecule pharmaceuticals and immunotherapy that target a single protein, known as amyloid, but if we think about Alzheimer's as a broader systemic breakdown, we need to turn to other molecular targets and explore alternate strategies, including gene therapies, or even digital therapies.

In my lab, we've been pursuing several novel approaches to Alzheimer's. One involves increasing the power of a brain wave frequency that is flagging in Alzheimer's patients, 40Hz, by stimulating the senses with light and sound flickering and clicking at that frequency. It's an unconventional idea, but we and other groups are finding not only in Alzheimer's mice but also in patients with Alzheimer's that this systems neuroscience approach safely produces several therapeutically meaningful benefits, including reduced brain atrophy and preservation of cognitive function.

Notably, the development of this potential digital therapeutic has required the collaboration of a wide gamut of actors: MIT scientists and engineers, hospital physicians, philanthropists, investors, and volunteers from the community, whom we've marshaled via a collaboration called the Aging Brain Initiative.

Still, a more expansive scientific search is not enough. A huge innovation gap for many diseases, Alzheimer's included, results from the so-called valley of death, in which novel discoveries, though promising, are nevertheless seen as too new for companies or investors to assume the risk of developing further. One collaborative opportunity for Greater Boston's universities, hospitals, and biotech firms would involve creating a public-private "de-risking" consortium. Such an effort would combine resources both to pool the most promising intellectual property coming out of academic labs and conduct the testing needed to make worthy advances ready for commercial development. Success or failure would ride on the whole team, not just on a lone player. And with a broad coalition of stakeholders, it would also spread the financial risks associated with early stage commercialization.

Moreover, innovations that would benefit from broader collaboration and de-risking are not limited to therapies. Clinicians, patients, engineers, businesspeople, and scientists could all advance a parallel ecosystem of technology development. Imagine how artificial intelligence and robotics could be harnessed to create assistive technologies for people with Alzheimer's and the loved ones charged with their care. Technology can also accelerate the scientific and medical enterprise. For instance, as we grapple with immense data sets emanating from genomic, epigenomic, proteomic, and metabolomic research, AI can help us find new patterns and pathways.

The need for big change in how we think about Alzheimer's is also an opportunity for Greater Boston to become a global leader. The region has all the scientific, educational, technological, medical, financial, and industrial infrastructure necessary to foster a more collaborative "hub-like" approach. With a more expansive mode of thinking, we can bridge the old innovation gaps and cross new valleys of discovery to deliver meaningful progress toward the end of Alzheimer's.

Li-Huei Tsai is the director of the Picower Institute for Learning and Memory at MIT and the lead investigator of the Aging Brain Initiative.

## Notes

1. Jonathan Vespa, "The Graying of America: More Older Adults Than Kids by 2035," U.S. Census Bureau, March 13, 2018, https://www.census.gov/library/stories/2018/03/graying-america.html.

2. Lauren Medina, Shannon Sabo, and Jonathan Vespa, "Living Longer: Historical and Projected Life Expectancy in the United States, 1960 to 2060," U.S. Census Bureau, February 2020, https://www.census.gov/content/dam/Census/library/publications/2020/demo/p25-1145.pdf.

3. Paula Span, "For Older Adults, Home Care Has Become Harder to Find," *New York Times*, July 24, 2021, https://www.nytimes.com/2021/07/24/health/coronavirus-elderly-home-care.html.

4. "Selected Long-Term Care Statistics," Family Caregiver Alliance, updated February 2015, https://www.caregiver.org/resource/selected-long-term-care-statistics/.

5. Matthew McGough et al., "How Does Health Spending in the U.S. Compare to Other Countries?," Health System Tracker, February 9, 2023, https://www.healthsystemtracker.org/chart-collection/health-spending-u-s-compare-countries/#item-spendingcomparison_health-consumption-expenditures-as-percent-of-gdp-1970-2019.

6. Jared Ortaliza et al., "How Do Health Expenditures Vary across the Population?," Health System Tracker, November 12, 2021, https://www.healthsystemtracker.org

/chart-collection/health-expenditures-vary-across-population/#item-while-health
-spending-increases-throughout-adulthood-for-both-men-and-women-spending
-varies-by-age_2016.

7. Kulleni Gebreyes et al., "Breaking the Cost Curve," Deloitte, February 9, 2021, https://www2.deloitte.com/us/en/insights/industry/health-care/future-health-care -spending.html.

8. "Alzheimer's Disease Fact Sheet," National Institute on Aging, updated April 5, 2023, https://www.nia.nih.gov/health/alzheimers-disease-fact-sheet#:~:text=Alzhei mer's%20disease%20is%20currently%20ranked,of%20dementia%20among%20 older%20adults.

9. Maja Beckstrom, "Alzheimer's Research: The Setup and Setbacks," APM Reports, October 15, 2019, https://www.apmreports.org/story/2019/10/15/alzheimers-research -history-timeline.

10. "Reducing the Impact of Dementia in America," The National Academies Press, 2021, https://nap.nationalacademies.org/read/26175/chapter/1.

# 9
# Housing

## Aging in Community

With a supportive housing and senior care ecosystem and experienced leadership, Massachusetts can serve as a beacon for the nation.

Amy Schectman and Elise Selinger

When it comes to aging well, where we live—and how and with whom—has an outsized effect on our well-being. Even before COVID-19, doctors and scientists identified loneliness as the biggest public health threat to aging well. It accelerates the rate of physical decline,[1] doubles the rate of dementia,[2] and increases the prevalence of stroke and heart attack.

To establish a thriving longevity hub in Massachusetts, those of us developing community-based housing must build more opportunities for older adults to overcome isolation: to live—and age—as part of a community.

This past year, we saw the benefits of such an approach firsthand in 2Life Communities, where we manage over 1,300 affordable apartments in Greater Boston. Our apartments—strategically situated in village-center locations in Brighton, Newton, Framingham, and Brookline—are designed to enable older adults to age in community: to live full lives of purpose and connection to the world just beyond the doors of their supportive, dynamic residences.

For older adults in the state, the height of the coronavirus pandemic was difficult, but for the adults living in a community, not as isolating nor deathly as it would have been had they lived by themselves. In terms of physical health, while 9 percent of Massachusetts residents contracted COVID-19, only 4.6 percent of 2Life's residents did, and less than 1 percent tragically died from it.

Housing is a primary social determinant of health—a fact Massachusetts has taken seriously for decades. The state has been a national leader in affordable housing and community development since the 1960s. The Section 8 rental assistance program, for instance, was invented here, and we have the most extensive network of state-supported public housing in the country. We also have a network of community-based organizations that has grown from various independent grassroots efforts to a mature system for housing production that responds directly to local needs.

More recently, the state has instituted guidelines, based on 2Life's aging-in-community design practice, for developers who use state subsidies about how to create adaptable apartments that accommodate seniors' needs as they age.

But despite Massachusetts' past and present leadership, the gap between supply and demand for senior affordable housing remains vast. (When 2Life opened a new 61-unit affordable community in 2019, we had almost 1,000 applicants.) With such high housing and other living costs here, many low-income older adults cannot pay for basic necessities, never mind dine out or participate in cultural activities that keep people connected. According to UMass Boston's Elder Economic Security Index, in 2019, Massachusetts was first in the country in the percentage of single older adults and third behind Vermont and New York for couples without economic security to afford basic costs of living.[3]

Aging in community may offer one answer to that shortfall. The approach combines affordably priced housing with engaging programs, including fitness, wellness, education, and cultural activities. It also provides key pillars of support, such as 24/7 on-site staff response to emergencies, help accessing entitlement benefits to ensure basic needs are met, tech support, and arranging transportation. These services allow people to remain in their community, minimizing isolation even as new needs emerge. Crucially, this level of care and support can be provided at a fraction of what it would cost to provide these same supports to residents living in single-family homes, to say nothing of what it costs to house someone in a nursing home.

What will it take to make aging in community available to everyone? The state needs more subsidized housing and must pay attention to inequities in the current distribution. Black, Indigenous, and people of color older adults are too familiar with inequities in housing and care. The racial wealth gap has grown over the past 30 years, and the oft-cited $8 median net worth of Black Boston households leaves no financial resources for housing or care. Community-based housing developers need to center the needs of communities of color as we develop more affordable supportive housing for all older adults.

Still another huge gap remains. There is a vast middle class that has too much money to qualify for subsidized housing but not enough to afford private offerings aimed mainly at wealthy elders. We will soon be introducing a new offering, Opus, to begin to fill the middle-market gap in Greater Boston. At Opus, every resident will volunteer their time and talents in order to share the activities they love most with their neighbors. This will help keep costs down and residents' sense of purpose up, which has been shown to reduce even minor cognitive losses.

Thanks to its network of high-capacity, mission-driven, community-based housing organizations, Massachusetts is poised to become a leader in creating a nationally recognized aging-in-community approach to housing. And with Housing Choice now law,[4] there is a real chance for the state to accelerate housing production.

The affordable housing tradition is rich in our region. With our supportive housing and senior care ecosystem and experienced leadership, we can serve as a beacon for the nation. Building on this foundation, we can work to deepen local knowledge, keep up with changing needs, and accelerate our production to meet demand with a laser-sharp focus on equity. We just need the will to make it happen.

Amy Schectman is the CEO at 2Life Communities and former president of CHAPA. Elise Selinger is the real estate innovation manager at 2Life Communities.

## Smaller Is Better

In the Green House model, residents live in houses of just 10 to 12 people, each with their own room and bathroom.

**Renee Lohman**

In Massachusetts and elsewhere across the country, there is insufficient senior housing, and what exists is usually too expensive. Far too often, institutional housing options for elders lead to impersonal living conditions for residents and impersonal working conditions for staff—to the detriment of both. Those working conditions, combined with low pay, have created a shortage of people who want to work with elders, particularly those trained to staff the nation's nursing homes. At a median salary of just $13.14 per hour,[5] the certified nursing assistants in this country are expected to provide care every day to sometimes as many as 30 frail elders. It's no wonder that there is high turnover and a dearth of employees to care for our nation's elders.

One solution may be to shrink senior housing: to "go small" in terms of physical structures and prioritize the human relationships at the heart of elder housing. In one such approach, put forward by the Maryland-based nonprofit Green House Homes, residents live in houses of just 10 to 12 people, each with their own room and bathroom. The administrative bloat involved in such small settings is generally smaller than in larger buildings and creates not only efficiencies that can be passed on to residents and workers, but also a greater opportunity for staff to develop personal relationships with the residents under their care.

The Green House Project envisions homes in every community where elders and others enjoy excellent quality of life and quality of care; where their families and staff engage in meaningful relationships built on equality, empowerment, and mutual respect; where people want to live and work; and where all are protected, sustained, and nurtured without regard to the ability to pay.

My discovery of this model began during my own search for long-term care for my mother. Unimpressed by the skilled nursing homes I toured in Massachusetts, I began a quest to find an alternative that I knew had to exist. My colleagues from the Robert Wood Johnson Foundation helped introduce me to the Green House concept, which its founders had based on a senior housing tradition originally developed in Denmark. I was soon touring Green House campuses across the country, from Detroit to Louisville to East Greenwich, Rhode Island, and to my childhood hometown of Cincinnati.

I reside in Barnstable, which, with a median age of 54, is one of the oldest counties in the United States. With the help of friends and family, I set about to build a company, Navigator Elder Homes, that could scale the Green House model locally, fulfilling the housing gap while replacing the older institutional model. Today, we're fortunate enough to have been awarded several new Green House model development projects, including a major elder housing development project on Martha's Vineyard. Funding for the project comes from a combination of individuals and organizations, as well as through a loan from the federal rural development program of the Department of Agriculture.

Perhaps the greatest evidence in favor of the smaller, more hands-on model is how well it's fared during the COVID-19 pandemic. The Kaiser Family Foundation reports that over the past year, more than 170,000 nursing home residents in the United States died of COVID-19. One study, by researchers at the University of North Carolina at Chapel Hill, has found that the Green House model has led to far fewer cases and deaths from COVID compared with larger nursing homes.[6]

In building a Longevity Hub in New England, the innovation challenge is not always to invent the future locally. It also involves casting a wider net, finding inspiration hundreds or thousands of miles away, and bringing it back home to develop it in New England. If enough people adopt this approach—importing innovation—we can benefit from the world's experience not just in housing but also in all aspects of later life.

Renee Lohman (1957–2022) served as president and CEO of Navigator Elder Homes of New England and Navigator Homes of Martha's Vineyard.

## Where Will We Live as We Age?

What would it take for the city of Boston to prioritize policies designed to enable seniors to afford to remain in their own homes and communities?

**Gina Morrison and Susan McWhinney-Morse**

The concept that Boston could possibly become the Silicon Valley of aging is a fascinating idea. There are, however, questions to be addressed and misconceptions that need to be put aside before we can claim the title. For example, where and how will the older generation live as we age? Who will provide support when needed? Is there the political will to help us answer these questions?

As of July 2019, people aged 65 and over represented nearly 12 percent of Boston's population[7]—and that number is growing steadily.[8] According to a 2018 AARP survey, 76 percent of Americans aged 50 and up stated that they wished to remain in their own homes, or at least their own communities, as they aged.[9] Yet the same survey revealed that only 59 percent felt that they would be able to age in place. Respondents cited obstacles including uncertainty about how to access support and services, and how to maintain a sense of community, with increasing age.

Twenty years ago, a group of my Beacon Hill neighbors banded together to address some of these issues. Determined to remain in our own homes and convinced that healthy aging is best realized when we are able to remain in control over our own lives and design how we live, we created a member-driven organization in downtown Boston to support aging in place. Called Beacon Hill Village, it has successfully provided its members with the support, knowledge, and stimulation to age well and safely in their own homes and community. It provides essential services such as transportation and grocery delivery; referrals to service providers; and educational, cultural, and social activities.

But, as it stands, aging in place is not doable for everyone. It's expensive to live in Boston. According to the Massachusetts Association of Realtors, the 2019 median cost of a home in Boston was $690,000 and, at $10.67 per $1,000 of assessed home value, property taxes are higher than the national average. The median cost of a one-bedroom rental unit as of March, meanwhile, was $3,083.

As a result, many residents find it hard to age in their longtime homes and communities. According to UMass Boston research,

Greater Boston ranks among the worst US metro areas in terms of elder economic security;[10] 63 percent of older adults in the region have insufficient income to afford their living expenses without assistance, and many fall into the unfortunate gap between economic sustainability and qualifying for means-based assistance.[11]

What would it take for the city to prioritize policies designed to enable seniors to afford to remain in their own homes and communities? What would it take for city agencies and the business community to work together with representatives from senior communities to address not only affordability but also how to effectively deliver services and supports at the neighborhood level? For instance, could Boston help fund and spawn the development of member-driven villages in neighborhoods across the city?

These questions are worth addressing, if only because Boston has so much to offer its older generations: first-rate medical care, great neighborhoods with local businesses and restaurants, and a vast array of cultural and educational institutions. There are also diverse housing options, including single-family houses, double- and triple-deckers, condominiums, high-rises, and blocks of apartment buildings. Boston is also a walking city with beautiful parks and great shopping centers. The transportation system is largely accessible to an older population.

Today, the Beacon Hill Village concept has swept across the country. There are more than 300 such ventures in the United States and seven overseas. It shows what can happen when people who are determined to solve a problem come together to do just that. This is an excellent example of age-friendly ingenuity, born in Boston, that has spread around the world.

But we have only just begun to see the possibilities of what can happen when not only enterprising older adults but also the government, local residents, and local businesses unite to accomplish a single goal. With hard work and fresh, creative approaches to the thorny issues surrounding housing and ageism, Boston could well become the Silicon Valley of aging—and even more important, a better home for all of its residents.

Susan McWhinney-Morse is the founder of Beacon Hill Village and a board member. Gina Morrison served as its executive director from 2019 to 2022.

## Community-Centered Senior Living Works for Seniors and Communities

The objective of community-centered living is to integrate residents into the wider population and to welcome everyone into a life-enhancing assembly.

**Joseph Carella**

The coronavirus pandemic shined a spotlight on nursing homes in Massachusetts, with more than 5,500 residents dying of COVID-19 (down from 6,722 after the state revised how it reports deaths in long-term facilities[12]). The deaths underscored the risks for residents who live in a communal setting, especially for those who share a room. A design developed decades ago for hospital-like efficiency, the shared room can contribute to substandard care and a dehumanizing, undignified end of life. It must disappear.

This will require investment in new models that support seniors' right to thrive in life-enhancing environments that are far superior to conventional institutional living. This funding initiative must motivate the developers and owners of nursing homes to create private living spaces for residents. It must also motivate them to include an invitation to "community-centered living" in their nursing home redesign of common space.

Private rooms alone will not modernize the outdated eldercare housing model. To avoid opening a building that is obsolete on day one, each developer should envision the senior living residence as community-centered, a gathering place for neighbors of all ages.

It is crucial to incorporate into senior housing common spaces that invite neighbors of all ages to join each other and create a life-enhancing sense of connectedness and purpose. Age does not erase a person's individuality and ability to grow and thrive. Community-centered living, a dynamic in which people of all ages and backgrounds interact, breaks down walls of separation. It promotes vibrant interconnectedness. This is the objective of community-centered living: to integrate residents into the wider population and to welcome everyone into this life-enhancing assembly.

The Scandinavian Charitable Society of Greater Boston successfully brought community-centered living to the Scandinavian Living Center in Newton. The physical and social design of the Scandinavian Living Center model challenged the all-too-common "out of sight, out of mind" attitude that many people hold about elders. The center was able to integrate the lives of its residents and their neighbors in the wider community. Before the pandemic, more than 2,000 neighbors from Greater Boston (not counting family and friends of the residents) came through the door every month to participate in communal activities, including lectures, movies, community club meetings, and art exhibits. Members of more than 40 organizations discovered the advantage of making this elder community their gathering place and headquarters. The opportunity to meet neighbors every day filled residents' need for human connections.

Of course, COVID shut down these opportunities, at least for a time. Yet in doing so, it only reinforced the importance for community-centered living in our lives, and the urgency to fund the necessary space.

Government and business leaders should support the construction and renovation of community-centered senior housing environments—and begin to think about nursing homes in the same way we consider schools: as a public trust. The best schools and best senior housing will lead to the best communities.

There should also be a review of the Hill-Burton Act.[13] Passed in 1946, this legislation provided funding for an eldercare infrastructure considered advanced at the time. Seventy-five years later, elected officials need to envision the outcomes that can be achieved by updating the act so that funding creates a landscape that brings neighbors of all ages together in a welcoming, community-centered living setting.

At all levels of government, citizens raise money to erect and maintain needed physical infrastructure such as military installations and government buildings. A funding source must be created that supports the full spectrum of nursing home developers and owners.

The benefits of funding senior residences that are committed to community-centered living are twofold. First, the need for stand-alone communal gathering space in towns and cities decreases. Second, the need to overregulate institutional-style senior living environments diminishes; visitors provide oversight and accountability.

Over time, the construction of community-centered senior housing residences will become a society-wide money saver. Why? Because the construction of community-centered living decreases duplication of capital and effort. When specific senior housing owners and developers refuse to accept Hill-Burton style funding, the market interest in their outdated facilities will decrease. Their institutional-style buildings will close from lack of demand by a community that insists on a better way.

This straightforward way to fund supportive elder housing is a win-win proposition for developer/owners and consumer/residents. And the operational isolation that leads to strict regulation, lonely living, and poor care decreases significantly overnight.

Society must offer all residents the dignity of private personal living. However, if developers renovate solely to create a private room for every resident, each new nursing home will be outdated the hour it opens. They must also include common spaces that meet the need for intergenerational, multicultural connection between and among residents and their neighbors. Imagine the day when skilled nursing residences in every American city and town become a life-enhancing destination.

Joseph Carella is the executive director of the Scandinavian Living Center.

## Architecture Plays a Key Role in Reimagining Care Solutions

A simple yet innovative concept combines stable housing, intergenerational care, social integration, and neighborhood revitalization.

**Marisa Morán Jahn and Rafi Segal**

Even before the coronavirus pandemic, older adults and people with disabilities were already beginning to feel the start of the nation's imminent care crisis. The problem is twofold: On the one hand, the high cost of care is financially out of reach for 80 percent of the middle class[14] and altogether inaccessible to lower-income families; on the other hand, there are not enough caregivers to meet the existing demand of aging baby boomers.

Without the daily help of caregivers, older adults and those with disabilities suffer preventable injuries or missed medication. These care deficits result in costly hospital visits paid for by patients, their insurance companies, or taxpayers. In an interview, Ai-jen Poo, director of the National Domestic Workers Alliance, painted a picture of the urgency for new solutions: "Every single family could be in a state of crisis by the year 2050 when 27 million of us are going to need some form of long-term care just to meet our basic daily needs. It's a situation that will impact the entire economy and shake up every family unless we do something drastically different."[15]

Two root causes contributing to this care deficit can be addressed through both policy and how we design our cities and homes. First, because caregiving has been historically and structurally devalued, today's caregiving industry is characterized by low wages and high turnover. With an income averaging $20,000 or less a year,[16] caregivers face acute economic and housing precarity. Second, isolation is a top challenge for older adults as they lose mobility, leading to a rapid decline in physical and mental health. So, too, caregivers working in individual homes face disproportionate health risks from tasks like lifting an older adult out of bed.

In response to the growing need for care solutions, we joined forces with real estate developer and urban planner Ernst Valery and healthcare and finance expert Ellen Itskovitz to establish Carehaus, the nation's first care-based co-housing project.

As a new type of residential building for older adults and those with disabilities, along with caregivers and their families, Carehaus is a simple yet innovative concept that combines stable housing, intergenerational care, social integration, and neighborhood revitalization.

Architecture plays a key role: All residents would live in independent units clustered around common spaces that support shared meals, child care, and activities such as art workshops, fitness, physical therapy, financial literacy courses, and gardening. Carehaus's design for both independent living and clustered or "congregate" care would make caregiving more efficient and safer: Caregivers could take turns keeping an eye on both elders and children in common spaces while also having their own private apartments.

In exchange for their labor, caregivers would receive good wages along with subsidized meals and housing for their families, child care, and other benefits. As a co-living community, Carehaus would be able to pass on cost savings—resulting from lower energy consumption, shared meals, care, and housekeeping—to residents in the form of consistent quality care and good wages for caregivers.

Founded on the belief that art and storytelling enable us to live our fullest, stimulate the senses, and should be accessible at each stage of life, Carehaus will integrate the arts into its DNA—in its arts programming offered to all residents young and old,[17] in its interiors, where art narrates specific histories, and its exterior design, which inspires us to revalue aging and care.

We are building the first Carehaus in a historically underserved neighborhood of Baltimore. As we look at other sites and cities where this model of intergenerational care-based co-housing would thrive, we would adapt Carehaus size and form to meet local needs, challenges, and opportunities. Given Greater Boston's world-class medical facilities, strong leadership among domestic workers and care advocates, and a growing population of older adults, Carehauses throughout Massachusetts could harness the power of architecture and art to inspire new ways of how we live and care for one another.

More broadly, as we rebuild our nation's care infrastructure in this moment of economic recovery, we need to consider how the design of our cities and homes can enable the active participation of caregivers, elders, and people with disabilities in our democracy.

Marisa Morán Jahn is an artist/filmmaker who teaches at The New School and MIT. Rafi Segal is an architect, associate professor of architecture and urbanism at MIT, and director of Future Urban Collectives.

## Notes

1. "Medicare Spends More on Socially Isolated Older Adults," AARP Public Policy Institute, Harvard University, Stanford University, November 2017, https://www

.aarp.org/content/dam/aarp/ppi/2017/10/medicare-spends-more-on-socially-isolated
-older-adults.pdf.

2. Robert S. Wilson et al., "Loneliness and Risk of Alzheimer Disease," *Archives of General Psychiatry* 64, no. 2 (2007): 234–240.

3. Jan E. Mutchler, Yang Li, and Ping Xu, "Living Below the Line: Economic Insecurity and Older Americans Insecurity in the States 2016," UMass Boston, September, 2016, https://scholarworks.umb.edu/demographyofaging/13/.

4. Jon Chesto, "Housing Choice Bring the Biggest Changes to Massachusetts Zoning Laws in Decades," *Boston Globe*, February 8, 2021, https://www.bostonglobe .com/2021/02/09/business/housing-choice-brings-biggest-changes-massachusetts -zoning-laws-decades/.

5. "CAN Salary—What to Expect," Registered Nursing, updated January 22, 2023, https://www.registerednursing.org/certified-nursing-assistant/salary/#:~:text=CNA %20Salary%20Per%20Hour,-As%20an%20entry&text=For%20aspiring%20nursing %20assistants%20who,%2410.24%20and%20%2419.02%20per%20hour.

6. Sheryl Zimmerman et al., "Nontraditional Small House Nursing Homes Have Fewer COVID-19 Cases and Deaths," *Journal of the American Medical Directors Association* 22, no. 3 (2021): 489–493.

7. "QuickFacts," U.S. Census Bureau, https://www.census.gov/quickfacts/bostoncity massachusetts.

8. Jan E. Mutchler et al., "Aging in Boston," City of Boston, Spring 2014, https:// www.boston.gov/sites/default/files/document-file-05-2017/2014-aging-boston.pdf.

9. Joanne Binette and Kerri Vasold, "Home and Community Preferences: A National Survey of Adults Age 18-Plus," *AARP Research* 10 (2018).

10. Steven Syre, "Elder Index at Work: Helping Boston's Age-Friendly Plan Take Aim at Economic Insecurity," UMass Boston, March 25, 2021, https://blogs.umb .edu/gerontologyinstitute/2021/03/25/elder-index-at-work-helping-bostons-age -friendly-plan-take-aim-at-economic-insecurity/.

11. Jan Mutchler, Yang Li, and Nidya Velasco Roldán, "Living Below the Line: Economic Insecurity and Older Americans Insecurity in the States 2019," November 2019, *Center for Social and Demographic Research on Aging Publications*, 39.

12. Robert Weisman and Kay Lazar, "Mass. COVID-19 Death Toll in Nursing Homes Drops by 1,200 as the State Adopts a New Way to Report Long-Term-Care Deaths," *Boston Globe*, April 15, 2021, https://www.bostonglobe.com/2021/04/15/metro /covid-19-death-toll-is-about-drop-state-adopts-new-way-report-long-term-care -deaths/.

13. John Henning Schumann, "A Bygone Era: When Bipartisanship Led to Health Care Transformation," *NPR*, October 2, 2016, https://www.npr.org/sections/health-shots/2016/10/02/495775518/a-bygone-era-when-bipartisanship-led-to-health-care-transformation.

14. Paula Span, "Many Americans Will Need Long-Term Care. Most Won't Be Able to Afford It," *New York Times*, May 10, 2019, https://www.nytimes.com/2019/05/10/health/assisted-living-costs-elderly.html.

15. Ai-jen Poo, National Domestic Workers Alliance, https://www.domesticworkers.org/press/spokespersons/ai-jen-poo/.

16. Julia Wolfe et al., "Domestic Workers Chartbook," Economic Policy Institute, May 14, 2020, https://www.epi.org/publication/domestic-workers-chartbook-a-comprehensive-look-at-the-demographics-wages-benefits-and-poverty-rates-of-the-professionals-who-care-for-our-family-members-and-clean-our-homes/.

17. Barbara Bagan, "Aging: What's Art Got To Do With It?," Today's Geriatric Medicine, https://www.todaysgeriatricmedicine.com/news/ex_082809_03.shtml.

# 10
# Health

## The Future of Home Health Care Is Now

The healthcare industry now has powerful tools it can apply toward at-home health care.

**Heather Cox**

Ten thousand Americans turn 65 every day, adding to a population that will nearly double from 52 million in 2018 to 95 million by 2060.[1] Approximately 85 percent of them are managing at least one chronic health condition, and 60 percent have at least two.[2] One of the most important steps an aging society like ours can take then is simply to make the healthcare experience better for such patients, in terms of both improved outcomes and reduced complexity.

The healthcare industry now has powerful tools it can apply toward these goals. Thanks to the careful and judicious parsing of population-level data, frequently aided by machine learning—technology that uses data to make predictions to enable better informed decisions—it's become possible for providers to offer per-sonalized care strategies for each individual patient. New approaches to at-home health care, such as urgent care in the home, are making the patient experience more convenient than ever. These developments have the potential to transform the time that patients spend in contact with the healthcare system as well as their resulting outcomes.

However, a major challenge remains: making all the disparate parts of such a system—including health determinants like food and housing—work together. To solve that puzzle would be to identify a new way forward for the world's aging populations. The good news is that the solutions are getting closer each day.

Humana, a care delivery and health plan administration company, has used artificial intelligence to identify and personally reach out to customers who may need greater assistance in accessing health care. This effort revealed insights into their greatest needs as well as the powerful influence of social determinants of health. Many people shared that access to nutritious food was a serious issue. As a result, Humana has delivered more than 1.5 million meals to seniors across the country. Similarly, after hearing that many were struggling with loneliness from social distancing, Humana partnered with organizations like Papa to help mitigate the isolation by connecting seniors with younger caregivers.[3]

Data are making the healthcare journey more personal by addressing social determinants of health, but they are also revealing important insights about how and where older Americans want to receive care. Surveys revealed that 80 percent of older Americans prefer getting care in their homes.[4]

And thanks to a slew of innovative companies such as Dispatch-Health, Heal, and Kindred at Home, care in homes is becoming not just possible but also increasingly normalized. When Humana member John, who has multiple chronic conditions, was having trouble catching his breath, the nurses from healthcare services company Kindred at Home called DispatchHealth, a company that delivers acute, hospital-level care in the home, which performed a chest X-ray revealing he had pneumonia. Saving him a costly emergency room and potential hospital visit, Dispatch and Kindred's coordinated care also helped him get the medication he needed from his local pharmacy.

For John, managing his conditions requires in-home visits from health professionals. But other patients may not need or want the same in-home care. That's why health plans must create a robust, coordinated ecosystem of traditional in-home and remote options for care. A combination of insights into patient needs and comprehensive offerings to meet them will help create the quality of care older adults deserve.

The coronavirus pandemic only added to already growing patient demand for opportunities to connect with healthcare providers remotely. As a result, telehealth saw a 32 percent utilization rate, jumping from less than one-third of a percent before the pandemic. Telemedicine, along with other digital tools like remote monitoring and telepsychiatry services, is also helping reach older Americans. Remote monitoring tools like a heart rate monitor can keep providers tapped into the day-to-day health needs of their patients, and telepsychiatry services hold great promise for helping seniors access critical mental health care from where they want it—at home.

From in-home visits to video appointments, multipronged approaches are creating a path for older Americans to have a personalized, holistic healthcare experience. And it's only the beginning. Every day, industry-leading researchers and talent at places like the MIT AgeLab and Humana's Studio H in Boston are collaborating to create more innovative care options for older adults.

Such digital tools are not replacing doctors and traditional care options. The trend in healthcare innovation is not to replace human-to-human interactions, but rather to add to them by making healthcare services more convenient for patients.

Exciting digital developments in health care come with an industry-wide responsibility to advocate for the 42 percent of older

Americans who lack adequate broadband access at home.[5] Initiatives like the FCC's Emergency Broadband Benefit, an effort to provide affordable internet services to connect eligible homes,[6] are crucial in ensuring no one is left behind.

Another responsibility the industry must continue to own is the ethical management of data. As people find themselves interacting more with digital health tools, it's important they know their data are protected. Establishing a foundation of trust is essential to leveraging data to create better experiences.

With the number of baby boomers turning 65 each day, there's no time to wait—the healthcare industry must invest in personalized, integrated care to help meet older adults' health needs. By committing to such an approach, the health system can provide the quality care we will all need to manage our health in the decades to come.

Heather Cox, former chief digital health and analytics officer at Humana, is president of Sapphire Digital.

## Life Expectancy Depends on Where You Call Home

The coronavirus pandemic has been a wake-up call, not just to the looming threat of infectious disease but also to the many social determinants of health that dictate who suffers and who prospers.

Michelle A. Williams

American life expectancy fell by nearly a year and a half in 2020[7]— the sharpest one-year decline since World War II. A chilling statistic for sure, but one with a clear explanation: COVID-19 led to a profound increase in excess deaths,[8] particularly among Black and Hispanic residents.

What's more complex—and just as alarming—is the trend that emerged long before the pandemic took hold.

After decades of remarkable progress, US life expectancy has remained relatively stagnant since 2010, even dropping slightly between 2014 and 2017.[9] Today our lifespans lag behind those in other high-income nations by an average of five years.[10] That's despite having the highest healthcare spending per capita in the world.[11]

Reversing this trend is critical.

Contrary to what the term implies, life expectancy tells us something even more significant than how long a person might expect to live. It's a key indicator of overall population health, which can be compared across time. More broadly, it points to the overall quality of life in a given place.

A decline in life expectancy—or even a plateau—means that premature deaths are on the rise. In the United States, that reality can be attributed to a range of crises, from rampant substance use disorder to obesity and the rise in infant mortality and chronic conditions like diabetes and cardiovascular disease (all of which put people at higher risk of hospitalization and death from COVID-19).[12]

And it tells a powerful story about inequities across society.

Look no further than our own backyard. Here in Massachusetts, a relatively wealthy, well-educated state with near-universal healthcare coverage, people have a longer life expectancy than the vast majority of other Americans, at an estimated age of 80.1 years old[13] (compared with 77.3 in the nation as a whole[14]). But zoom in a little closer and the picture isn't nearly as encouraging.

Life expectancy varies widely depending on exactly where you call home[15]—not just what town but what neighborhood. For example, people in the Back Bay are living close to 90 years. But take the T a couple of stops to Roxbury and that number plummets to closer to 60 years. This devastating gap is a reflection of growing income inequality—and systemic discrimination that has siphoned opportunities for health and wellness from marginalized communities for decades.

Our city isn't an outlier in this respect. All across the country, life expectancy is lower in areas where a large share of people didn't graduate from high school, lack health insurance, and are low-income or unemployed.[16]

These disparities aren't simply a matter of healthcare access, though there's no question that affordable, high-quality care is essential for maintaining good health. They are primarily driven by other aspects of life. It is widely documented that the conditions in which we live, work, and play, known as the "social determinants of health," account for 80 to 90 percent of overall health and well-being.

We see this all too vividly in rural America. Chronic financial strain and the erosion of opportunity in recent years have led to an uptick in what we call "deaths of despair,"[17] including overdoses and suicide. Noncollege-educated middle-aged white Americans, particularly those who are no longer in the labor market, are especially prone to these tragedies.[18]

Then there are the vast and enduring health consequences of structural racism. To understand how they manifest today, one need only look at the disparities between predominantly white and predominantly Black neighborhoods in everything from education and income to pollution exposure, access to green spaces, nutritious food, and affordable housing. This is to say nothing of physical and emotional wear and tear caused by racism itself.[19]

The pandemic has not only laid bare these long-standing injustices; it has also exacerbated them. People in underserved communities have a higher risk of COVID-19 exposure where they live and work, have worse access to testing and vaccines, and are more likely to have underlying health conditions that make the virus more deadly.[20] And they are more likely to face future health consequences from the prolonged isolation, educational disruption, and economic downturn that have accompanied this crisis.

That said, there are reasons to be hopeful.

The past 17 months have been a wake-up call, not just to the looming threat of infectious disease but also to the many social determinants of health that dictate who suffers and who prospers. And that awakening can be a tipping point for change.

Dismantling health inequities will take significant investments in our social infrastructure, like expanding access to high-quality early childhood education, affordable housing, and efficient public transportation. It will require us to enact policies that address racial and economic inequality, from eliminating mass incarceration to promoting wealth-building through initiatives like "baby bonds"[21] and investing in revitalizing historically underserved neighborhoods through programs such as the National Community Reinvestment Coalition.

All of this change will take partnerships across sectors—between not just lawmakers and health officials but nonprofit and business leaders, community organizers, and storytellers as well. But imagine, if we come together to seize this moment, we can ensure all people—from the Back Bay to Roxbury and all across the country—can live longer, healthier lives for generations to come.

Michelle A. Williams, who served as dean of the faculty at the Harvard T.H. Chan School of Public Health from 2016 to 2023, is a professor of public health and international development at the Harvard Chan School and Harvard Kennedy School.

## Notes

1. Mark Mather, Paola Scommegna, and Lillian Kilduff, "Fact Sheet: Aging in the United States," Population Reference Bureau, July 15, 2019, https://www.prb.org/resources/fact-sheet-aging-in-the-united-states/.

2. "Talking with Your Older Patients," National Institute on Aging, https://www.nia.nih.gov/health/talking-your-older-patients.

3. Erum Ahmed, "How Tech Cos Like Papa Can Boost SDOH Uptake for Health Insurance Companies," Insider Intelligence, August 9, 2021, https://www.insider intelligence.com/content/how-tech-cos-like-like-papa-boost-sdoh-uptake-insurance -companies?_sm_au_=iVVkSsD6KWF4kbRFWTW4vK0p3MfC0.

4. "2018 Home and Community Preferences Survey: A National Survey of Adults Age 18-Plus," AARP, August 2018, https://www.aarp.org/content/dam/aarp/research /surveys_statistics/liv-com/2018/home-community-preferences-survey.doi.10 .26419-2Fres.00231.001.pdf.

5. "Aging Connected: Exposing the Hidden Connectivity Crisis for Older Adults," Aging Connected, January 27, 2021, https://agingconnected.org/wp-content/uploads /2021/05/Aging-Connected_Exposing-the-Hidden-Connectivity-Crisis-for-Older -Adults.pdf.

6. Emergency Broadband Benefit, Federal Communications Commission, updated May 25, 2023, https://www.fcc.gov/broadbandbenefit.

7. Elizabeth Arias et al., "Provisional Life Expectancy Estimates for 2020," NVSS, July 2021, https://www.cdc.gov/nchs/data/vsrr/VSRR015-508.pdf.

8. Krutika Amin and Cynthia Cox, "COVID-19 Pandemic-Related Excess Mortality and Potential Years of Life Lost in the U.S. and Peer Countries," Health System Tracker, April 7, 2021, https://www.healthsystemtracker.org/brief/covid-19-pandemic -related-excess-mortality-and-potential-years-of-life-lost-in-the-u-s-and-peer-countries/.

9. Betsy McKay, "U.S. Life Expectancy Fell by 1.5 Years in 2020, the Biggest Decline in Generations," Wall Street Journal, July 21, 2021, https://www.wsj.com/articles /u-s-life-expectancy-fell-by-1-5-years-in-2020-the-biggest-decline-in-generations -11626840061.

10. Steven H. Woolf, Ryan K. Masters, and Laudan Y. Aron, "Effect of the Covid-19 Pandemic in 2020 on Life Expectancy across Populations in the USA and Other High Income Countries: Simulations of Provisional Mortality Data," BMJ 373 (June 24, 2021): n1343, https://doi.org/10.1136/bmj.n1343.

11. Matthew McGough et al., "How Does Health Spending in the U.S. Compare to Other Countries?," Health System Tracker, February 9, 2023, https://www.health systemtracker.org/chart-collection/health-spending-u-s-compare-countries/#item -spendingcomparison_health-consumption-expenditures-per-capita-2019.

12. Steven H. Woolf and Heidi Schoomaker, "Life Expectancy and Mortality Rates in the United States, 1959–2017," JAMA 322, no. 20 (November 26, 2019): 1996–2016, https://doi.org/10.1001/jama.2019.16932.

13. Elizabeth Arias et al., "U.S. State Life Tables, 2018," National Division of Vital Statistics, March 11, 2021, https://www.cdc.gov/nchs/data/nvsr/nvsr70/nvsr70-1 -508.pdf.

14. Arias et al., "U.S. State Life Tables, 2018."

15. Emily Zimmerman et al., "Social Capital and Health Outcomes in Boston," VCU Center on Human Needs, September 2012, https://societyhealth.vcu.edu/media /society-health/pdf/PMReport_Boston.pdf.

16. Robert A. Hummer and Elaine M. Hernandez, "The Effect of Educational Attainment on Adult Mortality in the United States," *Population Bulletin* 68, no. 1 (June 2013): 1–16; Steffie Woolhandler and David U. Himmelstein, "The Relationship of Health Insurance and Mortality: Is Lack of Insurance Deadly?," *Annals of Internal Medicine* 167, no. 6 (September 19, 2017): 424–431, https://doi.org/10.7326/M17 -1403; Raj Chetty et al., "The Association Between Income and Life Expectancy in the United States, 2001–2014," *JAMA* 315, no. 16 (April 26, 2016): 1750–1766, https://doi.org/10.1001/jama.2016.4226; James N. Laditka and Sarah B. Laditka, "Unemployment, Disability and Life Expectancy in the United States: A Life Course Study," *Disability and Health Journal* 9, no. 1 (January 1, 2016): 46–53, https://doi .org/10.1016/j.dhjo.2015.08.003.

17. Casey B. Mulligan, "Deaths of Despair and the Incidence of Excess Mortality in 2020," National Bureau of Economic Research, December 2020, https://www.nber .org/papers/w28303.

18. Carol Graham, "America's Crisis of Despair: A Federal Task Force for Economic Recovery and Societal Well-Being," Brookings, February 10, 2021, https://www .brookings.edu/research/americas-crisis-of-despair-a-federal-task-force-for-economic -recovery-and-societal-well-being/.

19. Michelle J. Sternthal, Natalie Slopen, and David R. Williams, "Racial Disparities in Health: How Much Does Stress Really Matter?," *Du Bois Review: Social Science Research on Race* 8, no. 1 (April 2011): 95–113, https://doi.org/10.1017/S1742058X 11000087.

20. "What Is Health Equity?," Centers for Disease Control and Prevention, updated July 1, 2022, https://www.cdc.gov/healthequity/whatis/?CDC_AA_refVal=https%3A %2F%2Fwww.cdc.gov%2Fcoronavirus%2F2019-ncov%2Fcommunity%2Fhealth -equity%2Frace-ethnicity.html.

21. Annie Lowrey, "A Cheap, Race-Neutral Way to Close the Racial Wealth Gap," *Atlantic*, June 29, 2020, https://www.theatlantic.com/ideas/archive/2020/06/close -racial-wealth-gap-baby-bonds/613525/.

# 11
# Living Laboratory

## A Living Laboratory Must Close the Equity and Opportunity Gaps

As the nation recovers from the pandemic, we need to ensure that everyone can live a longer, healthier, more productive life.

Jean Accius

As we embrace the COVID-19 vaccine rollout and look toward an end of the coronavirus pandemic crisis, the thought of getting back to normal is on all our minds. But any desire to get back to normal must be accompanied by the recognition that normal excluded many in our pre-COVID world.

COVID-19 demonstrated the disparities embedded in our nation. The pandemic dealt major blows to many people and families, especially BIPOC (Black, Indigenous, and people of color) communities, individuals with unstable incomes, and older adults in long-term care facilities. Consider that nearly 95 percent of COVID-19 deaths have been of people aged 50 and older, and around 40 percent of all deaths have been among nursing home residents and staff, with

Black and Hispanic nursing home residents dying at three times the rate of other residents.[1] New data from the Centers for Disease Control and Prevention show that life expectancy in the United States declined by a full year in the first half of 2020[2]—the worst decline since World War II. More troubling, the average life expectancy decreased by 2.7 years for non-Hispanic Black people and 1.8 years for Latinos.[3]

There were disparities and inequities before the pandemic. These disparities did not happen by chance, and everyone is losing as a result. In fact, disparities in health and wealth stifle economic growth.

An AARP report found that discrimination against workers over the age of 50 cost the economy $850 billion in 2018.[4] The economic contribution of the older population could increase by $3.9 trillion annually in a no-age-bias economy.

The Kellogg Foundation reports that closing the disparities gap would generate an additional $8 trillion in our GDP by 2050,[5] an increase in additional federal tax revenues by $450 billion, and in state and local tax revenues by $100 billion annually. As the nation starts to recover from the effects of the pandemic, we need to ensure that everyone has the opportunity to live a longer, healthier, and more productive life. This is not just a moral imperative; it's also an economic necessity.

Boston can pioneer the modern merger of moral imperative and economic growth, and drive equity and opportunity. Government, academic, business, and nonprofit leaders know that we cannot plan for or work within a longevity economy that provides goods, services, and experiences for only those who have means or access.

If the region is going to be the Silicon Valley of aging, it needs to embed the principles of equity as a core strategy for growth and innovation. Boston is a city of both wealth and poverty. It is burgeoning in its diversity. But the wealth disparity must be addressed, and people of color must be included and empowered in helping to co-create the solutions. A community doesn't need to be told what their challenges are, nor should it have a solution thrust upon them without their input.

Since the economic downturn is directly related to the pandemic, efforts to rebuild the economy must likewise be multifaceted. Older Americans' contributions are transforming markets and sparking new ideas across every sector of the economy and will play critical roles in the effort to rebuild the economy.

More specifically, as states face immediate economic challenges due to the pandemic, it is a critical time to recognize its growing aging population as part of a strategy for economic recovery and growth. According to the AARP Longevity Economy Outlook, the 50-plus population accounted for 37 percent of Massachusetts' population, yet contributed 44 percent—or $244 billion—of the state's total GDP in 2018.[6] By 2050, that figure will more than double to $767 billion.

People aged 50 and over also play a significant role as part of Massachusetts' workforce. By 2030, workers over age 50 are projected to number 1.3 million, representing 34 percent of the state's total labor force—that means 2.4 million jobs in Massachusetts will drive employment growth across all age groups and industries.

While there is promise for the future of those 50 and older in this longevity economy, we must be mindful of the chasm of disparities in our culture. As a society, we are missing out because many people are being left behind. Improving longevity means not just improving the healthcare and long-term care systems, but also addressing systemic disparities in terms of community living options, longevity, workforce challenges, and the growing digital divide. To maximize the longevity dividend and create opportunity for all, we must act now to eliminate the widening disparities that stifle economic growth and prosperity and rob people—particularly communities of color—of the opportunity to live longer, healthier, and productive lives.

We must be intentional to close the opportunity gaps that impact all of us. We must listen, ask questions, build trust, and include the very communities' we are seeking to help. Rather than thinking about overcoming these obstacles as a measure of success, we need to think about removing or preventing them altogether.

Inequality, in any form, hurts us all, not just those who are primarily affected. The removal of barriers and prevention of new ones will determine how we can fully leverage the longevity dividend. Solutions, products, and services need to build wealth, strengthen health, and provide economic opportunity for everyone.

We must act with purpose and lead others to do the same. By leveraging the asset that is the aging population in this era of unprecedented change and uncertainty, we can create economic growth and societal benefits—now and for the future.

Jean Accius is president and CEO of Creating Healthy Communities. Previously, he was the senior vice president for global thought leadership at AARP.

## How Massachusetts Can Become a Living Laboratory for Aging

Let's measure what's going on in cities and towns so we can identify how a community's aging circumstances change over time.

**Elizabeth Dugan**

In a country growing rapidly older,[7] New England has the potential to become a kind of living laboratory for all things related to aging. Several of the nation's oldest states and communities are here, and it is in our regional DNA to innovate. We are also home to many professionals who can establish New England as a global Longevity

Hub—academics, biomedical researchers, financial service providers, technology designers, venture capitalists, housing developers, and experienced government and private sector leaders with a vision of what is possible. Many have not focused their attention on aging yet but, given the potential in this area, they should.

Historically speaking, population aging is new and presents a growing, largely untapped resource. Aging is something we all have in common, and we can leverage that collective reality to create moon-landing levels of advancements. We need a mindset that sees the older population as a solution and opportunity, not a burden or cause for panic.

One of the keys to seizing this opportunity is to measure what's going on in our cities and towns and identify how a given community's aging circumstances change over time. This goes far beyond simple head counts of how many are over 65. It requires granular information on a community-by-community level to really be effective.

My research team at the Gerontology Institute in the McCormack Graduate School of Policy and Global Studies at the University of Massachusetts Boston has been creating such tools for nearly a decade, with support from the Tufts Health Plan Foundation. We started in Massachusetts, collecting detailed data, most recently in 2018, about older adults living in every one of the Commonwealth's 351 cities and towns, and we then produced similar information for Rhode Island, New Hampshire, and Connecticut. All this information can be found in our Healthy Aging Data Reports, available at healthyagingdatareports.org.[8]

We collect community information about important elements of life like transportation, housing, employment, safety, civic participation, wellness, health services utilization, chronic disease, mental and behavioral health, community support, and the economics of aging. Our research suggests that social factors contribute a great deal to elder community health, some of them complex (increased public safety and walkability, for example) and some as simple as always using microphones in public meetings to make sure those with hearing impairments can fully participate. This is good news because it means we can change things for the better, if we have the will and grit to do so.

Snapshots of healthy aging for a community or state are helpful. But information collected repeatedly over time is even better in that it shows where we've been, where we are, and the direction we're headed. In Massachusetts, the results show clear trends and quantify how the state is aging. Our older population is getting larger both in sheer numbers and as a percentage of the total population. The "young-old" set of residents—those 65 to 74 years old—is an increasingly larger part of the elder population. The older population has also become more diverse in terms of race, ethnicity, and LGBTQ status.

Our work has shown how much the circumstances of older people in different communities can vary. A single, inflexible idea will rarely meet a need or solve a problem everywhere. Widely available technology can help older adults continue to live independently, whether it makes our homes more manageable, monitor our health, or allow us to remain connected to family, work, or volunteer opportunities. But most of the things older adults need or want in order to live a better life—services, mobility, jobs—depend on local solutions.

For example, one common issue for older adults is the need for better transportation options. But the kind of innovation that would make a difference in larger cities—such as greater access to bikes and safe bike paths—won't work as well in rural areas. Solutions need to take into account local demographics, infrastructure, and economics. The Healthy Aging Data Reports reveal the disparities from one community to the next and can guide our actions and investments.

We need to invest in educational programs that will build the workforce for the Longevity Hub and help a younger generation imagine the future of aging.

Finally, we need to stoke political energy to generate and sustain the movement to create a more age-friendly society. We can cultivate the kind of technological and practical innovation that will serve a growing older population that we'll all be part of someday—if we're lucky. Let's do the work now so that in 50 years we can look back and see another revolution we led and prospered from. As the Longevity Hub, Massachusetts can be a model for the rest of the nation and the world.

Elizabeth Dugan is an associate professor in the Department of Gerontology at the McCormack Graduate School at UMass Boston.

## Notes

1. AARP Nursing Home COVID-19 Dashboard, Public Policy Institute, updated May 18, 2023, https://www.aarp.org/ppi/issues/caregiving/info-2020/nursing-home-covid-dashboard.html.

2. Elizabeth Arias, Betzaida Tejada-Vera, and Farida Ahmad, "Provisional Life Expectancy Estimates for January through June, 2020," NVSS, February 2021, https://www.cdc.gov/nchs/data/vsrr/VSRR10-508.pdf.

3. Laurel Wamsley, "American Life Expectancy Dropped by a Full Year in 1st Half of 2020," NPR, February 18, 2021, https://www.npr.org/2021/02/18/968791431/american-life-expectancy-dropped-by-a-full-year-in-the-first-half-of-2020#:~:text=The%20average%20U.S.%20life%20expectancy,year%20from%2078.8%20in%202019.

4. "The Economic Impact of Age Discrimination," AARP, 2020, https://www.aarp.org/content/dam/aarp/research/surveys_statistics/econ/2020/impact-of-age-discrimination.doi.10.26419-2Fint.00042.003.pdf.

5. "Business Case for Racial Equity," W.K. Kellogg Foundation, https://www.wkkf.org/resource-directory/resources/2018/07/business-case-for-racial-equity.

6. "The Longevity Economy® State Profiles," AARP, 2020, https://www.aarp.org
/research/topics/economics/info-2020/longevity-economy-outlook-states.html.

7. Mark Mather, Paola Scommegna, and Lillian Kilduff, "Fact Sheet: Aging in the
United States," Population Reference Bureau, July 15, 2019, https://www.prb.org
/resources/fact-sheet-aging-in-the-united-states/.

8. Healthy Aging Data Reports, https://healthyagingdatareports.org.

# II
# Global Hub Candidates

# 12
# Dubai

**Alyaa AlMulla**

In 2010, the United Arab Emirates announced a forward-looking national agenda that established long and healthy life as a top state priority:[1] a vision of equitable, healthy longevity for all Emiratis. This was followed by a set of overarching strategic plans, called Centennial 2071, that the UAE intends to achieve by its 100th birthday. Included in this comprehensive list is the goal of making the UAE the best place in the world for older adults to call home.[2] The UAE has already taken a number of discrete steps to this effect by leveraging several natural and earned advantages. It has the wealth, the enabling environment, infrastructure—and most importantly, the political wisdom and mindset—to emerge as a regional longevity hub that supports its long-lived society with good health and wealth.

In just the past 50 years, the UAE was able to create an advanced economy that today attracts and retains top global talent and international investment. It has been ranked first regionally in the Global Innovation Index for six consecutive years,[3] and continues to promote new innovation as the country continually adapts and changes: accelerating reforms, regulations, and policies dedicated to improving people's lives. Its economy continues to grow while its private, NGO, and public sectors push forward work centered around human advancement, prosperity, and well-being, in pursuit of the prerogative originally set by the country's late founder, Sheikh Zayed Bin Sultan Al Nahyan.

One very telling measure of a country's well-being is how its residents live as they grow older. In the UAE, aging takes many different pathways among its heterogenous population. Over two hundred nationalities reside in the country, most of which are found in the country's young and middle-aged visiting working population. These residents bring in their own behavioral and lifestyle norms, including different ideas of how and where aging should take place. The resulting complexity makes it challenging for the government and businesses to tailor interventions for the aging population, but also opens avenues of opportunity.

The UAE's overall population is experiencing a demographic transition to an older composition, due to decreases in its average fertility rate and increases in its lifespan. As of 2018, it has a low fertility rate of 1.4 children per woman, down from 6.6 in 1970. UAE's citizens, who make up 11 percent of its population, still have a fairly high fertility rate (3.5, as of 2020), but this figure, too, is declining quickly.[4]

The UAE's residents' lifespan, meanwhile, keeps increasing. Like many advanced economies, the UAE benefited from its economic growth over the past half-century, which has enhanced health, education, and quality of life: both for citizens and non-citizen residents. As a result, life expectancy has risen from 51 in the 1960s to 80 as of 2019:[5] a great achievement of economic and public health measures.

As a result of these forces, as of 2020 there are more UAE residents over age 50 than under 10; by 2030, the 50-plus will outnumber all children and teenagers. These are demographic parameters the likes of which the UAE has never seen in its history, and which will come with benefits as well as challenges.

Chief among the challenges is the need to meet the UAE's growing lifespan with a longer health span. The UAE's healthy life expectancy, at 66 years,[6] is above the world's average, but still lower than most prosperous nations. In order to achieve its goal of becoming an ideal place in which to grow old, the UAE will need to invest in steps to rectify this fact. The UAE has the relative advantage, however, of having a majority young and middle-aged population, which means it has more time than other nations to prepare for its demographic future.

To promote long and active longevity while becoming an attractive destination where healthy living is a lifestyle, the UAE's government is investing in preventative health and biotech research and development, while at the same time taking a balanced approach toward supporting aging adults.[7] This focus on collaboration—between government, business, NGOs, and the residents of the UAE—has created the conditions for a unique regional hub of innovation around aging.

## Hub Origins

The cabinet of the UAE—the country's chief executive body—has a dedicated mandate to anticipate future megatrends and design scenarios for how the UAE can evolve resiliently. Population aging is one such megatrend. A constellation of factors related to the UAE's aging population has spurred its government to invest in longevity innovations, both in the form of direct funding and by providing other incentives to non-state actors.

Today's young workforce is tomorrow's older population. The UAE, meanwhile, has one of the world's lowest retirement ages: a minimum of 49 for its citizens and 55 (or after 15 years of service) for expatriates—although it's often possible in practice to work beyond these set ages. Soon there will be a need to incrementally stretch the working age to match the growth of the lifespan. One answer may be a multi-stage life approach:[8] rethinking jobs and careers to offer flexibility for individuals to opt in and out of work throughout their lives. To that end, the UAE has adopted and tested a 4.5-day working week to offer better work-life balance and improve the well-being of its workforce. A more innovative, flexible, and resilient pension system—including the financial products and investment models involved—tailored to emerging longevity needs, may help boost economic productivity while improving the lives of older adults.

Without a healthy workforce, meanwhile, there can be no healthy longevity economy. Diabetes, cardiovascular disease, and obesity pose ongoing problems in the UAE. In 2019, for instance, it was estimated that obesity and overweight cost the UAE $11.67 billion USD.[9] Thirty-eight to 41 percent of the country's school children aged 13 to 17 are overweight, and 17 to 24 percent are obese.[10] The UAE's adult rate of diabetes, at 16.3 percent, is higher than that of most countries.[11]

To combat these and other issues, in 2016, the UAE commenced its National Program for Happiness and Wellbeing. Today the program continues to look at the aging population, for instance by promoting an active aging lifestyle through such interventions as the Dubai Fitness Challenge 30X30, an annual citywide fitness challenge that includes a special track for older athletes.

## Longevity Innovations

The UAE is home to a variety of companies and projects that, taken together, speak to a growing level of regional energy around and investment in later life. The seven cities comprising the Federation (Abu Dhabi, Dubai, Sharjah, Ajman, Umm Al Quwain, Ras Al Khaimah, and Fujairah) each have different, yet complementary, competitive advantages in such spheres as trade, logistics, tourism, finance, energy, real estate, and technology. For the past decade, the different cities have been working to attract investments across healthcare services, pharma, biotech, wellness, and health tourism.

Abu Dhabi and Dubai are particular leaders in attracting health tourism. Dubai announced in 2014 the development of different well-being clusters that will cater to longevity and aging well. These will add to its well-established Dubai Health Experience: a health tourism product that supports a patient's seamless journey from the moment they contact Dubai for the purposes of medical tourism until their full recovery. This announcement was followed in 2016 by the announcement of Dubai's biggest wellness cluster: the WorldCare Wellness Village, which focuses on preventative health in an effort to design solutions and meet the demands of the country's changing demographics. Similarly, Abu Dhabi has a growing health tourism industry, featuring international hospitals and medical facilities, and as well as active medical and life sciences research. In Abu Dhabi's Kizad Life Science Park, for instance, the entire pharmaceutical value chain is centered in one location. Its aim is to provide incubation, incentives, support, and dialogue with regulators. As of 2022, the UAE plans to triple Kizad's research and development spending by 2031.

The UAE has grown increasingly attractive for longevity investments in the private health sector as well. For instance, Mubadala, an investment company, collaborated with Group 42, an artificial intelligence and cloud computing company, to set up a biopharmaceutical manufacturing campus in Abu Dhabi to develop innovative therapeutic products and vaccines. In work also centered on Abu Dhabi, the UAE partnered in 2021 with several private-sector operators to launch the Emirati Genome Program, an effort to provide data for preventive and personalized healthcare and to improve the health of future generations.

Financial innovation, too, finds a home in the UAE—especially Dubai. The first regional saving scheme launched by the Dubai International Financial Center (DIFC) in 2021, called the DIFC

Employee Workplace Savings (DEWS) Plan, serves 1,187 local firms and, as of 2021, has more than 19,182 employees enrolled. Replacing the end-of-service gratuity that employees once received at the end of their employment, the new plan aims to regulate how organizations save and invest their employees' money, to grow their wealth over time. Adopting this global best practice brings more stability and adds to the wealth span of the many foreign employees who would like to stay and grow older in the UAE.

On a policy level, one of the world's most remarkable investments in an older society is the UAE's new Golden Visa scheme,[12] which seeks to attract individuals aged 65 and above to live in the UAE. Instead of working to mitigate the proportion of older people in the population, like many other aging countries, the UAE has in effect decided to double down on their potential. Alternatively, older expats can enroll in the "Retire in Dubai Program," which offers a special Dubai Retirement Visa to those who meet certain economic criteria, such as a sustainable amount of income, property ownership, or an eligible bank deposit in Dubai. In addition to these incentives, the UAE offers a favorable tax system for older adults, with no tax on personal income. Also, as one of the safest countries in the world that boasts good weather more than six months per year, it is simply attractive to retirees on its own merits.[13]

With its new visa schemes, the UAE expects an influx of older adults and retirees making the country their home, which will create a new portfolio of needs and demands to be served by the public and private sectors—and thus new opportunities to create markets quickly and at scale.

## Unique Advantages

The UAE has a number of attributes that have led to a disproportionate amount of localized energy in longevity innovation, including the government's prioritization of longevity concerns, a culture of innovation (especially in the healthcare sector), a culture of heeding the concerns of older people, and the free flow of ideas both into and within the country.

One important contributing factor is the availability and affordability to consumers of the UAE's advanced healthcare and well-being sector, which has long been a priority in the annual government budget's allocation. As of 2021, 41 percent of the budget is allocated for people's welfare and advancement through the social sector, including health and education.[14] Today the UAE boasts more than 45 government-funded and 98 private hospitals,[15] offering a wide range of specializations empowered with cutting-edge technologies.

In addition to such direct health interventions, The UAE has been a pioneer in prioritizing happiness and well-being in its national agenda. In 2016, the country appointed its first Minister for Happiness and Wellbeing;[16] today, various government plans have to contend with people's well-being and happiness as an outcome measured with key performance indicators. Also in 2016, in recognition of the fact that workplaces impact people's well-being and longevity, the UAE established its National Program for Happiness and Wellbeing to drive organizations and industries to improve the lives of their employees.

Counterintuitively, the relatively youthful wealth distribution of the UAE also contributes to its forward-looking attitude when it comes to age. It is true that, as in many countries, personal wealth in the UAE is concentrated among older people, but many young and middle-aged people in the UAE are doing better financially than in other countries. According to a recent HSBC survey, the UAE's millionaires, with an average age of 35, are among the world's youngest.[17] When such individuals invest in aspects of the longevity economy, they are investing in their own future.

Also key to the UAE's approach to population aging is its culture of innovation, which led its prime minister, His Highness Sheikh

Mohammed Bin Rashid al Maktoum, to refer to the country in 2019 as a "living lab" where "the impossible becomes possible."[18] One of the most visible manifestations of this spirit is in real estate development. This sector has grown exponentially the past two decades, leading to the construction of exceptional buildings and landmarks including the world's tallest building, the Burj Khalifa; and the world's biggest man-made island, Palm Island. Entrepreneurialism also finds the infrastructure and agglomerative advantages it needs to grow in government-supported business districts and working spaces, as well as the UAE's 40 multidisciplinary free zones, where foreign investors and expats can have full ownership of companies. These include the Jabal Ali Free Zone, Dubai International Financial Center, Dubai Internet City, the Dubai Healthcare City, twofour54, and the Dubai Design District.

Meanwhile, to make the UAE even more attractive for businesses, a wave of new business-friendly programs and reforms were introduced in the wake of COVID-19. These included a variety of special visas for businesses with flexible criteria, such as the "freelancing license" introduced in 2022 to encourage businesspeople and entrepreneurs to conduct business in the UAE while residing in any location worldwide for up to five years. Additionally, to help small businesses ideate and grow, the UAE supports different accelerators focusing on sectors including biotech, health tech, fintech, insurtech, regtech, and Islamic fintech; as well as transportation and logistics, smart cities, AI, and the Internet of Things.[19]

## Connectivity

In addition to the above examples, the UAE has one other advantage in its push to develop as a longevity hub: its role as a regional, global, and generational crossroads.

One global competitive advantage the UAE maintains is its aviation sector, which provides rapid connectivity to different countries and continents through its two major airports in Dubai and Abu Dhabi—home bases for Emirates and Etihad Airways, respectively. Regionally, the country's seven cities are well connected through modern highway infrastructure, and their proximity to each other makes it easy for people to commute, permitting them to choose where to live depending on factors such as natural amenities and standard of living. Mobility between the seven emirates will be enhanced further through the completion of the UAE's 1,200 kilometer freight and passenger railway project, Etihad Rail, the first of its kind in the region, under construction as of 2023.

The ease of regional mobility in turn enables two further areas of connectivity that are vital to the UAE's longevity hub: cross-sectoral and intergenerational connectivity.

Firms in the UAE benefit from talented and skilled workforces thanks in great part to the UAE's 79-strong-and-growing list of institutions of higher education, including global universities like NYU and Sorbonne University in Abu Dhabi. The resulting wide range of specializations and research environments offers continued opportunities to upskill and reskill employees to meet changing employment market demands. Reskilling creates the opportunity for workers from one industry to cross-pollinate assumptions and practices to another. Universities also offer opportunities for different industry, government, and NGO entities to come together and compare approaches and concerns.

Crucially, research conducted at the UAE's universities, or by the government in concert with university researchers, can help inform products and policy. For instance, seven out of ten people in Abu Dhabi report being happy, according to an annual study conducted by the Department of Community Development. The purpose of this study is to establish long-term data on well-being and happiness that feed into policymaking and reforms, which can in turn improve quality of life across the age span. Likewise, the Emirates Center for Happiness Research, part of the country's oldest university, UAE University, was initially funded by the government to carry out research on people's happiness and well-being, and provide solutions to governments, businesses, and NGOs.

Perhaps the most valuable form of connectivity within the UAE's longevity economy, however, is intergenerational connectivity. As in many MENA cultures, positive attitudes toward older adults have deep roots in UAE's society. Intergenerational connections have changed in recent decades due to younger generations' need to move to new work locations and the rise of nuclear families, but the UAE's transportation and communications infrastructure still permits visiting and care connections between different generations of families. The UAE's government housing model design, too, supports intergenerational living and connection by granting houses to family members within close proximity to one another, in order to help them maintain their co-living, care, and relations. Such continued proximity can also help younger people in the workforce maintain close knowledge of their elders' wants and needs.

## Conclusion

In Dubai's Museum of the Future, completed in 2022, visitors can metaphorically travel to the future in a time machine. The building—instantly iconic following its 2022 completion—is shaped like a ring standing on end and is covered in Arabic calligraphy. The museum is a permanent space featuring installations and displays of future technologies and innovations, offering both an experiential way to imagine the future and physical testimony to the investment the UAE is making in innovation, risk-taking, and entrepreneurialism.

My own father, Abdulla, is a colon cancer survivor and is now enjoying good health at the age of 80. He still enjoys working, having tried out retirement not once but twice. He says his job keeps him alive and going, plus he enjoys social interactions with colleagues. He benefits from the UAE's strong cultural respect for elders, and his employer is one of many that embraces a multi-stage life by looking at the full employee, beyond their age. My father also walks and moves throughout the day, monitors his food and eating habits, and consistently measures his blood pressure. Crucially, he also finds purpose every day.

The UAE is gearing up to create a population of older adults like my father: healthy, happy, and full of purpose. Making technology more age-friendly for all would help create equal opportunity for those who are elderly now; yet technology also needs to be made more user-friendly for users of all ages. Cohesive society and strong social relationships have been always a priority in this country, and the new longevity agenda takes this priority to the next level.

Longevity innovation in the UAE will be driven by the people's demands. The government and businesses are already preparing to respond: allocating more in terms of budgets and accelerator institutions, and creating more innovative services and products. New partnerships and approaches to organizational design with industry will help the government and the private sector scale up a healthy longevity economy together.

The United Arab Emirates is evolving quickly and organically to become a leading longevity hub in its region: embracing all ages in its call for healthy living and aging well.

Alyaa AlMulla is the founder of Longevity Think Tank, a policymaker, and a well-being and healthy longevity advocate in the UAE. She advises her government and private investors on improving the population's health span, well-being, and longevity economy through a public policy framework and lens. She led teams toward developing policies, programs, and partnerships that support the UAE government's Vision 2071. She led the workplace well-being effort in the UAE's National Program for Happiness & Wellbeing, where she developed an evidence-based framework for happiness and well-being in the workplace for both public and private sectors, improving overall well-being in organizations. She is a Visiting Senior Lecturer in the School of Psychology at the University of East London, where she teaches Positive Psychology & Positive Societies. Alyaa holds a master's degree in public administration from the Harvard Kennedy School of Government (HKS), Harvard University (2016). She was an academic fellow at the Oxford Institute of Population Ageing, Oxford University (2022). For two terms she was a member at the World Economic Forum's Future Council on Human Enhancement and Healthy Longevity.

## Notes

1. "Vision 2021," United Arab Emirates, 2021, https://www.vision2021.ae/en/uae-vision/list/united-in-prosperity.

2. "UAE Centennial Plan 2071," United Arab Emirates," June 1, 2017, https://Uaecabinet.Ae/En/Uae-vision.

3. Soumitra Dutta et al., *Global Innovation Index 2022*, WIPO, 2022, https://doi.org/10.34667/TIND.46596.

4. "Fertility Rate, Total (Births per Woman)—United Arab Emirates," World Bank, updated December 22, 2022, https://data.worldbank.org/indicator/SP.DYN.TFRT.IN?locations=AE.

5. "Life Expectancy at Birth, Total (Years), United Arab Emirates," World Bank, updated December 22, 2022, https://data.worldbank.org/indicator/SP.DYN.LE00.IN?end=2020&locations=AE.

6. "Average Healthy Life Expectancy," UAE National Agenda, Ministry of Health and Prevention, updated 2020, https://www.vision2021.ae/en/national-agenda-2021/list/card/average-healthy-life-expectancy.

7. "United in Responsibility," United Arab Emirates, updated 2018, https://www.vision2021.ae/en/uae-vision/list/united-in-responsibility.

8. Andrew J. Scott and Lynda Gratton, *The New Long Life: A Framework for Flourishing in a Changing World* (Bloomsbury: Bloomsbury Publishing, 2021), 143–164.

9. "Economic Impact of Overweight and Obesity, United Arab Emirates," Global Obesity Observatory, November 2022, https://data.worldobesity.org/country/united -arab-emirates-225/#data_economic-impact.

10. Najla Hussain Sajwani et al., "The Effect of Lockdowns and Distant Learning on the Health-Related Behaviours of School Students in the United Arab Emirates," *BMC Primary Care* 23, no. 1 (September 27, 2022): 253, https://doi.org/10.1186 /s12875-022-01856-y.

11. Fatheya Alawadi et al., "Emirates Diabetes Society Consensus Guidelines for the Management of Type 2 Diabetes Mellitus—2020," *Dubai Diabetes and Endocrinology Journal* 26, no. 1 (February 19, 2020): 1–20, https://doi.org/10.1159/000506508.

12. "UAE Cabinet Approves Executive Regulations of Federal Decree-Law on Entry and Residence of Foreigners," UAE Media Office, April 2022, https://www.mediaof fice.ae/en/news/2022/April/18-04/UAE-Cabinet-chaired-by-Mohammed-bin-Rashid -approves-law.

13. Law and Order 2022 Report, Gallup, accessed December 1, 2022, https://www .gallup.com/analytics/356963/gallup-global-law-and-order-report.aspx

14. "Federal Budget 2022," Ministry of Finance, United Arab Emirates, accessed December 1, 2022, https://mof.gov.ae/federal-budget-2022/.

15. As per 2017 statistics released by Federal Statistics and Competitive Authority, United Arab Emirates.

16. "National Program for Happiness & Wellbeing," United Arab Emirates, 2018, https://www.hw.gov.ae/en.

17. Jamila Gandhi, "World's Youngest Millionaires Live in the UAE, Reports HSBC," Forbes Middle East, February 12, 2020, https://www.forbesmiddleeast.com/money /banking-finance/worlds-youngest-millionaires-live-in-the-uae-reports-hsbc.

18. "Quotes—His Highness Sheikh Mohammed Bin Rashid al Maktoum," United Arab Emirates, 2019, https://sheikhmohammed.ae/en-us/Quotes.

19. "Business Incubators—The Official Portal of the UAE Government," United Arab Emirates, accessed November 7, 2022, https://u.ae/en/information-and-services /business/business-incubators.

# 13
# Louisville

**Bruce Broussard**

Louisville, the country's largest hot spot for businesses specializing in aging care, is arguably America's leading longevity hub. The beginning of Louisville's history as an aging-innovation epicenter can be traced back to the origins of Humana—formerly Extendicare—which was founded in 1961 as a nursing home. The company soon took off as a healthcare leader in what was to become the most rapidly expanding sector of the nation's economy.[1] Its founders extended its services to hospitals and officially renamed it Humana in 1974. That same year, BrightSpring Health Services set up shop in Louisville, and Almost Family was founded in the city just two years later: both providers of home- and community-based health services. Since then, Kindred Healthcare and other health-sector powerhouses have been drawn to Louisville as well, along with smaller innovative startups looking to collaborate, compete, and innovate.

Humana, now a leading health insurance company, today retains powerful access to capital and over 12,000 employees—more than any other regional employer—making it a center of gravity in Louisville's aging-innovation ecosystem. The culture of collaboration that's developed over the past several decades, however, has helped set up other major Louisville institutions like the University of Louisville and the City of Louisville as equally essential players in the region's innovation hub. Meanwhile, nearly 10,000 Louisville residents are working in the aging industry but not for Humana: a sign of how the city has become a magnet for a broad network of healthcare innovators and leaders.

Today, with not just Humana but also major companies including Kindred Healthcare, Atria Senior Living, and Signature Healthcare all headquartered within city limits, businesses partially or entirely devoted to the well-being of older adults are generating more than $50 billion in revenue[2] annually. Five of the top ten local employers, too—Humana, Norton Healthcare, Baptist Healthcare Systemic, University of Louisville, and University of Louisville Health—fall into this category. Together with the academic and public institutions, private industry leaders are striving to better understand and serve the 13 percent of Louisville's population[3] who are aged 65 and up. This heightened level of investment and innovative energy has, and will continue to have, major positive ramifications not just for Louisville's older population but for the larger world of aging adults.

## Aging Innovation in Louisville

Innovation for aging in Louisville is propelled by public-private partnerships and cross-industry collaboration. Perhaps the most notable recent event in this process occurred in 2017, with the formation of the CEO[C]—Louisville's Healthcare CEO Council—which is composed of 14 companies headquartered or founded in Louisville, all involved in providing care of some kind to older Americans. CEO[C] was founded on the principle that with a formal landing ground for aging-innovation collaboration, the council could solve problems beyond the scope of any one individual member company. While CEO$^C$ is based in Louisville, the organization has become a national leader in aging innovation, with member companies collectively representing over $120 billion in annual revenue, employing 475,000 nationally, and touching 8.5 million lives annually.

In addition to the CEO$^C$ member companies, many of the city's key institutions—including the Louisville Metro Government and the University of Louisville—are similarly committed to aging and care innovation in Louisville. During his tenure from 2010 to 2022, Louisville's longtime mayor Greg Fischer made aging innovation a special priority, for which work he received a national Age-Friendly award from AARP.[4] Whether it's the government seeking to promote economic opportunity for the city or grassroots public health advocates looking to advance health equity, there are few residents unaware of Louisville's commitment to aging care innovation.

Louisville's citywide dedication to aging innovation has developed steadily for nearly half a century. Today, this process is only gaining steam, now catalyzed by cross-industry convening forces like CEO$^C$ and Aging2.0 (see chapter 20, by Stephen Johnston)—the international aging-innovation organization recently acquired by the Council—as well as the local Thrive Innovation Center, Aging2.0's Louisville chapter, the Louisville Health Advisory Board, and the University of Louisville's Health Equity Innovation Hub.[5] With such forces aligned toward promoting quality of later life, Louisville can credibly lay claim to the title of a leading, world-class longevity hub of innovation for older adults and their loved ones.

## Achieving Longevity through Health Equity

The output of Louisville's concerted innovative energy is being felt in two key domains: by the local aging population, and nationally, in the larger world of health consumers.

While Louisville's longevity hub has been emerging since the late twentieth century, the past decade has seen a remarkable acceleration in terms of the city's aging and care innovation. A large part of this growth has come from a newfound attention to local health equity. Industry leaders have grown to recognize that every member of the aging population arrives with unique backgrounds, experiences, and needs—which are inextricable from such concerns as their social determinants of health, race, and ethnicity.[6]

Part of this new focus comes from necessity. The median household income for a Louisville senior is $33,516,[7] more than $14,000 below the national average[8]—the result, in part, of the stark geographic and racial health disparities among the local population. For example, people living in western, southwestern, and central Louisville, regions with majority-minority populations, have higher-than-average rates of chronic disease,[9] and Black Louisville residents are at higher risk for adverse health outcomes.[10] AARP Kentucky and the Louisville Metro Center for Health Equity, in a 2022 study of leading causes of death for the 50-plus population in Louisville, found that Black residents die of cancer at younger ages and had higher rates of infection and death from COVID-19 compared with white residents.[11] The study also found that factors like income, housing, transportation, food access, health care and social connection are leading to negative outcomes for Black residents.

The need for innovation and improvements to address health inequities and improve the quality of life for the entire aging population is a pressing concern for the city's stakeholders. Public, nonprofit, and private institutions, including such key players as Humana, the University of Louisville, the Kentucky Derby Festival, and Jefferson Public Schools, have engaged in targeted efforts to address these issues, often acting in partnership with one another. An important early part of this process consisted simply of understanding the scope of the local health-related need. To that end, Humana undertook a large-scale social-need screening effort, conducting 6,157,340 screenings in 2020. When the COVID pandemic struck, this trove of data allowed Humana to identify and provide assistance to food-insecure families.[12] Meanwhile, Humana's partnership with Kare Mobile, a new mobile dental clinic, provided top-level dental care in patients' homes for the same cost as a traditional dental visit. Because the company reaches local, predominantly Black populations who are at risk for high blood pressure, heart disease, and stroke, Kare Mobile also performs blood pressure checks, making it a key part of Humana's Louisville Community of Opportunity Initiative, aimed at removing obstacles to quality care by addressing social determinants of health.[13] Without collaboration with Humana, Kare Mobile would not be able to operate at this large scale.

Other examples of multiple sectors of Louisville institutions working together include the free social events held by the Derby Equity and Community Initiative (DECI),[14] which was created to address social determinants of health like social connectedness and financial security in a city where social isolation (31 percent of Louisville seniors live alone[15]) and poverty (29 percent of Louisville seniors have an annual income of less than $20,000[16]) can stand in the way of life-giving relationships. Similarly, during the early COVID pandemic, a public-private partnership among Jefferson County Public Schools, Norton Healthcare, Humana, and the state and local government opened a COVID-19 vaccine clinic at Whitney Young Elementary School, in an effort to reduce barriers preventing older Louisville residents from receiving their COVID-19 vaccine.

These sorts of community-level innovations represent the foundation of Louisville's longevity hub: a shared, cross-sector commitment to building a community where a connected, healthy later life is equitably available. In fact, such efforts and the organizations contributing to them have helped put Louisville among the top five most affordable cities for an early retirement:[17] a superlative, awarded by the finance website SmartAsset.com, determined partially by access to affordable health care. (Lexington, Kentucky—which, at just an hour's drive away, can be considered part of greater Louisville's innovative ecosystem—ranked first.) Meanwhile, in 2016, Louisville was a winner of the RWJF Culture of Health Prize,[18] awarded by the Robert Wood Johnson Foundation, which honors communities for their efforts to ensure all residents have the support system they need to live longer, healthier, and more productive lives. It is on this solid foundation of livability that Louisville's larger innovative engine finds its footing.

## Innovation Initiatives

In Louisville's care-centric business community, a handful of major corporations predominate, and either directly or indirectly, the region's innovative ecosystem tends to be connected to these businesses. New innovations often come from within these businesses, and—increasingly, in recent years—the business community has joined together with local nonprofit and government institutions to facilitate the region's vibrant entrepreneurial pipeline, as well as the local circulation of actionable innovative ideas.

The University of Louisville's Health Equity Innovation Hub, announced in early 2022, is one example of such a partnership.[19] The Hub is funded by a potential total investment of $25 million, including $10 million from the University of Louisville, $1.5 million from Humana, and up to $13.5 million from the Humana Foundation. The Hub is helping to create a talent pipeline to healthcare companies for underserved community members and customers by conducting outcomes-based research on population health issues.

In 2021, CEO[C] completed its acquisition of Aging2.0, a global organization of innovators in the aging care space and creator of Optimize, the US's leading annual conference of aging care innovators, providers, payers and capital partners, which will now be held in Louisville each year. The conference includes a pitch competition devoted to care technologies. For example, 2022 pitch winner Famileo is addressing social determinants of health like loneliness by using a digital technology that allows friends and family to send a weekly printed gazette to older loved ones.[20] With the help of CEO[C], Famileo is partnering with Signature and Trilogy Health Services, eldercare companies, to bring their innovative project to older Louisville residents and Americans at scale.

The CEO[C]'s acquisition of Aging2.0, with its over 130 chapters in 30 countries on six continents, represents a major step for Louisville onto the world stage of aging innovation. On top of this investment, CEO[C] also recently launched a $50 million fund dedicated to supporting companies that advance innovations in the aging space. Finally—possibly unique among regional longevity hubs—CEO[C] has created a data strategy that can ingest the vast data resources of member companies with the goal of bringing sophisticated data analytics to the aging-innovation space.

The Thrive Innovation Center, a nonprofit devoted to innovation for healthy aging, is yet another local institution connecting innovators with the market for positive change. This group interacts directly with Louisville's older adults to understand how new technology can address their needs. At Thrive's headquarters in downtown Louisville, older adults are engaging in trials with music and memory games, writing workshops, and virtual reality experiences. These trials have helped inform the development of immersive, virtual reality technology specifically adapted to seniors,[21] developed by Thrive and Samsung acting as partners. These tools are designed to help improve the quality of life of older Louisville residents experiencing conditions including chronic pain and anxiety, as well as Alzheimer's and other forms of dementia.

XLerateHealth, a healthcare accelerator company headquartered in Louisville, offers yet another pathway for the region's innovators.

It chooses seven startups to participate in its annual Louisville Accelerator Cohort bootcamp.[22] Incumbent providers like Humana are partnering with these types of smaller companies to leverage remote monitoring tools, such as a heart rate monitor, designed to keep providers tapped into the day-to-day health needs of patients.

## Meeting Older Americans Where They Are

The bulk of medical care for the older population in the US has historically taken place in hospitals and nursing homes, but today's healthcare innovators are adapting to reflect the fact that 80 percent of older Americans now say they would prefer to receive care in their homes.[23] Louisville has been at the forefront of private-sector efforts to respond to this demand.

In 2021 and 2022, Humana completed a suite of acquisitions and partnerships designed to bring care services into the home, starting with its acquisition of Kindred at Home, making it the country's largest provider of in-home nursing care.[24] With this infrastructure for home care in place, Humana further partnered with the companies Heal and Dispatch Health, who bring primary and urgent care to the home, respectively. The combination has proven synergistic. For example, when Humana member John, who has multiple chronic conditions, was having trouble catching his breath, Kindred at Home nurses called Dispatch, whose technicians performed a chest X-ray, revealing he had pneumonia, saving him a costly emergency room and potential hospital visit. This robust and coordinated home health system is helping seniors get the care they need efficiently and saving them significant expenses. With both Humana and Kindred headquartered in Louisville, health care remains the region's second-largest industry by employment.[25] Leaders across the country are turning their attention to the city and looking at the partnership as a model for delivering home health to patients at scale.

## Looking Ahead

From decades of work in Louisville, stakeholders in the city have learned important lessons about aging care innovation. The companies leading the way know that aging-related industries have only scratched the surface in terms of learning how social determinants of health are impacting patients, and they are seeing that older adults are still adjusting to the rapid influx of new digital tools. Leaders of the Louisville longevity hub are committed to correcting these and other shortfalls: generating cutting-edge solutions that make aging as comfortable, happy, and healthy as possible for older adults. Humana—a center of gravity in the hub—together with academic, private-sector, and public-sector partners, are on their way to creating a model for what the future of home-based care looks like. And with CEO$^C$'s acquisition of Aging 2.0, Louisville is making a name for itself in the aging-innovation space, both nationally and internationally. So long as both private and public stakeholders remain genuinely committed to aging innovation, Louisville will continue to stake a worldwide claim as a leading longevity hub.

There will be challenges ahead. As remote and hybrid work continue to become the new norm, for instance, Louisville companies like Humana and Kindred may need to think creatively about how to keep the innovative energy flowing, even while many workers are located physically outside the immediate geographic environs of Louisville. Another responsibility the industry must own with new advancements is the ethical management of data. As patients find themselves interacting more with digital health tools, it's important they know their data is in good hands. Establishing such a foundation of trust is essential to turning data into better experiences. Humana has already begun to address this issue: in 2020 it took the EqualAI pledge, promising to hold itself to the strictest ethical standards and commit to responsible applications, fair and inclusive actions, trustworthy and transparent technology, and private and secure systems. As peers in aging care nationwide make similar digital advancements, transparency and trust must come hand in hand.

The future of the Louisville longevity hub is bright. Building off the past decade of rapid innovation, major healthcare companies and startups alike have the unique opportunity to share discoveries with national health leaders and play a leading role in operationalizing an aging care movement that prioritizes health equity and home care. From smaller scale partnerships like Humana's relationship with Kare Mobile, to first-of-its-kind collaborations like CEO$^C$, what's happening in Louisville is scalable. Leaders in Louisville have the chance to be a voice for our aging society nationwide, and to show cities across the country what it can mean to truly take care of our aging loved ones.

Bruce Broussard is the president and chief executive officer of Humana Inc., one of the nation's leading healthcare companies, responsible for helping improve the quality of life for people with complex health issues—including seniors, individuals with disabilities, and those receiving assistance from government welfare programs. Humana also supports the health needs of military members and their families, as well as individuals who are covered under employer-sponsored health plans. The company provides an array of services ranging from insurance products to healthcare services such as primary care, home health, pharmacy benefits management, home delivery of prescription drugs, combined with solutions that address social determinants of health.

A ten-year veteran of Humana, Bruce was appointed CEO January 1, 2013, bringing to Humana a wide range of executive leadership experience in publicly traded and private organizations within a variety of healthcare sectors, including oncology, pharmaceuticals, assisted living/senior housing, home care, physician practice management, surgical centers, and dental networks.

Prior to joining Humana, Bruce was the chief executive officer of McKesson Specialty/US Oncology Inc. US Oncology was purchased by McKesson in December 2010. At US Oncology, Bruce served in a number of senior executive roles, including chief financial officer, president, chief executive officer and chairman of the board.

Bruce plays a leadership role in key business advocacy organizations such as the Business Roundtable, the Business Council, and the American Heart Association CEO Roundtable. He is a member of the board of directors of HP Inc., and a member and previous chair of America's Health Insurance Plans (AHIP). Additionally, Bruce serves on the board of the trust for the National Mall, a non-profit philanthropic partner of the National Park Service dedicated to restoring and preserving the National Mall.

## Notes

1. Chris Farrell, "Why Louisville Is Becoming America's Aging Capital," Forbes, January 8, 2018, https://www.forbes.com/sites/nextavenue/2018/01/08/why-louisville-is-becoming-americas-aging-capital/.

2. "Humana History," Zippia, December 14, 2021, https://www.zippia.com/humana-careers-5720/history/.

3. "Louisville, KY Senior Guide," SeniorCare.com, accessed August 18, 2022, https://www.seniorcare.com/directory/ky/louisville/.

4. Julia Huffman, "National Age-Friendly Award Presented to Mayor Fischer during Triad Meeting," Wave, May 10, 2022, https://www.wave3.com/2022/05/11/national-age-friendly-award-presented-mayor-fischer-during-triad-meeting/.

5. The Thrive Center, accessed August 18, 2022, https://www.thrivecenterky.org/; "Age-Friendly Louisville: About Us," Age Friendly Louisville, 2017, https://www.agefriendlylou.com/about-us; "Louisville Health Advisory Board," Louisville's Culture of Health, accessed August 18, 2022, https://www.louisvillecultureofhealth.com/louisville-health-advisory-board; Baylee Pulliam, "UofL, Humana, Humana Foundation Announce up to $25M Innovation Hub to Boost Health Equity for Marginalized Populations," University of Louisville, February 16, 2022, https://louisville.edu/sphis/news/uofl-humana-humana-foundation-announce-up-to-25m-innovation-hub-to-boost-health-equity-for-marginalized-populations.

6. Charron L. Long et al., "Health-Related Social Needs among Older Adults Enrolled in Medicare Advantage," *Health Affairs* 41, no. 4 (April 2022): 557–562, https://doi.org/10.1377/hlthaff.2021.01547.

7. U.S. Census Bureau, accessed August 18, 2022, https://www.census.gov/.

8. Emily Miller, "Average Retirement Income: Where Do You Stand?," Annuity.org, July 22, 2022, https://www.annuity.org/retirement/planning/average-retirement-income/#sources.

9. Lisa Gillespie, "New Data Show Stark Health Disparities in East, West Louisville," 89.3 WFPL News Louisville, March 4, 2017, https://wfpl.org/new-data-show-stark-health-disparities-east-west-louisville/.

10. "Report: Disparities Lead to Worse Health Outcomes for Many Older Louisville Residents," *AARP Bulletin*, May 1, 2022, https://states.aarp.org/kentucky/report-disparities-lead-to-worse-health-outcomes-for-many-older-louisville-residents.

11. "Report: Disparities Lead to Worse Health Outcomes for Many Older Louisville Residents," *AARP Bulletin*.

12. "Loneliness and Social Isolation Social Determinants of Health Issue Brief," Humana, October 2021, https://populationhealth.humana.com/wp-content/uploads/2021/10/SDOH-Issue-Brief_Loneliness_October2021-EXTERNAL.pdf.

13. "Humana Launches New Community of Opportunity Initiative to Advance Health Equity in Louisville's West End," *Humana News*, February 24, 2021.

14. "Derby Equity & Community Initiative," Kentucky Derby Festival, June 22, 2022, https://discover.kdf.org/derby-equity-community-initiative/.

15. "Louisville, KY Senior Guide," SeniorCare.com, accessed August 18, 2022, https://www.seniorcare.com/directory/ky/louisville/.

16. U.S. Census Bureau, accessed August 18, 2022, https://www.census.gov/.

17. Billy Kobin, "Retiring Early? This Study Says You Should Move to Kentucky," *Courier Journal*, October 2, 2018, https://www.courier-journal.com/story/news/2018/10/02/national-study-has-louisville-kentucky-among-most-affordable-early-retirees/1495434002/.

18. "Louisville, Kentucky," Robert Wood Johnson Foundation, March 4, 2022, https://www.rwjf.org/en/cultureofhealth/what-were-learning/sentinel-communities/louisville-kentucky.html.

19. Pulliam, "UofL, Humana, Humana Foundation Announce $25M Innovation Hub to Boost Health Equity."

20. "Expanding the Success of Famileo: Still Bringing Residents and Families Together!," Signature Healthcare, January 5, 2022, https://www.globenewswire.com

/fr/news-release/2022/01/05/2361975/0/en/Expanding-the-Success-of-Famileo-Still
-Bringing-Residents-and-Families-Together.html.

21. "HIMSS 2018: Tech & Aging—How Innovation Can Improve Senior Living,"
HealthTech, March 7, 2018, https://healthtechmagazine.net/media/video/himss-2018
-tech-aging-how-innovation-can-improve-senior-living.

22. "XLerateHealth Selects 7 Healthcare Startups for 2021 Louisville Accelerator
Cohort," Business Wire, August 3, 2021, https://www.businesswire.com/news/home
/20210803005112/en/XLerateHealth-Selects-7-Healthcare-Startups-for-2021-Louis
ville-Accelerator-Cohort.

23. "2018 Home and Community Preferences Survey," AARP, August 2018, https://
doi.org/10.26419/RES.00231.001.

24. "2021 Impact Report," Humana, 2021, https://docushare-web.apps.external
.pioneer.humana.com/Marketing/docushare-app?file=4707469.

25. "Employment Trends by Industry for Louisville Metropolitan Statistical Area,"
Economic Development, Greater Louisville Inc., September 2021, https://www
.greaterlouisville.com/economic.development/#tab-7.

# 14
# Japan's Urban Satellites

Jon Metzler

As measured by share of population 65 and above, Japan is the oldest country in the G7, and indeed the world.[1] Japan's population is not just growing older, but also more centralized around Greater Tokyo: the megalopolis at the country's center and the world's largest metropolitan area. As of October 2021, close to 30 percent of Japan's total population resides in the four capital-area prefectures of Tokyo, Kanagawa, Chiba, and Saitama.[2] This continues a decades-long trend of consolidation around the center.

This central region's share of population aged 15 to 64 trends higher than the rest of the country, in great part because young adults, many from one-child households, come to university in the big city. By dint of momentum, connections, and agglomeration of opportunity, they often stay. A US resident can think of Greater Tokyo as Washington, DC, New York, and Los Angeles rolled up into one: home to the nation's financial sector, media and entertainment industry, and national political system. The Tokyo metropolitan government also has its own large footprint. The co-location of industries and policy creates an economic gravitational force.

As a result, a visitor to Tokyo will see cranes, construction, packed trains—even post-pandemic—and come away with a sense

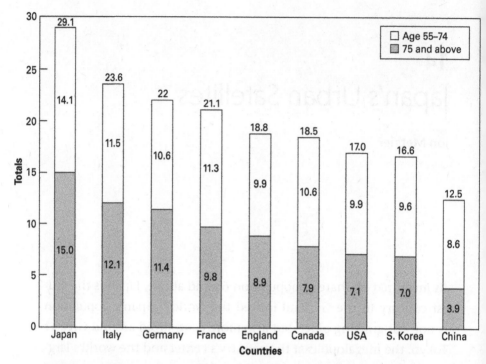

**Figure 14.1**
Longevity cohort: Percentage share of population age 65 and above for the G7 plus South Korea and China. (Source: Statistics Bureau of Japan data, September 2021. Ex-Japan data from World Population Prospects, 2019, https://www.stat.go.jp/data /topics/topi1292.html.)

of general vibrancy and high levels of consumption. First-time visitors, arriving with low expectations having read about Japan's "lost decades," are often surprised by the sight. As the famous quote attributed to a visiting British MP goes, "If this is a recession, I want one."[3] I have witnessed this effect multiple times in taking business students to Japan. The Japan they first experience in Greater Tokyo is bright, lively, and energetic: not the economically lackluster Japan they read about in Western business media.

A visitor to Japan's rural areas, however—even just an hour from Tokyo—will often witness a different set of economic and social signposts. Outside the country's bustling urban centers, there is evidence of depopulation: empty houses, perhaps a scarcity of children out and about, and civic assets or shopping arcades looking somewhat shopworn.

In April 2016, I visited Yuzawa, in Niigata Prefecture, about one hour away from central Tokyo by train. In winter it is a ski town with many small, steeple-roofed inns. I arrived in snowmelt season and the rush of the thaw was audible. The cherry blossoms were still in bloom given the northerly latitude. It was beautiful, but I couldn't help observing empty houses.

Depopulation and its impacts are by no means unique to Japan. It is a phenomenon seen worldwide, particularly after deindustrialization, which can leave empty houses and buildings in its wake. In aging countries that are home to a single megalopolis, like Japan or South Korea, simultaneous aging and population consolidation makes the impacts of aging most apparent in rural areas. Japan may be a bellwether of what could transpire in other aging nations whose economic geography revolves around a megacity.

Per October 2021 government estimates, just one prefecture out of Japan's 47 is still growing, albeit modestly, compared to 2020: Okinawa, a collection of islands about a three-hour flight from Tokyo. All 46 other prefectures shrunk from 2020 to 2021—even the four forming the Tokyo mega-region. For Tokyo itself, this broke a 26-year streak of growth, dating back to 1995.[4] Greater Osaka and Greater Nagoya, which, together with Tokyo, account for 53 percent of Japan's total population, also saw slight declines.

Even while shrinking in absolute terms, Greater Tokyo's relative share of national population grew by a tenth of a percent, to 29.4 percent. The modest rate of growth may have reflected the pandemic's slowing effect on the capital's population concentration. A number of prominent businesses, including titans such as NTT and Fujitsu, announced reductions in their Tokyo office footprints due to increased remote work. More than 300 major firms announced relocations of some of their headcount out of the capital city.[5] Telework also surged, both nationwide and in Tokyo in particular.[6]

Against the backdrop of Japan's continued population flows—toward Greater Tokyo, amid a general population decline, in the midst of experimentation with remote work—there are several examples of communities outside of Tokyo with aging populations that are bucking these prevailing trends. They are distinguishing themselves in a number of ways, such as securing new anchor employers, institutional investment, culture and quality of life, and also by being overt and intentional about what it means to age. These can credibly claim to be examples of longevity hubs. Individually, they are unique. Together, they tell a story of how communities can come into balance with the forces of aging and centralization.

## Defining Longevity Hubs

What constitutes a successful longevity innovation hub? There are a number of factors worth considering, in addition to classic metrics from cluster literature such as patent production and economic output. These might include population dynamics, as well as professional culture: the famous differentiator from *Regional Advantage*, AnnaLee Saxenian's pioneering study of the dynamics at work in Silicon Valley. Other potential distinguishing factors include the presence of major employers, governance and community engagement, quality of life, and institutional engagement with needs around aging.[7]

There is vital national context on why this matters. In the decades ahead, Japan's central government predicts greater consolidation of citizens ages 65 and above in midsize and larger cities, and a drop in this cohort's representation in smaller cities, particularly those with population below 50,000.[8]

From an efficiency perspective—of costs, infrastructure, and health care provision—this prediction perhaps presages difficult national decisions about where (and where *not*) to invest. It may also hint at conditions necessary for the success for a longevity hub outside the big city in countries like Japan: being in range of a large metropolitan area, for instance, and that city's amenities, economy, and healthcare systems.

Japan's renowned train system helps support this "satellite city" scenario. So too do two important, recent developments in Japan's economy: the rise of sharing services and telework. Together, these enable new varieties of age-friendly innovative and economic activity outside of the traditional confines of the capital city.

**Tech-Enabled Distributed Economy**

Telework in Japan has developed in a meaningful way since March 2020. In 2011, after the 3/11 triple disaster—the interrelated earthquake, tsunami, and nuclear accident at the Fukushima Daiichi Nuclear Power Plant—workers stayed home from the office for a week, but often without remote work tools such as laptops and VPNs, not to mention general acceptance of the idea of working from home. As a result, workers were functionally on standby until they could go back to the office. During that immediate post-earthquake week, I had a number of Skype calls with friends and colleagues in Japan who were, in essence, waiting for the call to go back to the office. This was the case even for firms in the tech and telecom sectors. (I had originally planned to be in Japan the day of 3/11 but had postponed the trip. Had I been, I would have been stranded at Narita Airport like a number of colleagues were.)

I happened to be visiting Japan close to nine years later, in January 2020, when the country's first Covid-19 patient was diagnosed. This time, unlike 2011, when the work-from-home order came, companies were more prepared. Importantly, the national government had adopted its Work Style Reform Act in June 2018: an attempt to bring about greater workplace flexibility, lessen overtime, recognize part-time work, and get people to actually use their vacation time.[9] At a practical level, this helped legitimize the notion of working somewhere besides the office, under a supervisor's watchful eyes. And thus in March 2020, when employees had to go remote, at least part of the time, the tools and infrastructure necessary—Zoom, Teams, Slack, VPNs, 4G/5G networks, and Wi-Fi—were available. I cannot emphasize enough how different my experience was working with Japanese colleagues in 2020 and 2021, compared to 2011. A large-sample survey by the Ministry of Land, Infrastructure, Transport and Tourism (MLIT) conducted in October and November 2021 and published in March 2022 supports this, showing that 27 percent of employees engaged in telework, and the share of teleworkers was highest in Greater Tokyo, at 42.1 percent, followed by the Greater Osaka region at 27 percent.[10]

Another important factor that has developed concurrently with remote work infrastructure is the adoption of sharing platforms. These include both international platforms like Airbnb and domestic platforms such as Spacemarket, and hybrid Japan-US operators like the translation firm Gengo (now part of Lionbridge). In 2016, I began research on Japan's sharing economy, and the growth of inbound tourism and its impacts, and from 2017 to 2020 I conducted in-country interviews of a variety of stakeholders: regulators, platform operators, platform suppliers (e.g., hosts), and investors.[11]

Why look at sharing platforms? Over the past 30-plus years, Japanese corporations have greatly increased their usage of part-time workers, with about 37 percent of workers occupying non-regular roles, often at 25 hours per week or less. Women—especially those returning to the workforce after taking time off for parenting—occupy a disproportionate share of this contingent workforce. In fact, only in the 25-to-34-year age bracket do more Japanese women work full-time than non-full-time. In the older age brackets, men, too, step into non-full-time roles. In the age 65-plus bracket, male non-full-time workers outnumber their full-time peers.

For the many Japanese workers and retirees already familiar with part-time or temporary work, sharing platforms offer an intuitive

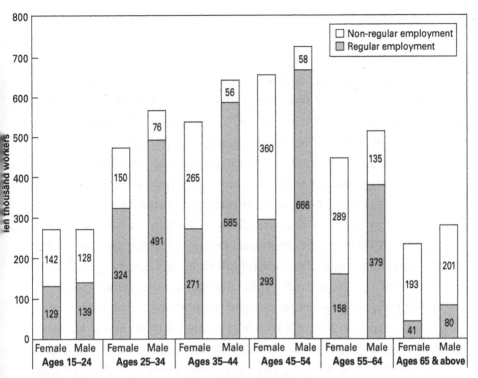

**Figure 14.2**
Japan's full-time and non-full-time workers, by age and gender. February 2021 data. Units in tens of thousands. (Developed based on Bureau of Statistics of Japan data. Table created in 2023 using 2021 data.)

outlet for those who have time, skills, or assets to contribute—across a wide variety of sectors. Japan's Sharing Economy Association segments sharing platforms into five categories, depending on what is being shared: Goods, Space, Mobility, Skill, and Money.[12]

Such firms offer routes for regions' older populations to participate in both the productive and consumer sides of the economy to an extent that might not have been possible in generations past. In many cases the older adults involved find themselves bringing their deep knowledge and decades of experience to bear on new challenges. Airbnb host Keitaro, whom I initially interviewed in August 2018, offers an example of an older Japanese worker who has found his way into the sharing economy. Keitaro retired from a Japanese multinational with experience working overseas: a career that equipped him with international exposure, experience dealing with visas, and a level of comfort with regulatory ambiguity.[13]

Prior to our initial interview, Japan's Tourism Agency; under the Ministry of Land, Infrastructure, Transport and Tourism (MLIT); had announced tighter rules around hosting on home-sharing platforms: limiting guest-nights to 180 per year, and requiring that short-term hosts either be co-resident or professionally licensed as inn operators, or else use a professional property management firm.[14] This led to a dramatic drop in listings on platforms like Airbnb. Following our interview, Keitaro obtained inn operating licenses so he could offer lodging full-time, 365 days per year.

Keitaro possessed both capital (property) and skills (language, hospitality, willingness to navigate regulations), and Airbnb provided a platform through which to monetize these assets. He even helped foreign guests go through the process of obtaining visas. He noted that as a retiree, one of his chief assets was the time and patience necessary to work with his local ward office and help them navigate a dramatic influx in tourists and significant changes in the nature of hospitality. Keitaro, who started hosting as a way to say thank you to international staff he had met over the years, expressed gratitude to Airbnb for providing a platform for community, new experiences, and meaningful income to supplement his pension.

The pandemic put a temporary stop to the rapid growth of inbound tourism, which had reached 31 million visitors to Japan by 2019,[15] but Japan has since taken incremental steps to once again welcome international visitors. Many tourists, foreign and domestic, are older adults. As of 2021, Airbnb Japan notes that 15 percent of its hosts in Japan are above age 60.[16] In a profile of older hosts, Airbnb Japan features Akiko Nakagawa, age 88 as of 2021, who is a "Superhost" on Awaji Island.[17] Her son, Kinya, who lives in Osaka, remotely helps his mother with her hosting business.

In addition to housing, underutilized resources in depopulated areas that are seeing new forms of use thanks to technology platforms include public and commercial spaces, retail spaces, and event halls. Spacemarket, founded in Tokyo in 2014, is a sharing platform that provides access to spaces for short-term use, such as for corporate offsites, remote work, fitness events, parties, wedding receptions—even *cosplay* photo shoots. Spacemarket is now public on the growth exchange of the Tokyo Stock Exchange. The company is also a member of Japan's Sharing Economy Association and helped facilitate multiple interviews with other association members over the course of my research.

Developments around telework and the sharing economy—especially with regard to older workers who may be retired from full-time work—together with high levels of connectivity in terms of both transportation and communications infrastructure, have created conditions to inject new vibrancy in regions outside Tokyo.

In four locations in particular, these shared conditions as well as unique local attributes and institutional investment have combined to nurture economic and cultural activity around aging. For these reasons, the following regions can each make their own claim to be a longevity hub.

## Four Longevity Hot Spots

### Okinawa

The island of Okinawa is known for its beaches and its American military presence—and for its physical and cultural distance from the capital. It is also home to a relatively new research university: the Okinawa Institute of Science and Technology (OIST), announced in 2001 and accredited in 2011. OIST is focused on graduate study in science and offers a five-year, English-language doctorate program in a tropical island environment. In its short history, OIST has injected about 1,350 staff and researchers, or close to 1 percent of Okinawa Prefecture's total population, into the island's economy. In 2019, the institute released a report indicating that every 100 yen spent on OIST had a total impact of 228 yen, 163 of which were captured within Okinawa. Previous OIST president Peter Gruss announced plans for a research park to be developed around the institute, akin to many famous research parks in innovation hubs around the globe, to supplement the area's current startup incubation space. Multiple Tokyo-area venture capital firms have since struck partnerships with OIST.

Aging is on the research agenda at OIST. In one notable research thread, OIST's G0 Cell Unit, led by professor Mitsuhisa Yanagida and working with researchers at Kyoto University's Geriatric Unit, has conducted research in frail and non-frail elderly patients to identify how different metabolites align with different aging markers.[18] As a next step, researchers are undertaking large-scale, deep phenotype analysis of human age cohorts.

Jack Moorman is a cofounder of US-Japan Medtech Frontiers, which hosts a series of healthcare-themed events connecting US and Japanese companies. He also advises a Ministry of Health, Labor and Welfare committee on assistive devices. He observes that the relative diversity of Okinawa's population, pleasant island climate, and inexpensive flights to the main islands of Japan align well with potential further development as a longevity hub.

As US Senator Daniel Moynihan once said, "If you want a great town, build a great university and wait 200 years."[19] Through the talent-attracting forces of capital and beautiful natural environs, an ecosystem of research innovation is developing around OIST on a shorter time frame.

### Awaji Island

Awaji Island, in the Seto Inland Sea, is part of Hyogo Prefecture, best known for the port city of Kobe. Awaji also functions as something of a gateway between the island of Honshu, home to most of Japan's large cities and 80 percent of its population, and the more rural island of Shikoku. Awaji has a population of around 120,000. In 1998, the Awaji Kaikyo Bridge connecting the port city of Kobe with the island of Awaji opened. This six-lane highway made getting to the island much easier.

Yasuyuki Nambu, chief executive of the major Japanese staff placement firm Pasona, is a native of Hyogo Prefecture. In 2008, in an effort to connect urban dwellers with agriculture, the firm started its "agriventure" service to train future farmers. (At one point, its Tokyo headquarters had a vertical farm in a former bank vault.[20]) It also began tourism operations on the island of Awaji. It then acquired buildings, including dormitories, formerly belonging to Sanyo Electric, itself acquired by Panasonic in 2009. Pasona has also developed amusement parks and hospitality facilities on the island.

On March 30, 2020, Pasona announced the Awaji Island Institute for Healthy and Happy Life, located at Awaji Yumebutai, a conference and hospitality center on the island designed by architect Tadao Ando and which opened in 2000, after the opening of the Awaji Kaikyo Bridge.[21] The institute recruited Dr. Hiroshi Kanazawa, an emeritus professor from Osaka University, as director. The institute disseminates information about diet and lifestyle oriented toward promoting the quality of aging life, not just longevity.

In April 2020, early in the pandemic, Nambu himself relocated to Awaji Island, and in September 2020, Pasona announced it would relocate 1,200 staff to Awaji: mainly in IT and back-office functions. This group represents about 1 percent of Awaji's population.

In the Clusters class I teach at the Haas School of Business, we talk about seed companies and anchor companies. Fairchild Semiconductor, which begat Silicon Valley's semiconductor industry, would be an example of a seed company: tremendously impactful, but not in itself large in terms of headcount. Intel, the largest of the "Fairchildren" and significant employer in California, Oregon,

Arizona, New Mexico, and soon Ohio, is an example of an anchor company.[22] In Pasona, Awaji has landed an anchor company that is itself in the staffing and training business, and thus can nurture additional seed companies. This is a win for the regional economy, and also seems symbolic of a shift.

In November 2022, Pasona hosted the Japan-US Well-Being Innovation Forum on Awaji, a health-tech event promoting partnerships between Silicon Valley companies and Japan. The event was held in partnership with Japan Society of Northern California.[23] Having committed to the island, Pasona is now investing in attracting relevant stakeholders to it.

Awaji and Okinawa each offer an example of how large organizations can have a major impact on regional economies. Next, we look at two resort towns that have done relatively well post-pandemic: Kamakura and Karuizawa. They have benefited from the combined impact of proximity to Tokyo; increased remote work; robust transit networks; and being pleasant, uniquely historic places to live.

### Kamakura

Kamakura, famous for its temples and Great Buddha bronze statue, is within an hour of Tokyo by car or train. As of 2020, 31 percent of the city's population is age 65-plus, making it older than the nation at large (28.9 percent 65-plus) or its surrounding prefecture, Kanagawa (25.7 percent). Unlike the town's surrounding prefecture, however, its population is not shrinking, and in fact grew by 0.2 percent in 2020, mainly due to people moving to the area.[24] Kamakura faces out onto Sagami Bay, in an idyllic area where the beach is within walking distance of historic temples.

Within Kamakura is the hillside neighborhood of Imaizumidai, home to some 5,000 residents. The area is a "new town" built in the postwar growth area. By foot, it's about 20 minutes uphill from Kamakura Station. The area's housing predominantly consists of well-maintained, single-family homes.

| Age bracket | not frail | pre-frail | frail | respondents |
|---|---|---|---|---|
| 65–69 | 64.6% | 26.2% | 9.2% | 65 |
| 70–74 | 59.4% | 30.2% | 10.4% | 106 |
| 75–79 | 58.7% | 29.3% | 12.0% | 167 |
| 80–84 | 38.7% | 37.1% | 24.2% | 124 |
| 85–89 | 36.5% | 34.6% | 28.8% | 52 |
| 90 and above | 25.0% | 25.0% | 50.0% | 8 |

Figure 14.3
Independent Imaizumidai residents, by level of self-declared physical "frailty." (Recreated from figures 2–7, Survey on Community Building for a Long-Lived Society, 2020. Accessed by the author at http://imaizumidai.org/eventnews-photo/syukei 20201223.pdf.)

On the street, many pedestrians can be seen walking with assistance from rollators. A survey conducted by the Imaizumidai neighborhood association in February 2020 (the "Survey on Community Building for a Long-Lived Society") indicated that 74 percent of respondents (658 households or 1,051 residents) were 65 or older, 52 percent were over age 75, and 14 percent were over 85. Just 8 percent were in their twenties. The vast majority of neighborhood residents reported living with other people; twelve percent of respondents lived alone.[25] The neighborhood's hyperdense longevity cohort has self-organized through its neighborhood association, which in addition to conducting surveys also publishes monthly newsletters and holds regular events, supported by member fees of 3,500 yen per year, or around $30.[26]

The same 2020 survey segmented residents by their level of independence and, for those not in need of official caregiving, whether they are "frail," "pre-frail," or "not frail."

Overall, it's a relatively active group of residents. Seventy-four percent get around by bus; 67 percent on foot. Still, 230 respondents described having fallen in the past year. As one might expect for a neighborhood with residents living well into their nineties, the share of residents receiving caregiving services (as designated by Japan's Long-Term Care Insurance) increases with older age brackets. Seventy-five percent of residents aged 90 and over receive some form of support from Japan's LTCI program.

In January 2017, the following stakeholders announced that a Living Lab would be launched in the Imaizumidai community: the city of Kamakura; the University of Tokyo Institute of Gerontology; Sumitomo Mitsui Bank; and TSKI, a local nonprofit supporting the Kamakura Imaizumidai community. TSKI also organizes some of the events promoted by the neighborhood association.

The Kamakura Living Lab states that it takes its inspiration from similar institutions in Europe, and Sweden in particular.[27] At its outset, the lab focused on getting customer (i.e., Imaizumidai residents) feedback on new product and service concepts targeting senior customers, and stated it hoped to expand activity to generate ideas about new modes of working and better ways of living healthily and happily. The lab is not a fixed installation; rather, a local community hall is used as needed to host events and programming.

The king and queen of Sweden visited in April 2018, accompanied by Hisako, Princess Takamado, a member of the Japanese Imperial Family.[28] The king and queen were shown a demonstration of an Itoki telework desk, a product tested at the Living Lab, and a "close call" reporting system being developed by an automaker. The Itoki telework desk is a multifunction desk meant to support people who have to toggle between remote work (from home) and caregiving or parenting duties.[29]

The Ministry of Health, Labor and Welfare began holding its annual Long-Term Care Insurance Summit in 2000. In 2018, the ministry rebranded the conference as the Summit for Promotion of Regional Prosperity, with the goal of promoting best practices for living well at the regional level. ("Regional" in such settings generally refers to "outside of Tokyo.") The event venue has rotated through various regional cities. In November 2021, Kamakura held the third annual summit, and featured panelists from the Kamakura Living Lab initiative, including representatives of Itoki; the mayor of Kamakura; professor Hiroko Akiyama of the University of Tokyo Institute of Gerontology; Fukiko Yano, a local chef and owner of Kamakura Dining, a local cooking school; and TSKI, the nonprofit supporting the Imaizumidai neighborhood association.[30]

### Karuizawa

Nagano Prefecture, home of the Japanese Alps and the site of the 1998 Winter Olympics as well as Japan's wine industry, takes great pride in having the nation's longest life expectancy, both for women and men.[31] It is also home to the resort town of Karuizawa, once a stop on the Nakasendo route connecting Edo (now Tokyo) and Kyoto during the Edo era. Karuizawa was "discovered" by Western missionaries as a cooler summer getaway in the 1880s, and the Canadian missionary Alexander Croft Shaw famously described the town as a "hospital without a roof."[32]

Today, Karuizawa is a small town with global reach. In 2019, this town of just under 20,000 hosted the G20 Ministerial Meeting on Energy Transitions and Global Environment for Sustainable Growth. Following the G20 summit, the town updated its Smart Community vision in an attempt to harness the power of information and communications technology to reduce its energy footprint and promote sustainability. It has updated that plan each year since.[33] The town hosted a meeting of the G7 foreign ministers in April 2023.[34]

A short train ride away from Greater Tokyo, life in Karuizawa permits day-trips to the office, or to downtown healthcare services. It is widely perceived as an upmarket, affluent destination, with unique historical associations and proximity to wine, lakes, and skiing. The town was the summer home of Nobel Prize for Literature laureate Yasunari Kawabata and the Meiji-era industrialist Saburosuke Mitsui, among other notables.

In 2021, the town grew by around 600 in population; as of this writing its share of population age 66 and above is 33 percent, up from 25 percent in 2010.[35]

The town is also home to a collaboration beginning in 2017 between Shinshu University of Nagano Prefecture, and the Research Center for Advanced Science and Technology (RCAST) at the University of Tokyo.[36]

As Dr. Katsuya Tamai, professor at RCAST UTokyo, describes it: "Karuizawa was known as an affluent tourism destination, but it also had resource shortages often seen in small towns. For example the hospital had one specialist in internal medicine for a town of 20,000." One goal for the Shinshu-RCAST collaboration was to make the town more attractive for doctors. As part of the universities' collaboration, an RCAST assistant professor moved to Karuizawa to be at the hospital on a part-time basis, and in so doing attracted three other doctors to go with him. Another result of the collaboration was that Professor Toshiro Fujita, emeritus faculty from Tokyo University and project professor at Shinshu University, took on the role of emeritus director of Karuizawa Hospital in 2021.[37] Fujita is known for his research on the relationship between salt and hypertension. Nagano Prefecture is known as a "blue zone" of heightened longevity—even within long-lived Japan—due in part to a local campaign to lower salt intake.[38]

Professor Tamai commented on the town's additional benefits from the perspective of RCAST: the short commute from Tokyo and greater outdoor space available, for instance, has permitted research that wasn't viable in the urban constraints of Tokyo.[39] He added that, of the various collaborations RCAST has pursued with regional universities, the partnership with Shinshu in Karuizawa is unique, in that RCAST may transfer a portion of its operations from Tokyo to the Karuizawa campus, due to the space available and pleasant working conditions.[40] He acknowledged the role that rapid train access played in creating favorable conditions for such collaborations, noting that not all towns are so blessed.

The parties updated their agreement in June 2022, and announced expansion of the collaboration to education and town development strategy. Here, Professor Tamai shared a new, somewhat surprising goal for the collaboration: improvement of local high schools, which would support the town's ability to attract talent from the city. This goal echoed an ambition, seen in surveys of longtime residents of both Karuizawa and Kamakura, to make their town attractive for their grandchildren. Having a strong local school system can help parents of working age commit to teleworking from the area while being nearer to their children's grandparents: a potential multiplier of efforts to recruit talent out of the big city.

## The Virtue of Multiple Longevity Hubs

The gravitational force of Greater Tokyo on Japan's young and middle-aged population means that the impact of aging shows up first outside of the capital. Several of these satellite communities—Japan's multiple longevity hubs—have made experimentation and research around the needs of older adults, and the opportunities they pose, a priority. These hubs share a few commonalities: robust transportation infrastructure, for instance. All the longevity hubs profiled in this article are well connected to major cities, whether by highway (Awaji), train (Karuizawa and Kamakura), or air (Okinawa). This connectivity enables visits to or from major cities for their amenities or to see loved ones. All are also harnessing information and communications technology in the form of broadband, remote work tools, and sharing platforms, which can empower local workers and hosts. Notably, none of these locations were purpose-built as retirement destinations. Rather, they are inherently attractive locations that also happen to be attractive to older adults. As a result, some are even growing in population, despite demographic headwinds.

Importantly, all four communities boast concerted institutional activity around aging. Whether in the form of universities or anchor employers, these attempts to innovate for national and global markets also serve to augment local economies.

Such efforts are not only signs of fresh life in the world's oldest country, but also may serve as indicators of the conditions necessary for communities in other countries with a capital megacity to develop regional hubs and cultures of innovation of their own. Japan has long served as a macroeconomic bellwether of what countries might expect as they age. Perhaps its patterns of economic and innovative geography, too, offer a preview for nations just behind it on the aging curve.

Jon Metzler is a continuing lecturer at the Haas School of Business at the University of California, Berkeley, where he teaches on competitive strategy; strategy for the networked economy; international business, including business in Japan; and clusters. Jon teaches at the undergraduate and MBA levels. His research interests include 5G and cybersecurity, sharing economies, aging and longevity, and regional clusters. Jon is also associated faculty for the UC-Berkeley Center for Japanese Studies. Jon has taught at Haas since 2014 and is a faculty mentor at Berkeley SkyDeck, the accelerator for Berkeley-affiliated startups. He is also a Senior Research Affiliate for the Berkeley APEC Study Center. He has lectured at Waseda Business School in Japan since 2018. Jon completed his MBA/MA-Asian Studies at the Haas School of Business. There he cofounded the Berkeley Asia Business Conference, and authored a thesis comparing the innovation ecosystems and new venture formation in Silicon Valley and Japan. His interest in clusters and regional advantage stems from this experience. Jon also has a BA from the University of Michigan.

Jon is a member of the board of directors for the Japan Society of Northern California, a 118-year-old nonprofit fostering connections between Northern California and Japan; he served as board chair from 2017 to 2020. Jon and his family make their home in the San Francisco area.

## Notes

1. "Statistical Topics, #129, Part 1: Senior Population," Ministry of Internal Affairs and Communications, Japan, September 2021.

2. "National Census of Japan," Ministry of Internal Affairs and Communications, Japan, October 2021.

3. As quoted in David Pilling, *Bending Adversity: Japan and the Art of Survival* (London: Allen Lane, 2014).

4. The year 1995 was an eventful one: it was the year of the Tokyo subway gassing; the Great Hanshin (Kobe) earthquake; and the year the yen spiked to 79 yen to the dollar, putting a crimp on Japanese exports. I was living in Yokohama at the time of the subway gassing and Kobe earthquake.

5. Alex K. T. Martin, "Tokyo Exodus: Is the Capital Losing Its Luster among Businesses?," *Japan Times*, December 19, 2021, https://www.japantimes.co.jp/news/2021/12/19/national/tokyo-exodus-remote-work/; Eri Sugiura, "The Great Tokyo Exodus," *Financial Times*, June 6, 2022.

6. "Japan's Uneven Teleworking Revolution," East Asia Forum, November 24, 2022, https://www.eastasiaforum.org/2022/11/25/japans-uneven-teleworking-revolution/.

7. For example, Richard Florida, *The Rise of the Creative Class, Updated Edition* (New York: Basic Books, 2019).

8. "4 地域別にみた高齢化 | 令和元年版高齢社会白書（全体版）—内閣府," 内閣府ホームページ," accessed July 9, 2023, https://www8.cao.go.jp/kourei/whitepaper/w-2019/html/zenbun/s1_1_4.html.

9. "閣法 第196回国会 63 働き方改革を推進するための関係法律の整備に関する法律案," accessed July 9, 2023, https://www.shugiin.go.jp/internet/itdb_gian.nsf/html/gian/keika/1DC8956.htm.

10. MLIT State of Telework survey, March 2022. N=40,000, of which 35,990 were employees, and 4,010 were self-employed.

11. Research was conducted with support from the UC-Berkeley Center for Japanese Studies. The San Francisco office of JETRO, under METI, also provided generous support in arranging interviews in 2017.

12. "Change Japan Through Sharing," The Sharing Economy Association Japan, https://sharing-economy.jp/en/.

13. The author thanks the team at Airbnb Japan, which arranged interviews with super hosts and provided space for interviews. The team also sat for multiple conversations from 2018 to 2022.

14. "住宅宿泊事業法｜観光産業｜政策について｜観光庁," accessed July 9, 2023, https://www.mlit.go.jp/kankocho/shisaku/sangyou/juutaku-shukuhaku.html.

15. "Trends in Visitor Arrivals to Japan," Japan Tourism Statistics, updated 2023, https://statistics.jnto.go.jp/en/graph/#graph--inbound--travelers--transition.

16. "In an Era of 100-Year Lifespans, Home Sharing Is a Way of Life for Seniors," Airbnb News, October 22, 2021, https://news.airbnb.com/ja/senior_host_2021_japan/.

17. Airbnb news, "In an Era of 100-Year Lifespans, Home Sharing Is a Way of Life for Seniors."

18. "Leaving Its Mark: How Frailty Impacts the Blood," Okinawa Institute of Science and Technology OIST, April 7, 2020, https://www.oist.jp/news-center/news/2020/4/7/leaving-its-mark-how-frailty-impacts-blood; "Frailty Markers Comprise Blood Metabolites Involved in Antioxidation, Cognition, and Mobility," accessed July 9, 2023, https://doi.org/10.1073/pnas.1920795117.

19. Paraphrased from Enrico Moretti, *The New Geography of Jobs* (Boston: Houghton Mifflin Harcourt, 2012).

20. "Pasona O2," Atlas Obscura, accessed July 9, 2023, http://www.atlasobscura.com/places/pasona-02.

21. The conference center was originally planned to open with the development of the Awaji Kaikyo Bridge. Yumebutai translates to "stage of dreams."

22. "Fairchild, Fairchildren, and the Family Tree of Silicon Valley," CHM, December 20, 2016, https://computerhistory.org/blog/fairchild-and-the-fairchildren/.

23. Japan Society, "2022 U.S.-Japan Healthcare Connection: Well-Being Innovation Forum in Awajishima," *Japan Society of Northern California* (blog), October 12, 2022, https://www.usajapan.org/2022-u-s-japan-healthcare-connection-well-being-innovation-forum-in-awajishima/. The author has been a board director of the Japan Society of Northern California since 2015.

24. Data available at https://www.city.kamakura.kanagawa.jp/soumu/toukei/documents/kamakuranojinnkoutosetai09014.pdf.

25. Accessed by the author at http://imaizumidai.org.

26. Monthly newsletters are accessible here: http://imaizumidai.org/4-7tayori.html.

27. Statement may be found here: https://www.city.kamakura.kanagawa.jp/kisya /data/2016/documents/living-lab-press.pdf.

28. "スウェーデン国王夫妻「鎌倉リビング・ラボ」視察に今泉台来訪," *NPO法人 タウンサポート鎌倉今泉台*" (blog), May 11, 2018, http://www.npotski.com/archives/2790.

29. Itoki sells a variety of work-from-home-oriented products: https://eshop.itoki .jp/shop/e/eTelework/.

30. 鎌倉市, "第3回地域共生社会推進全国サミットinかまくら," 鎌倉市," accessed July 9, 2023, https://www.city.kamakura.kanagawa.jp/chikyo/summit2020.html.

31. "「長寿日本一の秘訣は適度な毒」長野県民が実践する病気知らずの食事法 50年かけて短命から長寿に大変化," PRESIDENT Online（プレジデントオンライン）," February 6, 2021, https://president.jp/articles/-/42931.

32. "Karuizawa, Nagano Pref.," JapanGov, accessed July 9, 2023, https://www.japan .go.jp/g20japan/karuizawa.html.

33. "軽井沢スマートコミュニティについて | 長野県軽井沢町公式ホームページ," accessed July 9, 2023, https://www.town.karuizawa.lg.jp/www/contents/1499066054858/index .html.

34. "G7 Foreign Ministers' Meeting in Karuizawa, Nagano," Ministry of Foreign Affairs of Japan, accessed July 9, 2023, https://www.mofa.go.jp/ecm/ec/page24e _000391.html.

35. Data can be found at https://www.town.karuizawa.lg.jp/www/contents/15284 25604611/simple/r04_toukeisho.pdf.

36. "軽井沢プロジェクト・軽井沢臨床研究プロジェクト," 信州大学 社会基盤研究所," accessed July 9, 2023, https://www.shinshu-u.ac.jp/institution/rcss/project/karuizawa .html.

37. "名誉院長の紹介 | 軽井沢病院," accessed July 9, 2023, https://www.karuizawa hospital.jp/www/hospital/contents/1021000000017/index.html.

38. "Toshiro Fujita," RCAST, https://www.rcast.u-tokyo.ac.jp/en/research/people /staff-fujita_toshiro.html.l; Kirk Spitzer, "Longevity Secrets from Japan—How to Live Longer," AARP, accessed July 9, 2023, https://www.aarp.org/health/healthy -living/info-2014/longevity-secrets-from-japan.html.

39. Research involving UAVs was one example.

40. RCAST's website lists 14 regional collaborations; a University of Tokyo publication published in fall 2017 listed 32 regional collaborations.

# 15
# Milan

Emanuela Notari

Longer life is one of humankind's most important achievements. Thanks to advances in medicine, prevention, healthier home and work environments, and improved general well-being, average lifespans in most developed countries have reached lengths unheard of only a century ago.

In Italy, longer lifespans—as well as reduced fertility and a large, aging baby boomer generation—are causing the population to grow older at a rate never before seen. In economic and policy circles, this trend tends to be presented as a threat, since an aging population may saddle an unprepared country with a host of issues, including high eldercare and healthcare costs, pension liabilities out of step with revenues, and macroeconomic effects of a shrinking workforce and an increasing number of retirees. Indeed—across its physical, financial, and policy infrastructure—Italy's demographic future demands a broad set of updates. However, the need to reimagine aspects of life in Italy for a longer-living population is more than just a burden or obligation to be fulfilled. It is also an extraordinary chance. With its historical strengths in industries that track changing consumer demands closely, Italy has a unique chance to turn the seeming liability posed by population aging into an economic and social opportunity.

## Demographic Background

### Demographic Straits

Italy is Europe's oldest major economy by percentage of older adults.[1] Today, 14 million Italians, or 23.8 percent of the total population, are age 65 or over. This group is projected to reach 20 million by midcentury: thirty-five percent of a shrinking total population. Fourteen percent will be over 80.[2] In this future Italy, the current ratio of 1.87 seniors[3] for every young person under age 15 will rise to three seniors, and the ratio of three people of traditional working age for every senior (as of 2021) will settle at less than two-to-one by 2050.[4]

The aging of the Italian population is due in no small part to the lengthening of Italian lifespans. As of 2021, the country's average life expectancy is 82.4 years: ten years longer than half a century prior.[5] This figure is estimated to reach 88 years by midcentury.

It is not that instances of such longevity never occurred in the past. A reader of Italian history will often encounter individuals, usually belonging to wealthier social classes and less strenuous occupations, who outlived their period's average lifespan. Italy's modern life expectancy gains are more widely distributed, although significant differences still persist between rich and poor provinces. Italy's long-standing North-South divide, for instance, is not just a matter of wealth but also lifespan. In 2021, residents of the North could expect 1.7 more years of life than those in the South.

Italy ranks near Europe's average in *healthy* life expectancy, the average number of years someone can expect to live without irreversible limitations in their ability to perform activities of daily life. Both Italian men and women at age 65 can expect to live ten additional years in good health.[6]

Even if healthy life in Italy now often extends to age 75, however, the country's older population in need of care is growing. Italy's total count of non-self-sufficient seniors now stands at around

3.8 million: a number that, as of 2019, represents 28.5 percent of all Italians aged 65 and over, and which is projected to reach five million by 2030.[7] Of these older adults, 312,000 reside in an assisted living facility; the rest rely on voluntary family caregivers.[8]

Italy's growing need for caregivers is deeply interconnected with yet another factor making the country's population older: its low birthrate. At 1.25 children per woman, this figure is among the lowest in Europe, and markedly lower than the 2.9-child norm that prevailed at the birth of the baby boomer generation.

Today, having children requires greater resources than in the past. According to Centro Studi Moneyfarm, raising a child to age 18 in Italy costs around €140,000 in total.[9] Making matters more dire is an insufficient supply of public nurseries and kindergartens, as well as the fact that public funds for parents are restricted to low-income families, rather than universally aimed at all parents, as in other EU countries such as France. As a result of these and other factors, only 50 percent of working-age Italian women are employed, 61 percent of whom work part-time.[10] Due in part to a lower number of worked hours, Italian women bring home €57 for every €100 earned by men.

Further economic problems arise from the pension gap: the unfortunate fact that working Italian women, despite being longer-lived than men, receive 37 percent less income from occupational pensions.[11] (Women also rely on their husbands' pension and/or state social pensions.)

Countries such as France and Germany, experiencing the same demographic winter trend as Italy, have long since adopted policies to adapt to population aging. Their strategies support the reconciliation of women's family and work burdens. Other countries, such as Canada, have promoted selective immigration policies as a means to address labor shortfalls. Italy has done little in either regard: inaction that has exacerbated the nation's demographic and economic straits.

**Gender and Financial Sustainability**
When faced with the realities of aging, Italian individuals and the Italian state alike are united by a single need: sustainability. The nation's 1996 and 2011 pension reforms, which shifted the emphasis from defined-benefit to defined-contribution retirement plans, reduced the monthly check older Italians receive. Most Italians did not metabolize this reality, however, and still hold in their collective imagination the idea that the state will provide the income necessary for a rather comfortable old age, as it did for their parents and grandparents.

Many, thinking ahead to retirement, also mistakenly believe that life in old age will cost less than in middle age. In fact, costs can increase in the last decades of a long life, as an individual's health becomes more fragile while their needs increase.

Costs of longevity and population shrinking are therefore on the rise for both individuals and the state, undermining Italy's universal health system and pension system, and the sustainability of many individuals' longevity.

Because individuals are often inadequately prepared for their economic future, the Italian nation is underprepared as well. In Germany, for instance, it is mandatory for every citizen worker to have a health policy and a long-term care (LTC) policy, toward which the worker and the employer each pay 50 percent. In Italy, a country that has long relied on a universal health system and the family as a safety net, LTC insurance policies have an infinitesimal penetration. As a result, more than 10 percent of Italy's total population acts as an informal caregiver (a figure that does not include the country's one million professional caregivers). Seventy-five percent of them are women. Most caregivers are between age 45 and 55,[12] a range that is trending older. These women (and many men) often care for aging parents as well as their own adult offspring, who have been leaving home later in recent years. Meanwhile, the large subset of older Italians who need care is not limited to people who are extremely frail or unable to complete activities of daily living. The act of caring for elderly family members is frequently made up of a thousand small errands, financial support, attention, and supplementary household tasks.

After the age of 60, many of the care-providing Italians become full-time grandparents, about three-quarters of whom spend at least two hours a day caring for their grandchildren. According to SHARE (The Survey of Health, Ageing and Retirement in Europe), Italy is the country with the highest share of grandparents taking care of grandkids on a daily basis—33 percent. Older adults both receive and provide care; it is often older Italians aged 65 and above who take care of their non-independent cohabiting family members.

To further complicate matters, as of 2021, Italian women's life expectancy at 65 is around 3.4 years higher than men's.[13] This fact, combined with the two-year-average age difference within couples, means older women live an average of five to six years alone at the end of their life. These years are often the most demanding in terms of the need for care, an issue exacerbated by the fact that women enter later life with significantly less pension income than men. Eighteen percent of women aged 65 to 79 are entitled to no pension at all, and live off their husband's pension income or a social security check. Eighty-two percent of people who qualify for Italy's minimum subsistence supplement are women, numbering 2.5 million;[14] 600,000 more women receive another form of social supplement that is also conditional on having very low income.[15] Taken together, this means almost one in two women over the age of 65 are receiving no pension or a very low one, supplemented by anti-poverty measures. Although the presence of spousal income makes the situation somewhat better than it appears, overall, almost 50 percent of women in Italy are lacking in economic independence as they age.

Meanwhile, divorces have been increasing since 2015, when a new "fast divorce" law was approved.[16] The vast majority of marriages with one partner over age 60 are undergone by men entering a second marriage with a younger woman. Divorced women who are already advanced in years, meanwhile, are more likely to remain alone.

## Opportunities and Players

### An Opportunity Out of Necessity
Italians aged 65 and over own 40 percent of Italy's privately held wealth, a number out of proportion to their 23.8 percent share of the Italian population. Although this figure glosses over many nuances of economic diversity, as a group, older Italians are overall in good economic condition. At least half of them are in the younger, age 65-to-75 bracket; they often enjoy good physical and cognitive health, and remain active. The vast majority of older Italians (87 percent) live in houses they own;[17] and they often have defined-benefit pensions, little or no debt, and savings they accumulated earlier in lives where work seniority automatically brought economic growth. Most of them willingly spend on quality products, services, and experiences, and as many as half of Italians over 65 also contribute to the economic well-being of their adult children who face occupational uncertainty and consequent economic hardship.[18]

### The Beginnings of a New Market
Given the disproportionate wealth of older generations and its stable nature, one reasonable response from the private sector would be to churn out products and services according to older adults' needs and specifications. And indeed, a new silver economy, built on meeting and stimulating the true and emerging desires of older adults, is developing in Italy, with particular energy centered around Milan, the country's financial hub and business core that is perhaps best known for being the heart of the Italian fashion industry.

Areas of special activity include home healthcare, personalized medicine, digital consumer tech, and dedicated senior housing. Spreading word about this activity among the separate industries involved, meanwhile, is a growing group of Italian academic, NGO, and private-sector longevity experts, who communicate via articles, surveys, conferences, advisory activities, and other events. Taken together, this market can be said to be developing along three separate axes of discovery: scientific discovery and engineering, the discovery of Italian older adults by industry (foreign and domestic), and the discovery of traditionally youth-oriented products by older adults.

This last category has accelerated in the wake of the COVID-19 pandemic, which led Italian older adults to learn a variety of digital skills, including the use of Zoom for joining with relatives during lockdowns, buying groceries online for home delivery, shopping on Amazon and other online retailers, home banking, streaming television and movies, and engaging in telemedicine procedures.

The recent pandemic has also lent momentum to the field of precision medicine. Completely individually tailored treatments may be many years away, but in the nearer term Italy is strongly supporting gender-specific medicine. Globally speaking, until the late 1990s, medical and pharmacological research was conducted almost exclusively on male subjects, both human and animal.[19] As a result, women have long been treated with drugs designed for men, only in lower doses. This has potentially produced a mass of side effects, as well as a diagnostic and therapeutic generalization that is holding back improvements in later female life, which is potentially responsible in part for chronic conditions on the feminine side of longevity.[20]

In an effort to rectify this situation, Italy has taken a number of concrete steps, including the passage of a law in 2018—the first of its kind in Europe—requiring clinical trials of medical products to strive for adequate gender representation;[21] as well as Italy's Health

Ministry's 2020 establishment of a national observatory dedicated to gender medicine.[22] Northern Italy, in particular, is serving as a locus of activity in this ongoing work. In 2017, the State Center for Gender Medicine (Centro Studi Nazionale Salute e Medicina di Genere) was founded in Padova. With the launch of this center, the region has stepped to the forefront of European promotion of gender-specific research and medicine.

Longevity medicine also includes preventive treatments. SoLongevity,[23] a company born in 2019 from the partnership of clinicians and researchers from the three main hospitals of Milan, offers anti-aging medical advisory, treatments, supplements, and nutraceutical products, all aimed at boosting well-being during aging.

Italy's push into the neglected frontiers of gender medicine and opening its way into longevity medicine come at the same time that industry is making strides into neglected markets centered around the wants and needs of older adults. In this regard, Italy's housing and financial industries stand out.

**Senior Housing**
Housing is of direct relevance to both individual and social sustainability in an aging Italy. The homes of Italian seniors are largely very old and tend to lack energy efficient insulation, heating, and air-conditioning systems. One in four residential buildings with over two floors and at least one older resident has no elevator,[24] conditions that are especially prevalent in Italy's many historical centers. Many older adults' longtime family homes where they once raised their children are also larger than necessary,[25] which creates a burden in terms of maintenance and utilities costs. As a result of these and other factors, 48 percent of Italian over-65s' monthly spending is on their homes. The combination of expense, isolation, unfit interior design and layout that increase risk of falls, temperature extremes, difficult-to-manage outdoor spaces, and inadequate accessibility together make aging in place a challenge

for many Italians. In an early 2022 survey of Italians both under and over age 55, the Active Longevity Institute, which I cofounded in 2019, found that over 25 percent of respondents perceive that their home could be unfit to host them in safety and comfort when they reach a very old age—a share that rises to 44 percent among women under 55,[26] probably due to the fact that they themselves experience their parents aging and becoming frailer in unfit homes.

The first wave of companies recognizing opportunity in older Italians' housing needs came from outside Italy's borders in the form of two major French housing groups: Domitys and Over (a partner of Korian), which entered the Italian market in 2020. As the president of Over said in a 2021 interview, 20 percent of people in medical assisted living could easily live in senior housing if only it were an option in the Italian market.[27]

The Italian senior housing industry is in many respects in its early stages. As of 2022, the Italian state offers neither financial aid for senior housing residents and builders, nor regulation around what might be considered "senior housing." Now that the business case for senior housing has been made, however, new players are getting involved. These include private-sector projects, such as the one undertaken by the UK's Guild Living, which launched a partnership in 2022 with the architect German firm Specht Gruppe to develop new senior residences in Tuscany.[28]

A number of investment funds and organizations have also found their way into this space, often with some degree of involvement from the Italian state. These include Invimit SGR, an asset management company created by Italy's Ministry of Finance for the development of real estate funds, whose projects may include senior residences created through the improvement of publicly owned buildings.

The Aristotele Senior Fund is another such example: it is owned by the public pension company INPS as well as the private

Professional Pension Funds Inarcassa and Enpap, and managed by the real estate asset manager Fabrica SGR.[29]

Convivit is yet another such company, established from a partnership between the publicly owned Cassa Depositi Prestiti (83 percent of which belongs to the Ministry of Finance) and the private group Generali Welion (part of the bank/insurance group Generali Italia), whose goal is to develop senior housing and assisted living facilities. As of 2021 the company's plan included building 2,000 apartments in Italy by 2030.[30]

The confluence of public and private energy devoted to addressing the demand for senior housing will soon turn into properties for Italian (and foreign) seniors in need of a more comfortable, social, and safe place to live. The growing awareness of the silver economy's potential, meanwhile, will not stay confined to the housing industry.

New concepts of city districts that include a senior living are also emerging, like Milano4You, a new, 90,000-square-meter "digital" district that is being built just outside Milan to offer a housing concept where residents' lifestyle is supported by technology.

### The Financial Industry

In addition to backing new housing products, Italy's financial industry is beginning to find other ways to tap into older Italians' demand. A number of Italian banks and insurance companies; including BNL BNP Paribas, Zurich Insurance Group, Allianz, Generali, and Candriam; are now offering their financial consultants training on how to understand and fulfill the complex, emerging needs of longer-living clientele. Others, not necessarily in the finance domain, are training their employees on how to approach a mutigenerational place of work. Many of such companies rely on the assistance of Valore D, the first corporate association based in Milan promoting gender balance and an inclusive culture in the workplace.

Like many other countries, Italy has undergone a shift from defined-benefit to defined-contribution pensions, which transferred part of the longevity risk from the state to the individual. Under the new pension regime and current demographics, the market must accommodate not only supplementary pension funds themselves, but also such concerns as long-term care policies, accumulation plans, and health insurance—everything that can allow people to plan for the future by reducing longevity risks.

As it currently stands, the Italian financial planning sector has yet to largely shift from old life insurance models that mitigate the financial risks of death to new financial planning practices that limit the risk of outliving one's savings. Moreover, the expected increase in women's share of assets under management in Europe (from 30 percent to at least 45 percent by 2030)[31] will force the industry to reprioritize women's longevity planning: targeting the older women inheriting their husbands' wealth, and younger women making their own wealth through a career, as well as women's specific risks linked to the big longevity transitions, such as the loss or incapacity of a loved one, or the need for professional caregiving.

## New Longevity Welfare

Some Italian companies are developing new corporate welfare programs designed to positively impact senior workers and their families. According to recent Boston Consulting Group and Jointly research, 17 percent of Italian workers spend more than €10,000 a year for family members who need assistance, and 30 percent of working caregivers spend more than 14 hours a week assisting a family member.[32]

For instance, take ATM, Milan's municipal transportation company, which received accolades in 2022 for the steps it took to support gender balance and women's career-building, including the provision of corporate kindergartens not only for workers' children but also for their grandchildren. In 2023, the company plans to launch a special welfare program dedicated to the sustainability of female workers' longevity. The program's goal is to help the company's woman workers become aware of the specific risks they may encounter as they age, and to provide them with training and tools to protect their financial, physical, and human capital.

Other Italian companies, too, are paying attention to the specific needs of their senior workers and caregiving workers, and offering special benefits like flexible working hours and remote working, decentralized corporate co-working places, and corporate kindergartens. Companies that have taken such steps include Terna, one of the main players in electric power transmission with over 5,000 employees in Italy; Team System, which offers digital management systems for companies and professionals; and TIM, the main national telephone company, which offers their caregiver employees both a network of services on demand and a family manager call service.

Many companies, including TIM and others, develop these "new welfare programs," as they are known, with the help of specialized contractors like Jointly, a private benefit company, which is particularly engaged in turning corporate welfare into corporate well-being.

The need for assistance and care is also inspiring startups. These include Village Care, specialized in services and consultancy for caregivers; Ugo, created in 2015 and active in 10 Italian regions as of 2023, which provides accompaniment for errand-running, medical visits, and companionship; and Nipote in affitto (Grandson for rent), which helps older people overcome home IT problems.

But aging can also be a pleasure. This is what another startup claims and promotes. Cocooners, the first online community of people over 60, offers gatherings in various cities, trips, and even romantic dating.

## Convening Forces

With much of the innovative energy in its universities and business leadership focused on aging, the northern city of Milan and its
surrounding region offer especially fertile ground for Italy's silver
economy. The city hosts the Silver Economy Network (SEN) as part
of Assolombarda's Life Science Department (an association of biological and medical enterprises in Milan's larger region, Lombardy).
SEN's president, Mariuccia Rossini, is also the president of the
senior living company Over. At the beginning of December 2022,
SEN launched the Silver Economy Observatory in cooperation with
Lattanzio KIBS (a provider of services and strategic consultancy to
the public administration) and Comarch (which offers IT software
for communication service providers).

Milan is also where I cofounded the Active Longevity Institute
(ALI) in mid-2019. ALI offers consultancy services, lectures, training
on longevity planning for financial consultants, and surveys to test
specific issues and ideas on a proprietary panel of around 700 people.

Northern Italy—as well as, in the south, Rome—also hosts villages for people with Alzheimer's disease, including some designed
after Hogeweyk, a trailblazing Dutch facility. These include Mon-
za's Il Paese Ritrovato, Milan's Piazza Grace, and Roma's Villaggio
Emmanuele. Other standout communities in northern Italy include
Genova, which hosts the annual Silver Economy Forum on new
trends in the Italian silver economy; and Emilia Romagna, which
hosts a great deal of experimentation and variety in social housing.

## Conclusion

The needs of the older Italian population add up to more than
just a hazard threatening Italy and its inhabitants. Their economic
demand poses an opportunity: for a conscious and sustainable

management of the economic transition to an older and longer-living nation. As in many other countries, an Italian economy of longevity is now developing, aimed at satisfying the needs and ambitions of seniors who have the economic resources to purchase solutions designed deliberately with them in mind (and possibly with them acting as inspirative advisors). Building out the longevity market could increase GDP, provide jobs, and produce tax revenue that could help support the care services demanded by Italy's frail elderly population.

Italy, with its aging demographics; generally (if not universally) wealthy older population; advanced financial sector; and long tradition of innovation, design, and industry; has many of the ingredients necessary for a silver economy to bloom. But perhaps what sets the country apart is the unique value it places on style and beauty, especially as created through its major industries' close relationships with consumers.

Italy could potentially lead the silver market for the entirety of aging Europe by adding its native sense of beauty to products aimed at the older generations: taking this category far beyond the all-too-typical "beige and brown" devices that older adults tend to not actively seek out so much as merely tolerate. The Italian automobile market, for instance, already creates cars that manage to be thrilling and powerful—without compromising on their aging customers' comfort. The country's fashion, financial, tech, and housing industries, among many others, should pay attention to this tradition: providing for the fundamental needs of aging adults by satisfying their desire for high performance, beauty, and fun.

(It is not by chance that Italy was chosen to host the first European accelerator specialized in silver economy innovation, NextAge, founded by CDP Venture Capital Sgr, National Fund for Innovation.)

Italy's silver economy must be responsive. What each new wave of older adults considers "fun" or "desirable" has the tendency to change, especially as older adults' tech literacy updates with each new generation—even while the vital importance of such eternal constants as safety, comfort, accessibility, and affordability always remain.

It's not impossible to service all these requirements, but they do call for age-diverse perspectives in product and service design and—just as important—marketing and communication. As Gabriele Troilo of Bocconi University in Milan has said, Italian marketing suffers from *demographic isomorphism*: the tendency to identify one's audience or target group with oneself.[33] Marketing, advertising, and product design are all typically conducted by workers who are much younger than the standard age of retirement. Creating and marketing better products and services can inspire older consumers while fulfilling the full range of their physical and mental needs. Achieving this balance, however, will require deep knowledge of older consumers' wants, needs, and motivations.

Italy's population—already Europe's oldest—is poised to age like never before. Transforming this fact from a threat into an opportunity is still possible. To do so, government, private companies, local experts, academics, and NGOs must come together to identify and make the most of the possibilities offered by a longer life.

Emanuela Notari is a cofounder of the A.L.I. Active Longevity Institute, the first observatory of the aging Italian population, which offers surveys and advisory services for companies and government bodies seeking to address older markets. She offers advice, lectures, and writes articles on aging, especially longevity financial planning and the development of demographic intelligence in organizations. Her background includes a strong expertise in communication developed over a 20-year career in advertising, during which she served as General Manager of Young & Rubicam Milano, and CEO and President of Young & Rubicam México.

# Notes

1. "Countries with the Oldest Populations in the World," Population Reference Bureau, accessed January 31, 2023, https://www.prb.org/resources/countries-with-the-oldest-populations-in-the-world/.

2. Istat, Bes, 2021, 38.

3. Istat, 2022, http://dati.istat.it.

4. "Projected Old-Age Dependency Ratio," Eurostat, https://ec.europa.eu/eurostat/databrowser/view/tps00200/default/table?lang=en.

5. "Report indicatori demografici Anno 2021," Istat, 2021, 149.

6. "L'aspettativa di vita in Italia 1872/2020," accessed July 9, 2023, https://statisticsanddata.org/it/data/aspettativa-vita-italia/.

7. CERGAS Bocconi, 4° Rapporto Osservatorio, Long Term Care, 37.

8. Itinerari Previdenziali, Quaderno di Approfondimento, 2022, Silver Economy: Una Nuova Grande Economia, 20.

9. Centro Studi Moneyfarm, https://blog.moneyfarm.com/it/finanza-personale/quanto-costa-crescere-un-figlio-italia/.

10. Rapporto Annuale 2022, Istat, 2022, 115.

11. Inps, XXI Rapporto annuale Luglio 2022, 76–165.

12. Rapporto Annuale 2022, Istat, 2022, 173.

13. "Regional Demographic Statistics," March 2021, 2022 data, Eurostat, accessed 2022.

14. Infodata Sole 24 Ore on Istat, 2017, https://www.infodata.ilsole24ore.com/2019/02/18/pensioni-non-autonoma-ieri-non-autonoma-oggi-ed-un-costo-tutti/.

15. Infodata Sole 24 Ore on Istat, 2017, https://www.infodata.ilsole24ore.com/2019/02/18/pensioni-non-autonoma-ieri-non-autonoma-oggi-ed-un-costo-tutti/.

16. Moneyfarm/Smileconomy, Centro Studi Moneyfarm, October 2022, https://www.milanofinanza.it/news/moneyfarm-divorziare-nel-2022-costa-fino-a-60-000-euro-a-coppia-202210031111451268.

17. Itinerari Previdenziali, Quaderno Silver Economy, 2022, 40.

18. Itinerari Previdenziali, Quaderno Silver Economy, 2022, 21.

19. Europadonna, 2022, https://europadonna.it/2022/04/14/gender-bias-e-medicina-di-genere/.

20. Deb Colville, "Medicine's Gender Revolution: How Women Stopped Being Treated as 'Small Men,'" The Conversation, August 6, 2017, http://theconversation.com/medicines-gender-revolution-how-women-stopped-being-treated-as-small-men-77171.

21. Italy's Law Nr. 3 of January 11, 2018.

22. Sandra Zampa, "Gender Medicine: The Role of Institutions," *Italian Journal of Gender-Specific Medicine* 7, no. 1 (Spring 2021): 1–3.

23. SoLongevity, https://solongevity.com/.

24. Auser, Secondo Rapporto sulle condizioni abitative degli anziani in Italia che vivono in case di proprietà (su dati Istat), 2015, 30.

25. Itinerari Previdenziali, Quaderno Silver Economy, 2022, 56.

26. Active Longevity Institute, I senior e la loro casa, http://www.activelongevity.eu.

27. Investire, November 2021, 19.

28. "Joint Venture between Guild Living and Specht Group Italia for the Launch in Italy," *Guild Living Italy* (blog), November 8, 2022, https://www.guildliving.com/italy/blog/2022/11/08/joint-venture-between-guild-living-and-specht-group-italia-for-the-launch-in-italy/.

29. Fondo Aristotele, Generali Italia, https://www.fabricasgr.com/al-via-aristotele-senior-dedicato-al-senior-living/.

30. Generali Italia web page: https://www.generali.it/chi-siamo/comunicazione/comunicati-stampa/2021-convivit-senior-living, accessed July 13, 2021.

31. "Wake Up and See the Women: Wealth Management's Underserved Segment," McKinsey, June 23, 2022, https://www.mckinsey.com/industries/financial-services/our-insights/wake-up-and-see-the-women-wealth-managements-underserved-segment.

32. "Digitale, locale integrato. Il futuro del welfare in un paese che invecchia," Boston Consulting Group, June 2022.

33. "Se il marketing non vede al di là della propria età," Economy Magazine, March 24, 2022, https://www.economymagazine.it/se-il-marketing-non-vede-al-di-la-della-propria-eta/.

# 16
# Newcastle

Gregor Rae and Colin Williams

Newcastle upon Tyne, the northern English metropolitan area long known for its heavy industry and shipping interests, has for hundreds of years served as one of the UK's innovative hot spots. Historically, its major contributions related to the city's industrial economy: mining, ship building, steam engines, boilers, water pumps.[1] However, like Newcastle's celebrated 1829 locomotive *Rocket*—the zenith of light steam engine technology—a new, local innovative tradition has rapidly gathered steam.

The region has hosted a complex web of efforts concerned with solving the needs of an aging population—emerging from public, private, academic, and NGO sectors. Today, it can be considered a world-class cluster of such activity: drawing in investment, exporting ideas, producing knowledgeable professionals, and creating genuinely useful products, services, and design work for the local older population.

Unlike textbook, private-sector-led technology or industry hubs, much of this work has taken place in the interstices and connective fibers between various combinations of organizations, individuals, and government entities. This level of government and NGO interest and interconnectivity stems from a tension that has attended aging in the region since it first became an issue worthy of dedicated collaborative inquiry, starting with local, pioneering dementia research in the 1960s.

Is the aging population a market for businesses to serve, or is it a social matter for state health and social services to address? Newcastle's story demonstrates that this is a false dichotomy—at least in a country like the UK, much of whose health and social services are run at the local level, responsive to shifting needs on the ground in the community.

Today, Newcastle can be viewed as a model for how innovation can proceed for older adults, in the context of an engaged government dynamic with respect to health and social care. It has provided a nucleus for a snowballing level of investment as well as local tacit knowledge and excellence concerning the needs of older adults across communities. And it has functioned as an exporter of such knowledge to major, global companies, as well as other cities seeking to make similar strides for their own aging populations.

## Biomedical Beginnings

Newcastle's intense focus on aging-related innovation can be traced back to the 1960s, when a small group of distinguished medical scientists at Newcastle University began to probe dementia's tragic mysteries. These included Sir Bernard Tomlinson, Sir Martin Roth, and Garry Blessed: the first researchers to systematically examine the brains of older people with dementia. This team developed standardized bedside cognitive screening assessments for Alzheimer's disease, and made the groundbreaking discovery that the disease's cognitive declines correspond to the degree of pathology that can be observed in the brain.[2]

The work of these researchers and others not only constituted critical first strides in the modern scientific study of Alzheimer's disease, but also led to Newcastle becoming a world leader in research into aging and age-related illness.

In these early decades, medical and life sciences research of this sort accounted for the bulk of innovative Novocastrian activity around aging. The significance of this pioneering work and leadership was soon recognized by the UK Medical Research Council (MRC), who went on to fund the Neurochemical Pathology Unit at Newcastle General Hospital, allowing continued research into neurodegenerative disorders including Alzheimer's disease and other forms of dementia.

Another notable program from these early decades got its start in 1983, when one of the region's premiere higher educational institutions, Northumbria University (then a polytechnic), commenced its North East Age Research Longitudinal Study, which would go on to include input from over 3,000 research participants and run for more than 20 years.

In the mid-1990s, Newcastle's biomedical strengths began to translate into other forms of work around aging. In 1994, the impending closure of a number of General Hospital functions provoked the leader of the MRC unit, Professor Jim Edwardson, along with colleagues Oliver James, Ian McKeith, and John Bond, to promote the concept of the Institute for the Health of the Elderly: a self-described "institute without walls" intended to bring together researchers interested in gerontology across disciplines and departments. Edwardson became the founding director.[3]

Two years later, Edwardson commenced a collaboration with Tom Kirkwood, professor of biological gerontology at Manchester University, who was renowned for his groundbreaking *disposable soma theory* of cellular aging,[4] which he put forward with molecular geneticist Robin Holliday. They established the Joint Centre on Ageing: a venture shared between Newcastle and Manchester Universities.

In 1999, Kirkwood was appointed William Leech Professor in Medicine at Newcastle University: a step that effectively kicked off a new era of growth and development in Newcastle's embryonic lon-gevity cluster. Kirkwood acted as a human nucleus around which much of the snowballing growth of Newcastle's aging efforts began to adhere, and would personally go on to found a number of local laboratories and efforts around aging.

Meanwhile, in 2002 the Institute for the Health of the Elderly (the "institute without walls") morphed into the Institute for Age-ing and Health (IAH), a significant milestone in the development of Newcastle's aging-focused institutions. This organization grew rap-idly: procuring funding for a new building (2003's The Henry Well-come Laboratory for Biogerontology Research), followed by four more buildings on a rapidly developing campus concept. Today, these biomedical and integrated clinical research facilities form the foundation for Newcastle University's bold plans for the Campus for Ageing and Vitality: a planned "health innovation neighbor-hood" designed to bring together business, government, and resi-dents to solve problems around aging in areas including not just health but also leisure, learning, and employment.

In addition to his efforts dedicated to the life sciences, Kirkwood would also go on to found the more wide-ranging Newcastle Initia-tive on Changing Age: a research program at Newcastle University devoted to crosscutting themes including cellular mechanisms and chronic disease, as well as aging's relationship with policy, business, and the arts and culture.[5]

## Government Takes Note

It was in the context of Newcastle's hive of biomedical activity that actors in the private and public sectors (including this chapter's authors) began to consider the wider socioeconomic implications of aging. As investment and development around aging-as-an-opportunity has grown in Newcastle, these two sectors have tended to move together in something of a continual dance.

Newcastle's public sector's interest in aging emerged in the 1990s, when the city found itself confronted with a number of pressing problems common to cities the world over, including the threat posed by climate change, the need to spur local economic activity, an aging population, and disparate life outcomes among different sub-populations—manifest, in Newcastle's case, in stark differences in life expectancy and health outcomes in different parts of the city.

Somewhat more unique to Newcastle—or at least to cities of its size in the UK—was the question of how the government was preparing to deal with the care costs soon to be posed by the aging population. Unlike the bulk of healthcare funding provision in the UK, which is done at the national level courtesy of the NHS, social care for older people is a local affair. In Newcastle, this important work fell to the city council's Adult Social Care directorate, whose services accounted for the single largest spending object in the city's budget.

Any improvements in aging services—from helping Newcastle's elders age in place in their own homes, to better health outcomes, to more targeted in-home services—would potentially redound to the benefit of the city's budget. Somewhat less obvious than the economic opportunity in the care sector, however, was the vast expanse of opportunity in just about every other area of life aging touched.

Over time, the city government made a series of concerted efforts, often in partnership with other sectors, to explore these opportunities. In addition to the aforementioned life science developments, these included the "Competitive Newcastle" strategy: a ten-year economic development plan launched in 1999 by the city government that established a set of eight business areas, including aging-related life sciences, that the council would focus on to help nurture a competitive and innovative city.

By 2002, the action plan had resulted in around 5,000 jobs being created or safeguarded, almost 3,000 training places developed, over £6 million of funding secured, and around 200,000 square feet of physical infrastructure supported.

A number of European, UK, and regional economic development funds, active around this time, had a significant positive impact on the economy of Northeast England. Sources such as the Millennium Commission, the European Regional Development Fund, the European Bank and the Rural Development Program for England contributed to a multi-billion-pound investment. The regional development agency, One North East, invested over £3 billion alone into the regional economy over its lifetime.[6]

Newcastle has been a major beneficiary of such investment, and has responded through highly collaborative policies, processes, and partnerships designed to leverage maximum impact on key strategic themes—of which aging, well-being, and longevity have featured strongly.

A major part of Newcastle's development—and an indication of its age-friendly resilience going forward—is the city's commitment to sustainable grassroots community engagement. This is a Newcastle trait that surfaces regularly—in the 1970s regeneration of its Byker neighborhood, for instance, rated in 2017 by the Academy of Urbanism as the best community in the UK and whose architecture features in the UNESCO global list of outstanding twentieth-century buildings. Or consider the creation, in 2001, of the Elders Council of Newcastle, whose stated purpose is "to provide an effective voice for older people who are resident or active in the City of Newcastle upon Tyne."

Further evidence of this grassroots capacity across the city came in 2004 with the launch of Newcastle's Quality of Life Partnership, consisting of the Elders Council of Newcastle, Age Concern Newcastle, Help the Aged, Newcastle Healthy City, and Newcastle City Council.

Three years later, in 2007, the Elders Council launched its milestone document, "Everyone's Tomorrow: The Strategy for Older People and an Ageing Population in Newcastle upon Tyne," which set out a clear statement of intent and purpose of the age-inclusive manner in which the city could work. Today, the Elders Council continues with important age-friendly policy and strategic support work in housing, retail, transport, city planning, quality of life, and health and well-being.

## Business Synergies

By the early aughts, the private sector had begun taking a serious look at the aging-oriented activities of Newcastle's public and academic sectors. To the extent that this article's authors can claim to have participated in this process, a major part of it had to do with the one discovering the contributions of the other.

In 2002 Gregor Rae's Scottish research-based consultancy, BusinessLab, had produced a prospectus for "ActiveAge," a collaborative, public-private research consortium established to consider the implications of aging for business and the wider economy. Newcastle invited him to come talk about it.

In decades prior, Rae had been researching economic turnarounds in Europe and North America, where he examined stepchange programs in Massachusetts, California, North Carolina, Texas, and Alberta. His particular focus was on the impactful collaborations forged in these regions between government, business, and academia to stimulate positive socioeconomic change. He had been applying the learning from these case studies to communities in the UK, and he was extremely interested in the approach adopted by Newcastle.

Colin Williams, meanwhile, had been working as Director of Transformation in Newcastle City Council's directorate of Adult Social Care, leading a program of service improvement and redesign. An important part of Williams's work focused on pushing forward a citywide aging-innovation agenda and leveraging the council's influence and connectivity through its key partnership with the NHS, the Universities, and the NGO sector. Working alongside the

Director of Adult Social Care, Ewen Weir, Williams was also interested in external aging-related programs that could help to build stronger strategic economic alignment with other organizations in Newcastle and beyond. ActiveAge, he decided, seemed a good potential fit.

According to Rae, Williams's insights, influence, connections, and commitment embodied the key factors for success that had surfaced from his North American case studies. Williams represented a focal point of vision and influence within city government that, in a city that can sometimes feel more like a village, could inspire a willingness in individuals to take projects under their wing, and bring them to higher levels.

Rae's early conversations with Newcastle coincided with the development of relationships on the other side of the Atlantic that have since endured over 20 years. In 2001, Rae learned of a new research lab at the Massachusetts Institute of Technology investigating the design of the driving environment for the 100-year-old female driver. This was the catalyst for a visit—the first of many—to MIT.

That 2001 visit to the MIT AgeLab convinced Rae that population aging was about opportunity—and that the numbers involved should be of intense interest to business and government. Joseph Coughlin, the founding director of MIT AgeLab, was significantly further down the road in terms of defining the opportunities involved, so Rae invited him to the UK launch of ActiveAge to share his perspectives with business and government leaders through a series of city-based seminars.

Newcastle was not originally part of the ActiveAge launch plan. However, word had reached Herb Kim, CEO of Codeworks—a new, UK-enterprise-agency-designated "Centre of Excellence" for Newcastle's digital industries—that a national aging-related program was in the offing. By coincidence, Codeworks' Assistive Technology Lab was also preparing to release the findings of a new research study into issues facing, and surrounding, older people.

Codeworks joined ActiveAge as a Programme Partner and agreed to jointly stage a conference in the Newcastle Civic Centre, at which Coughlin of the MIT AgeLab would be the keynote speaker. Of real significance to ActiveAge, this milestone event was also hosted by Newcastle City Council whose active participation turned a spotlight onto the flourishing ecosystem of world-class, aging-related expertise, innovation, and economic opportunity across the city.

The council also attracted the involvement of other key partners. Foremost among them was Newcastle University's Institute of Ageing and Health, led by Tom Kirkwood; along with the Newcastle upon Tyne Hospitals NHS Foundation Trust.

Both Newcastle University and Newcastle City Council quickly became founding partners of ActiveAge in Newcastle. They were followed by the Newcastle upon Tyne Hospitals NHS Foundation Trust, a major economic player in the region and one of the most successful Foundation Trusts in the UK.

With a head of steam rapidly building, Newcastle soon became the international hub for ActiveAge partners and programs, and the nucleus for an expanding global collaborative network of business, government, and NGO-sector leaders.

Around this time a new project was shaping up with the potential to raise Newcastle's international profile in aging innovation. In 2006, IAH commenced an extraordinary study to find out what life is really like for citizens aged 85-plus. The six-year, £3 million, Newcastle 85+ study was transformational: opening up a wealth of new knowledge into extreme longevity.

Williams, for his part, was seeking partners to deliver something unexpected for his comprehensive program driving improvements in performance and service delivery for Newcastle's Adult Social Care directorate, still the largest spending department in the local authority. Adult Social Care became Newcastle's point of connection for the ActiveAge consortium.

In the years that followed, representatives from organizations such IBM, BT, Intel, GE, Microsoft, and Cisco all established relationships in Newcastle: efforts to explore opportunities in integrated health and social care data systems, and home-as-platform solutions. (To this day, these issues continue to resemble holy grails for health and care agencies, and age-conscious tech firms.)

In 2016, on a trip to relate Newcastle's story to care leaders at that year's LeadingAge summit in Washington, DC, Williams saw an opportunity for shared learning, operational insights, and executive development with like-minded organizations and individuals in Newcastle and the US. Forging a relationship with LeadingAge and its members soon became a strategic priority for Newcastle. Then, in 2016, a new opportunity arose in the form of an invitation from the not-for-profit *Vitalocity!* Consortium of leading senior care and senior housing providers to participate in a bid for the Chicago-based MacArthur Foundation's "100&Change" grand challenge. The *Vitalocity!* Proposal positioned Newcastle as a global open learning lab for addressing the causes of social isolation and trialing and showcasing solutions.

By 2018, the age-friendly narrative that had become a constant refrain in many of Newcastle's conference rooms, irrespective of sector, had evolved into a "longevity economy"-oriented cluster-based framework. Influencing this evolution were Coughlin's 2017 book of the same title, the UK's 2017 Industrial Strategy with its focus on "The Ageing Society" as one of four Grand Challenges,[7] and the maturing of an exceptionally well-aligned public-sector triumvirate comprising the city council, the universities, and the NHS Foundation Trust.

As it became clear that private-sector conversations in northeast England were mirroring similar deliberations within Greater Boston and New England, Newcastle began to explore opportunities for collaboration with others who wanted to consider how a robust longevity-economy ecosystem could support economic development in the mode of a "Silicon Valley of agetech."

A multi-partner project team was mustered in Newcastle and exploratory meetings were held in Massachusetts and Newcastle, and a collaborative Memorandum of Understanding was signed with LeadingAge. But before plans could further develop, the global COVID-19 pandemic struck.

## Newcastle as Exporter

The impact of Newcastle's aging innovation has been felt both locally and globally. The Newcastle Story, as it's become known, has spread via a variety of organizations and partnerships. These include LeadingAge partners and members in the US and China; Global Coalition on Aging partners in the US, Taiwan, and Indonesia; master classes and workshops for the International Federation on Aging's delegates and partners in Europe; briefings and presentations for the WHO in the UK and Ireland; and reports, presentations, and workshops for partners and interested parties in Denmark and Canada.

The city's relationship with Microsoft Corporation has been particularly fertile. Around 2007, thanks to a Bill Gates–hosted, corporate "Think Week" on the topic, aging became a key focus for Microsoft. By 2008, Gary Moulton, a senior product manager out of Microsoft's Trustworthy Computing Group, had met a team from Newcastle, visited the city, and joined the ActiveAge consortium. Gary subsequently embedded himself in the city for six months and became a popular and active member of the ActiveAge community of interest.

The company's main open question concerned market development. Where were the commercial opportunities and potential interaction sites in the aging-related market? Part of this question concerned older adults themselves, and what was holding them back from adopting technologies that could solve problems in their lives. Another part concerned government services. For a company hoping to identify serviceable local government needs in the aging sphere, Newcastle's web of public and private relationships in these areas provided fertile ground for exploration.

Microsoft went on to use Newcastle not only as a testing ground but as a proof-of-concept benchmark that they would showcase in demonstrations around the world. Newcastle, through ActiveAge, was soon regularly selected to represent Microsoft's maturing insights into the impact of, and opportunities presented by, older IT consumers and their families.

This momentum strengthened through 2010 due to a close and productive collaboration between Newcastle and the newly formed, New York–based Global Coalition on Aging, whose CEO, Michael Hodin, played an active and valuable role in energizing the international network and helping to promote the Newcastle Story in places such as Kuala Lumpur, Taiwan, and San Francisco.

For Newcastle's partners, the city became a valuable repository of world-class research, a hub for collaboration, and an unparalleled seam of knowledge and expertise that could be mined over a coffee in the heart of a wonderful city.

In recent years, the go-to place for visitors, partners, students, and entrepreneurs interested in aging has become the Catalyst building on the Helix campus: the home of the National Innovation Centre for Ageing (NICA) under the inspired leadership of its director, Nicola Palmerini.

This £350 million inner-city research campus, built on the former site of a redundant brewery of Newcastle's iconic Brown Ale, is testimony to the vision, collaboration, decision-making and quality of management that underpins the city. From the moment in 2014 the UK Chancellor confirmed Newcastle as the successful bidder to host the UK's new National Innovation for Ageing, the city's collaborative ethos was mobilized to support the development program.

Today the Helix, with the Catalyst and NICA at its heart, offers a regional, national, and global resource for thinkers and doers from around the world, concerned with the future of aging and longevity.

One important group also located there is VOICE—Valuing Our Intellectual Capital and Experience—a unique market intelligence resource founded in 2007 by James Edwardson and the social gerontologist Lynne Corner, who is now also the chief operating officer for NICA.

In 2016, VOICE became a NICA sister organization, working hand in hand with NICA to provide an integrated research and market intelligence resource, representing Newcastle's (and indeed the UK's) crown jewels in terms of an aging and innovation capability that allows businesses to access pools of older adults for product and market testing and ideation.

Now a core offering from NICA, VOICE's role is unique: a franchisable, scalable market intelligence service inextricably linked to a longevity economy thought leader, supported by the neighboring National Innovation Centre for Data, based in one of the most iconic city campuses in the UK, with access to two of the UK's most respected universities nearby.

The capacity of the city to sustain a longevity leadership role going forward would appear to have been significantly strengthened by the combined leadership of NICA and VOICE, channeling new energy into aging intelligence. As we write these words, the page is now being turned to the next chapter of the Newcastle Story, with NICA's announcement of a new global initiative: the City of Longevity conference series, which is intended to promote healthy aging and longevity in the urban environment. In 2023's inaugural conference, Newcastle will play host to representatives from aging cities around the world.

A major, recent contributor to Newcastle's emerging longevity innovation economy has been Newcastle-based Northstar Ventures. This boutique VC firm is working with other partners to bolster early stage investment fund capacity in the region by steadily building "Venture North," a £100 million, early stage fund with an emphasis on social, as well as economic, impact.

Northstar is targeting four broad investment themes including healthy aging: a high-growth, high potential market largely untapped by VC finance. With around 40 coinvestors, the focus is on university spinoffs with preferred access to commercialization for a dynamic cluster of six Northeast universities.

To reinforce Northstar's capacity in these areas, the company has been recruiting an investment team of experts that combines scientific, operational, financial, and mergers-and-acquisitions skills.

US-based entrepreneur Dominic Endicott, for example, recently joined Northstar as a Founder Director of the Venture North Fund, and the company widened its geographic reach to include London and Boston.

In a sense, Newcastle in itself, and the tacit knowledge it contains for how to respond to an aging population in an economy where free enterprise must find ways to collaborate with multiple levels of government, is serving as an export engine. In its long history as a peripheral city, Newcastle has had to fight for every opportunity it's realized. Today the city is carefully reinvesting to sustain a good quality of life for its aging population, and to support its larger civic aspirations. In a world of aging cities, it will continue to serve as a prototype. Newcastle is a powerful example of a well-oiled machine of diverse parts—including institutions hailing from all sectors, and citizens of all ages—which, by working together, can move forward at full steam.

Gregor Rae is a UK-based entrepreneur and founder of numerous for-profit and not-for-profit enterprises in design, education, energy, media, research, regeneration, and competitive strategy. An architectural graduate of the Robert Gordon Institute of Technology, he cofounded BusinessLab, a research-based consultancy that has served as the platform for a series of international collaborative research programs focusing on demographic change, digital business, web-enabled public services, the learning organization, and social capital. He is also a long-standing student and practitioner in the field of social and economic step change in city-regions around the world.

Colin Williams has over 30 years' experience as an operational and transformation leader in the UK, working across central and local government and the NHS to promote and strengthen social and economic well-being. Most recently, Colin has worked with and for partners on a succession of transformation programs in the city of Newcastle upon Tyne. There, he designed and led a successful improvement and service transformation program for the city's social care provision; led a program to design and operationalize new partnership arrangements for health and longevity, as well as economic growth and prosperity; coordinated the creation of a number of international partnership arrangements; and led a series of initiatives that contributed to development of a globally significant cluster of longevity economy assets in the city.

## Notes

1. Robert Carlson, *The Liverpool and Manchester Railway Project 1821–1831* (Fairfield, NJ: Augustus M. Kelley, 1969).

2. Mark W. Bondi, Emily C. Edmonds, and David P. Salmon, "Alzheimer's Disease: Past, Present, and Future," *Journal of the International Neuropsychological Society: JINS* 23, no. 9–10 (October 2017): 818–31, https://doi.org/10.1017/S135561771700100X; Gordon Morris and Tom Kirkwood, *An Age of Wonders: The Story of the Newcastle 85+ Study* (Newcastle: Institute for Ageing and Health/Newcastle University, 2014).

3. J. A. Edwardson and T. B. L. Kirkwood, "The Institute for Ageing and Health, University of Newcastle, UK," *Experimental Gerontology* 37, no. 6 (June 2002): 749–56, https://doi.org/10.1016/s0531-5565(02)00016-5.

4. T. B. Kirkwood and R. Holliday, "The Evolution of Ageing and Longevity," *Proceedings of the Royal Society of London. Series B, Biological Sciences* 205, no. 1161 (September 21, 1979): 531–46, https://doi.org/10.1098/rspb.1979.0083.

5. "Newcastle Initiative on Changing Age," *Health Europa* (blog), February 19, 2018, https://www.healtheuropa.com/newcastle-initiative-changing-age/84338/.

6. *"Annual Report and Accounts 2011–2012: HC 159,"* One North East, June 14, 2012, 9.

7. "Industrial Clusters in England," GOV.UK, September 22, 2017, https://www.gov.uk/government/publications/industrial-clusters-in-england.

# 17
# São Paulo

**Layla Vallias**

The "Girl from Ipanema" has reached her mature phase. The song, written by Tom Jobim and Vinícius de Moraes in 1962, became an international hit, introducing Brazilian bossa nova to the world. Bossa nova was more than just a musical genre, however. As the historians Lilia M. Schwarcz and Heloisa Murgel Starling write in *Brasil: Uma Biografia* (Brazil: A biography), it was "a way of expressing the best of what the country had to offer, and the confirmation of its viability: a modern, cosmopolitan, sophisticated, beautiful, free Brazil." This new perception of the nation only contributed to a sense that had been growing since before World War II, perhaps most concisely articulated by the Austrian novelist and biographer Stefan Zweig in the title of his utopian 1936 book: *Brazil: Land of the Future.*

Zweig, who immigrated to Brazil from Vienna by way of England and New York, was passionate about the explosive culture, exuberant nature, and optimism he discovered in his new home. He foretold a future in which the giant of the South would prove a fertile ground for innovative and prosperous projects, made by the hands of an eternally youthful people. What he and the most daring demographers of his day did not imagine, however, was that Brazil would age so rapidly. Today, Brazilians can expect to live more than twice as long as their ancestors in 1900, and the country has 55 million people over 50 years old, representing 25 percent of the total population.[1]

The girl from Ipanema herself is an example of this new, silver country. Helô Pinheiro, the muse who, at the age of 17, inspired the song's composers, is now 77. Today, she is a digital influencer with almost half a million followers on Instagram. She is now a different sort of muse, offering an image of aging in Brazil that is no less optimistic than Zweig's youthful vision: a blend of maturity, culture, style, and technology.

Brazil isn't just aging faster than midcentury experts expected; it's aging faster than most other nations, both today and in the past. While France took 145 years to double the share of its population over age 65 from 10 percent to 20 percent, Brazil will do so in 19 years: from 2011 to 2030.[2]

The country already has more grandparents than grandchildren; more adults over the age of 50 than under 18. Every 21 seconds, a new Brazilian enters their fifties.[3] Two points explain much of this phenomenon. In 1988, the country adopted public policies that ensured access to medical care through the Unified Health System (SUS). That same year, it also instituted a family planning program ahead of other developing countries.

As a result of the country's healthcare system as well as technological advances, life expectancy has increased by an astounding 34 years since 1945, to almost 77 today.[4] Brazil's birth rate, meanwhile, was 5.8 children per woman in 1975, but it soon plummeted from these midcentury heights.[5] "The projection was that the country would only reach 1.7 children in the middle of the 21st century," says Jorge Felix, a longevity and population aging researcher at the University of São Paulo. "But it arrived before that: in 2018."

These changes to the picture of the Brazilian family happened quickly, not only as a consequence of the availability of contraception, but also due to changes in mass culture.

In Brazil, television dramaturgy has played a major role in disseminating new norms concerning family planning and female empowerment. In his study *Novelas e Fertilidade: Evidências do Brasil* (Soap Operas and Fertility: Evidences from Brazil), Inter-American Development Bank economist Alberto Schong analyzed the content of 115 soap operas broadcast by TV Globo, the largest TV network in Latin America, between 1965 and 1999. He points out that in the period since the 1970s, when Brazil's fertility rate dropped more than 60 percent, the presence of television devices in households increased more than tenfold, ultimately making their way into more than 80 percent of homes. In 62 percent of the scripts of those telenovelas since 1965, the main female characters had no children, and 21 percent had only one child. The nuclear families in national soap operas were happy, rich, and small: a portrait that influenced women of different socioeconomic backgrounds.

This history offers a window into Brazilian culture, in which the norm-setting power of entertainment and cultural products can serve as the starting point for social change.

As Brazil encounters the downstream effects of its fertility shift in the form of population aging, products developed with the 50-plus cohort in mind—especially cultural products—may continue to play an outsized role in determining the country's future path.

## The Construction of a New Way of Thinking

Television plays a crucial role in the circulation of social ideas, particularly in developing nations with a strong oral tradition, such as Brazil. In the face of the aging of the country, the construction of a new way of thinking has started to be stitched together by communities and interdependent support hubs. These have a central element known in Brazil as *Economia da Gambiarra*: a unique, grassroots kind of sharing economy. The term refers to the tendency, born of necessity, for people to share creative solutions with one another as a response to the dearth (or absence) of resources coming from formal bodies, such as governmental institutions.

One product of this tendency is the movement known as Envelhecimento 2.0.[6] This Brazilian group came together due to a combination of love and pain: the love and determination to transform the country into a more dignified and fair territory for older people; and the pain of being an invisible cause encumbered with barriers such as the lack of resources offered by companies and governments, and also lack of coverage in the media. It was founded in 2013 by Willians Fiori: the host and creator of GeroCast (the first podcast in Brazil on the longevity theme), a professor of graduate studies in gerontology at Albert Einstein Hospital in São Paulo, and manager of Professional Relations at Bigfral, Brazil's leading source of personal products for older adults. The group was born with the goal of bringing together and enhancing projects, businesses and information about longevity in the country. With more than 200 members from companies, institutions, and governmental bodies, it has become the main channel for exchange between thinkers, opinion makers, and doers in the longevity ecosystem. It is where Brazil's biggest aging-related initiatives take place.

In an organic way, the hub works interdependently. Informal and accessible, it operates through a WhatsApp group with 256 individual members. To join it, one needs to be recommended; Fiori, the founder and community manager, evaluates applicants based on their interests, ability to be an active participant, and values. It is not enough to merely have an interest in the theme of active aging; it is important to be an activist who gets involved to make change happen. On a daily basis, members exchange the pains and delights of working within longevity. At first, it was a group consisting mostly of health professionals, but gradually professionals from other fields were invited to join. Today there is a great diversity among geriatricians, gerontologists, occupational therapists, psychologists, professionals from nongovernmental organizations, marketing professionals, administrators, journalists, and entrepreneurs.

## Project Examples

Among the countless projects that were born and grew in Envelhecimento 2.0, the study "Tsunami60+" and "Longevity Startup Search" are two major highlights.

One of the great challenges of Brazil's longevity ecosystem was the lack of data that could prove and make tangible what this group of experts was witnessing both in their everyday lives and in their work with the elderly. The only source of available, relevant data was the Brazilian Institute of Geography and Statistics (IBGE), which would provide baseline numbers about Brazil's older population, but not deeper information about who the Brazilians over 50 were, and what they wanted and needed. With this in mind, the consulting company Hype50+ (now Data8), in partnership with the social business Pipe.Social, decided to create Tsunami60+: the first major study on the economics of longevity in Brazil. As soon as the project started, however, a problem arose: how to find a database of older Brazilians? Until then, no other research institute had done such a broad survey of people between 50 and 90 years old, from all regions of the country and income.

That was when the group Envelhecimento 2.0 came into the picture. Without resources to back the project financially, the members actively supported it in other ways. More than 100 organizations shared the research link, and the result was impressive: over 2,500 Brazilians aged 55 and above participated in the study. Assigning numbers to what had been mere anecdotes changed the way business viewed Brazil's longevity economy.

Armed with statistical data, Tsunami60+ won coverage in the mainstream media and exposed the new face of Brazilian maturity.

The following examples are just a few, but represent the impact of the study in the Brazilian business market. Banco Mencantil do Brasil created a marketing campaign that featured Fábio Jr., a popular singer immortalized by his song "20 and Something," which he updated to "50 and More" to honor the silver population. QuintoAndar, the largest housing platform in Brazil, which was created to simplify the lives of those looking for a new home—initially, primarily millennials—realized the potential of the huge silver market, since over 70 percent of the country's homeowners are aged 50 and above. It decided to fund an unprecedented research effort into how older Brazilians live, whose results were published in 2022 on the new platform Habitar 55+, dedicated to exploring different ways of living of a maturing society.

Tsunami60+'s greatest impact may have been cultural. In 2022, TV Globo, the world's largest producer of telenovelas, launched the soap opera *Um Lugar ao Sol* (A Place in the Sun), in which the protagonist Rebeca—played by the 58-year-old Andréa Beltrão—was responsible for several striking scenes in favor of healthy, vibrant aging. The character spoke about menopause, ageism, work, and intergenerational relationships, encouraging thousands of Brazilian women to initiate a conversation about aging. According to the TV network's data, at its peak of popularity, the soap opera was viewed by almost 16 million people every day, garnering a 35 percent viewership share. Representation matters: In Brazil, a country mostly consisting of people of mixed race, only 7 percent of TV ads feature an older person. Of those, 96 percent of the women depicted are white with straight hair, and 4 out of 10 have white hair.[7] Protagonists like Rebeca, a character based on the challenges and dreams of diverse Brazilians over 50, can make a genuine change.

The other research initiative that deserves attention is the Longevity Startup Search, whose first edition was published in 2018. At that time, there was no single, actionable database of significant actors in Brazilian agetech. With the support of the international aging entrepreneurship organization Aging2.0, the Longevity Startup Search mapped 141 agetech initiatives and 81 businesses in Brazil.[8] Of these, five companies were selected to receive mentoring and media coverage. Only two years later, in 2020, the pharmaceutical company NeoQuímica, in partnership with the social impact business accelerator Yunus Social Business, Hype50+ (now Data8), and Pipe.Social, launched NeoAcelera, a startup acceleration program focused on agetech. That same year, using the same methodology as in 2018, the partnership mapped 343 agetech businesses: an indication that the number of tech entrepreneurship concerned with aging is rising rapidly.[9]

## A Pulsating Market

The availability of data about Brazil's longevity economy has helped clarify its possible business dimensions, innovation potential, and social impact; while raising the profile of entrepreneurs at the forefront of solutions to the challenges of aging. Today, the longevity economy already represents over 20 percent of the Brazilian consumer market and still, four out of ten Brazilians over age 50 say they feel invisible in their relationship with traditional brands and companies. This is still a new market, growing at a fast pace and with a range of opportunities for entrepreneurs from all over the country. Of the total number of business initiatives surveyed in the more recent Longevity Startup Search research, 65 percent are for elderly care and management, assisting both familiar and professional caregivers. Twenty-two percent are for older adults' engagement and purpose; 17 percent are for lifestyle, and 9 percent are for mobility and movement. Other categories included technologies to support challenges in mental health (8 percent), financial health (5 percent), and end of life (1 percent).

Nearly two-thirds of solutions categorized in the study—64 percent—were developed in the Southeast of Brazil, especially in the vicinity of São Paulo, a region that has the largest GDP in Latin America and the 10th largest in the world.[10] These are often young, small businesses. (44 percent had existed for two years or less; 93 percent had teams of 19 members or fewer.) In the majority of cases, a woman is either the leader or co-leader of these businesses, a surprising outcome considering male leadership is still the norm in Brazil. In 2017, 63 percent of the businesses described didn't have any revenue, a rate that fell to 44 percent in the 2020 study.[11] This development suggests Brazilian agetech is growing not only in scope but in profitability.

The two Longevity Startup Searches boosted awareness and education about longevity, especially among those who sign the checks: venture capital funds. In 2021, two startups from the Brazilian agetech ecosystem received major investments. Maturi, a work and entrepreneurship platform for Brazilians over age 50, raised R$250,000 ($50,000 USD) in seed capital to develop its B2B solution. Meanwhile, Janno, an end-of-life platform, raised R$500,000 ($100,000 USD) from family and friends; and MaisVívida, an edtech company that teaches technology skills to older adults, received a R$150,000 ($30,000 USD) grant from BossaNova Investments, the biggest early stage venture capital firm in Latin America. Although such investments are still small relative to other sectors, these initial venture bets show that funds have begun to keep an eye on the national longevity market.

## A Silver Future

Longevity hubs in aging countries tend to benefit from the significant involvement of institutional actors: civil society organizations, private initiatives, academia, investment funds, and government.

Brazil's ecosystem includes some of these: civil society, private companies (which increasingly understand the importance of serving silver consumers), and renowned academic organizations. These include the Fundação Dom Cabral (Dom Cabral Foundation), which created FDC Longevity, a think tank for studies on longevity management; and Fundação Getulio Vargas (Getulio Vargas Foundation), which has developed an executive training course for the longevity economy. Until very recently, however, Brazil's longevity ecosystem has had to do without support from investment funds; and it is still lacking in terms of government backing and support.

Despite still having a long way to go, Brazil's network of longevity innovators stands out among other Latin American countries. In 2022, inspired by the idea of uniting Latin countries in favor of longevity, Data8 produced a new study, in partnership with NoPausa, a "menotech" firm that promotes information about menopause; OpinionBox, the first online market research institute in Brazil; and Pontes, a bureau of innovative solutions throughout the region. They created Tsunami8 Latam:[12] the largest study of maturity in Latin America ever conducted, with more than 20,000 adults over age 45 interviewed in Chile, Mexico, Brazil, Argentina, Uruguay, Peru, and Colombia. Following the Tsunami60+ recipe, the study's findings reached important organizations including: IDB (Inter-American Development Bank), El País (the largest newspaper in the country), Grupo Sura (a multi-Latin financial company), the government of Chile, and Universidad de San Andrés, in Argentina. Tsunami8 Latam presented the local aging revolution as a thriving opportunity, and became a starting point for further consolidation of the ecosystem. Examples of the study's impact can be found in Pensar en Grande,[13] a project that supports agetech entrepreneurs created by Endeavor Uruguay, IDB, and Xeniors (a nonprofit Uruguayan association of national scope and international reach). The study also inspired Junta Plateada, or the Silver League: a network

of activists in the region, brought together by IDB, that is using Tsu-
nami8 Latam data in its decision-making.

As one of the world's fastest-aging countries, Brazil adds invaluable effort and experience to the development of the larger Latin
American longevity ecosystem. Today, Latinos aged 60 and above
consume over $2 trillion USD annually,[14] and want to be seen
and heard.

Their voices very soon will be impossible to ignore. In 2030, they
will represent 27.5 percent of the total population—and by 2090,
36.4 percent—according to the UN's 2022 Revision of World Population Prospects.[15] By this point, Latin America will be more silver
than Europe and the United States of America. This will entail a
huge cultural and economic shift for countries that are still considered the land of youth. How will companies and governments
realign their understanding about retirement, lifelong learning,
health, user experience, and housing? Will there be enough pro-
aging products and services for Latin America's 50-plus population?
The challenges are great, but so are the opportunities in a region
that is maturing at a rate never before seen. In an aging world, Latin
America's longevity economy is not just the place to invest; it is the
place to be.

Layla Vallias, a Forbes Under 30 honoree, is the cofounder of the
Hype50+ and Data8 longevity economy research institute in Bra-
zil and Latin America. Layla coordinates FDC Longevidade and has
launched four studies in partnership with Fundação Dom Cabral.
In 2018 and later in 2021, she was responsible for Tsunami60+, the
biggest behavioral research about Brazilians over 50 in the country.
In 2022, she led the internationalization of the project—Tsunami8
Latam—a survey with over 20,000 participants in Mexico, Uruguay,
Argentina, Colombia, Peru, Brazil, and Chile. A TedX and SXSW
speaker, since 2020 she has been a member of Lemann Foundation Leaders Community and Latitud. A marketer with a certificate

in digital marketing from New York University, she worked at Endeavor Brasil in product design.

## Notes

1. "Projection of the Population of Brazil and the Federation Units," Brazilian Institute of Geography and Statistics, December 16, 2022, https://www.ibge.gov.br/apps /populacao/projecao/.

2. "FDC Longevity—Society," Dom Cabral Foundation and Data8, February 21, 2022, https://materiais.hype50mais.com.br/download-fdc-longevidade-sociedade.

3. "+50 Longevity Calculator," SeniorLab and Longevity Expo+Forum, December 16, 2022, https://contador.longevidade.com.br/.

4. "Complete Mortality Tables," Brazilian Institute of Geography and Statistics, accessed December 16, 2022, https://www.ibge.gov.br/estatisticas/sociais/populacao /9126-tabuas-completas-de-mortalidade.

5. "Fertility and Dynamics of the Brazilian Population," United Nation Population Fund, October 2018, https://brazil.unfpa.org/pt-br/publications/fecundidade-e-dina mica-da-populacao-brasileira-folder.

6. Although *Envelhecimento 2.0* translates to "Aging 2.0," this Brazilian movement is not directly affiliated with the Aging2.0 organization discussed in chapters 13 and 20.

7. "Todxs 2020," Heads and Women UN, April 2021, http://www.onumulheres.org .br/wp-content/uploads/2021/04/UA_TODXS9_Final-PORT.pdf.

8. Mariza Tavares, "Longevity Business, the Next Market Frontier," *Globo.com*, May 6, 2018, https://g1.globo.com/bemestar/blog/longevidade-modo-de-usar/post/2018 /05/06/negocios-da-longevidade-a-proxima-fronteira-do-mercado.

9. Estadão Team, "Accelerator Invests BRL 150,000 in Game Startup for Older Audiences," Estado S. Paulo, December 16, 2020.

10. "Brazilian Industry in Figures," National Industry Confederation, May, 2022, https://www.portaldaindustria.com.br/estatisticas/industry-in-figures/.

11. "FDC Longevity—Business," Dom Cabral Foundation and Data8, February 21, 2022, https://materiais.hype50mais.com.br/estudo-fdc-longevidade-negocios.

12. "Tsunami8 Latam," Data8, NoPausa, OpinionBox and Pontes, published April 7, 2022, https://materiais.hype50mais.com.br/tsunami-latam.

13. "Pensar en Grande," Endeavor Uruguay, IDB and Xeniors, accessed December 16, 2022, https://www.pensarengrande.com.uy/.

14. "Silver Economy: A Mapping of Actors and Trends in Latin America and the Caribbean," Inter-American Development Bank, April 2021, https://publications .iadb.org/en/silver-economy-mapping-actors-and-trends-latin-america-and-caribbean.

15. "World Population Prospects 2022," Population Division of the Department of Economic and Social Affairs of the United Nations Secretariat, July 15, 2022, https:// population.un.org/wpp/.

# 18
# Tel Aviv

**Keren Etkin**

For a nation of its size, Israel has made disproportionate contributions in the tech sector. In the specific realm of tech innovation for older people and their loved ones, Israel's influence is even more profound, giving it a reasonable claim to the title of world-leading longevity innovation hub.

How did this small Mediterranean country become a global leader in technology for older adults? What is the "secret sauce" that enables Israeli AgeTech companies to have such an outsized impact, and distribute their products to millions of older users worldwide?

The answer is complex: inseparable from Israel's unique demography and history. Its older population is burgeoning, but at the same time its fertility rate, by far the highest in the OECD, makes issues like worker-to-retiree ratios less pressing than in other wealthy countries. Its size, too—roughly the land area and population of New Jersey—means the domestic market for its innovations is relatively small. Nevertheless—or perhaps because of these factors—a concerted, interconnected, often outward-facing cluster of innovative activity aimed at older adults and their loved ones has developed in Israel.

There are three important pillars supporting this activity: Israel's long-standing commitment to care for its growing older population, its outsized level of innovative business activity, and its academic research traditions.

To understand the first of these, we need to look into Israel's past, long before the digital revolution was underway. The roots of Israeli innovation in aging can be traced back to more than 100 years ago, before the State of Israel was even established.

## Three Pillars of Israel's Aging Innovation

### Demography and Care

As of 2019, life expectancy in Israel is 83, higher than the OECD average of 81.[1] The number of people over the age of 65 in Israel is just above one million, and they account for roughly 12 percent of the population. With an average of 2.9 children per woman, Israel has the highest fertility rate in the OECD, making it the organization's fastest-growing country, and the third most densely populated.[2]

One reasonable, partial explanation for Israel's high life expectancy is the state's public healthcare system, which requires every resident to have a subsidized health insurance plan with one of four national healthcare providers. Another possible explanation is Israel's state-funded long-term care, which enables roughly 25 percent of people over the age of 65 to receive at least a few hours a week of in-home, non-medical care, paid for by the state. One plausible, additional factor is the fitness boost Israelis gain by participating in their country's mandatory military service.[3]

Israel's efforts to provide for its older population date back to well before the country's founding, beginning with the nonprofit established in 1914 as the Joint Distribution Committee, and today called JDC-Eshel (sometimes referred to as "The Joint").

The Joint was established by American Jews in an effort to provide humanitarian relief to Jews in Israel during World War I. Today, more than 100 years later, the JDC is considered a global expert in developing innovative services for community-dwelling older adults.

In 1949, when Israel was struggling to meet the needs of 100,000 sick, disabled, and elderly Jewish refugees who had flooded into the young nation, the JDC and the Jewish Agency established Malben: a care agency that laid the foundations for Israel's modern welfare system. Malben was ahead of its time in understanding that not every older adult wanted or needed institutional care. In addition to senior living facilities and nursing homes, it built apartments for independent older adults who wished to reside within the community. Eventually, Israel's Ministry of Health took over Malben's activity, and the global JDC decided to focus its efforts in Israel on the aging population.[4]

JDC's division for optimal aging (JDC-Eshel) was established in 1969 as a collaboration between the Joint and the Israeli government. It describes itself as "Israel's social R&D incubator, developing comprehensive responses to the complex challenges facing its aging population."[5] JDC-Eshel's work represents a unique cross-sector collaboration. It works closely with the Ministry of Health, the Ministry of Labor and Social Affairs, the Ministry for Social Equality, the Ministry of Finance, the Prime Minister's Office, and the National Insurance Institute, as well as with municipalities and nonprofits throughout the country.

## Innovation

Despite being a young nation with a population of less than 10 million, Israel has managed to make a name for itself in the realm of global tech innovation. Inventions like the USB flash drive, community-powered navigation (Waze, acquired by Google in 2013), and driver-assist and autonomous driving technology (Mobileye, acquired by Intel in 2017)—along with the fact that Israel is home to the world's highest number of tech companies per capita—have garnered it the nickname "Startup Nation."[6]

Like Israel's care traditions, its commitment to technological innovation dates back to its early years. The governments of Israel understood long ago that innovation, specifically technological innovation, was an engine for economic growth and enabling high standards of living. In 1965, the Israeli Innovation Authority (or IIA; it was originally named the "Chief Scientist's Office") was established as an independent, publicly funded agency with a mission, as the modern IIA puts it, to provide "a variety of practical tools and funding platforms aimed at effectively addressing the dynamic and changing needs of the local and international innovation ecosystems."[7] The IIA today serves early stage startups, established tech companies, academic groups requiring assistance in commercializing their ideas, and global organizations looking to partner with Israeli techmakers.

### Aging Research

Academic research is a major pillar of Israel's longevity hub. Israel has eight state-funded research universities and multiple aging-focused research centers spread throughout the country. Some of the universities (for example, the Hebrew University in Jerusalem) have launched "tech transfer" companies for the purpose of commercializing academic research, and the IIA has also taken steps to support this type of activity.

The list of Israel's research institutes exploring various aspects of aging includes the JDC-affiliated Myers-JDC-Brookdale Institute for applied social research, which contributes to national efforts to develop policies and services addressing the challenges faced by older adults and those who care for them.[8] The Minerva Center on Intersectionality in Aging (MCIA) (Haifa University), meanwhile, was founded as a research and implementation project related to marginalized old persons.[9]

Several of Israel's universities have gerontology departments that focus on research as well as knowledge dissemination, and there are also multidisciplinary and interdisciplinary research centers that combine geriatrics and gerontology, such as the Herczeg Institute on Aging (Tel Aviv University) and the Center for Multidisciplinary Research in Aging (Ben Gurion University).

Additionally, there are various research centers focused on longevity and life extension (sometimes called "anti-aging" research). Notable examples include the Sagol Institute for Longevity Research (Weizmann Institute of Science) and the Healthy Longevity Research Center (Tel Aviv University).

Importantly, Israel's multiple aging and longevity-focused research centers offer the private sector a wealth of technical and leadership talent. Israel's tech companies often have researchers from leading universities as part of their founding team or seated on their advisory boards.

## How Do These Pillars Lead to Innovation for Aging?

Today, much of Israel's innovative activity for older adults is taking place both through entrepreneurial pipelines aligned with and supported by the IIA, and through care practice and policy innovation aligned with dedicated public and private organizations, such as JDC-Eshel.

JDC-Eshel's focus is on developing innovative services for older adults who are aging in place. It works in a "develop and release" model: initiating and developing new services for older adults within the community, piloting them for three to five years, and then handing them over to local or national organizations—government or nonprofit—to expand and run on a national level. From inception, then, every new program developed by JDC-Eshel is expected to have an "exit strategy."

Some of the services that were developed by JDC-Eshel that are now available at the national level include, but are not limited to, social clubs that offer recreational activities, supportive communities, and adult day centers. Some of these services were invented in Israel, while others are global innovations that were adapted to fit the needs of local Israeli older adults. Many of these services are operated today by local nonprofits for the elderly, which JDC-Eshel helped establish throughout Israel.

In 2021, JDC-Eshel published its 5-Year Strategic Plan for Optimal Aging in Israel (2021–25), with the stated purpose of "maximizing a person's independence and autonomy during the aging process," as well as delaying dependence "with respect to health, social and economic risk, and in accordance with the indicators for optimal aging."[10] These indicators include health, sense of purpose, and economic resilience; the plan also asserts that digital literacy is a "cross-cutting predictor that influences all metrics." Guided by this national map of indicators, as of 2022, JDC-Eshel offers new models regarding issues including digital literacy, navigating post-retirement, and age-friendly cities, which can be adapted for and implemented by local organizations across Israel.

Serving older adults falls under the mandate of the IIA, too, and so the IIA provides funding to tech companies that aim to improve their lives. In 2022 the IIA partnered with Israel's National Insurance and published a call for proposals to promote technology solutions for the elderly.[11] They have also partnered with Canada's Centre for Aging + Brain Health Innovation (CABHI) on a program "intended to accelerate the evaluation and adoption of innovative products and services that address the needs of aging adults and the challenges presented by an aging population."[12]

These threads supporting aging innovation are of crucial importance to present and future Israelis of advanced age. But the type of innovation with the greatest import for Israelis as well as populations beyond Israel's borders takes place when such traditions

—around care and awareness of older adults, of tech creation—come together, frequently with the help of convening institutions such as universities.

The geography of Israel is conducive to such kismet. Most of its major research centers are only an hour or two away from each other by car, and from the major business hubs of Tel Aviv, Jerusalem, Haifa, and Beer Sheva. On top of physical accessibility, the institutions that facilitate cross-sector collaborations make it easy to not only transfer knowledge but also to collaborate on academic studies, and to test the efficacy of AgeTech solutions developed "in the wild" by startups.

## AgeTech: Tech for Older Adults and Those Who Care for Them

For a country with a smaller 65-plus population than most other OECD nations, Israel has a remarkably diverse AgeTech ecosystem, with dozens of startups working on a wide variety of technologies—from robotics and IoT to virtual reality and interactive games. These startups use cutting-edge technology to tackle some of the biggest challenges posed by aging, including post-retirement challenges, loneliness and social isolation, and fall prevention.

Essence Smart Care, for instance, which developed fall detection and health-monitoring technology for older adults and people living with chronic conditions, has millions of devices installed worldwide.[13]

VR treadmill technology maker "GaitBetter," which has developed technology for gait training and fall prevention, has featured in 18 peer-reviewed studies exploring its ability to reduce falls and outperform standard, treadmill-based therapy.[14]

Mobileye, which develops autonomous driving technology, was cofounded by the Israeli computer scientist Amnon Shashua, then a faculty member at the Hebrew University of Jerusalem.[15] This technology, which is installed in new cars by many of the world's major automakers, including BMW, Audi, and General Motors, can prevent crashes, and is therefore of direct importance to the health of older drivers and pedestrians.[16] It has also been adopted by commercial fleets with older drivers, such as a taxi company in Japan.[17]

ElliQ, the social robot created by Israel's Intuition Robotics, was chosen by the New York State Office for the Aging (NYSOFA) to be distributed to 800 older adults as a way to tackle loneliness.[18] It was shown to decrease feelings of loneliness for 80 percent of its users.[19]

Despite these examples, AgeTech companies represent only a fraction of the thousands of tech companies that currently operate in Israel. Meanwhile, some of those who operate here never launch their products in the local market. The challenge now facing Israel's longevity hub is twofold: to double or triple the number of tech companies that tackle the challenges of aging, and to make these solutions available not just globally but locally as well.

## Agetech Challenges

### Funding

At this time of writing, there are numerous Israeli VCs that have backed Israeli AgeTech companies, but only one VC in Israel that exclusively invests in AgeTech companies: Mediterranean Towers Ventures. While it is easier to raise funding for AgeTech in 2022 than in 2015 simply because there are more funds and fewer start-ups being established,[20] this space would benefit from more early-stage funding to help companies gain initial traction. Perhaps a major exit by an AgeTech company (similar to the 2018 example, in the US, of BestBuy's acquisition of GreatCall) could raise the profile of the entire ecosystem in the eyes of potential investors.

**Tiny Home Market**

How it is possible for Israeli startups to aspire to achieve unicorn status or to go public when they have such a small market available to them? One answer is to go global. Award-winning Israeli IoT companies, such as Essence Group, which serves millions of older end users,[21] distribute their products around the world rather than just locally.

Israeli tech companies have long used Israel as a "beta" site: a place to test new products and services before venturing out into bigger markets like the United States. In fact, some products that are developed locally never become commercially available here—at least not for consumers. Sometimes, the nature of the product means that creating a localized version and adapting it to the requirements or regulations of the Israeli market isn't economically viable.

Take, for example, ElliQ, the social robotic companion that I had the privilege of participating in building during my time at Intuition Robotics. ElliQ expresses herself not only via voice but also using body language, LED lights, sound effects, and content displayed on a screen. She has multiple features that require speech, and since she can currently only speak and "understand" English, ElliQ can only be used by English-speaking users. On top of that, since the company aimed to launch ElliQ in the United States from the start, we created a robot that spoke English in an American dialect, could tell culturally appropriate jokes, and check the score of last night's (American) football game.

Not all of ElliQ's features are culture-specific: video calling and messaging, for instance, can certainly be used by any English-speaking user. Yet if the company were to release this product in any other market, it would have to adjust not just the content and language, but possibly body language and other aspects as well.

Localization can require a lot of resources, depending on the type of product you're building. Are text or speech involved in any of its interfaces? Is it subject to regulation? Does it move? Getting to product-market fit is challenging as it is, and trying to do so in multiple markets at the same time increases the level of complexity. Since Israeli startups have to think globally, and startups in general require focus, some Israeli companies choose to forgo launching in Israel altogether.

As a result of these concerns, when faced with the question of whether or not to launch the product in Israel, companies have to decide whether there's a business opportunity here. Those building consumer-facing products have to assess how many of Israel's older adults they can reasonably reach, through which distribution channels, and how much customer acquisition will cost.

## Startup Nation Meets the Welfare State

Since Israel has subsidized mandatory health insurance, every older adult has a "membership" with one out of four healthcare providers. These providers all have innovation departments that are ready and willing to pilot new technologies, with the purpose of distributing them to members. One example of successful distribution in this model is Tyto Care, which is distributed in Israel by Clalit: the largest healthcare provider in the country, serving more than 4.5 million people.[22] Tyto Care is an Israeli startup that makes telehealth visits more effective by allowing the physician to perform a remote examination of the patient's body and vitals, including their temperature, throat, lungs, and ears.[23]

The National Security is another institution with a very wide reach. It has access to every older adult in Israel because it is in charge of distributing the country's old-age pension, as well as Israel's publicly funded long-term care benefit, which is currently distributed to just under 300,000 older adults.[24] Older adults who are eligible for this benefit can choose whether to receive a monetary stipend or to receive services, which can include care at home or in an adult day center. The only piece of in-home technology currently included in this array of services is a personal emergency response system ("panic button").

As of 2018, only 2 percent of Israelis over the age of 65 live in long-term care facilities.[25] Most prefer to age in place, for which the LTC benefit has been a critical source of support for more than three decades. Despite this program's reach, however, a 2022 joint task force from the ministries of Welfare, Health, and Treasury found that Israel has twice as many severely dependent older adults, compared to European countries.[26] Perhaps Israel's high dependency numbers, on one hand, and its tech sector's home-market challenges, on the other, can mitigate one another. One way to help this process along would be to expand the variety of tech that recipients of Israel's LTC benefit can choose from. This change might not only improve outcomes but also create an incentive for startups to launch their products in the local market. The local AgeTech ecosystem has much to offer, and it is possible to incentivize companies to not only develop their products locally but also distribute them locally.

There are multiple factors contributing to the success of Israel's longevity hub, including a legacy of Jewish innovation in aging, government support for tech innovation, a strong research and tech transfer tradition, and an entrepreneurial spirit driven by the needs of an emerging nation. Last, I would like to consider two cultural factors: chutzpah, and zero degrees of separation.

In her 2019 book *Chutzpah: Why Israel Is a Hub of Innovation and Entrepreneurship*, Inbal Arieli argues that chutzpah—an approach to surmounting challenges using directness, creativity, and risk-taking—is the secret sauce that made Israel a global leader in tech innovation.

Additionally, I would argue that there's another secret ingredient to Israel's longevity hub: zero degrees of separation.

Stanley Milgram's famous paper "The Small World Problem" concluded that on average, any two random strangers in the United

States can be linked by five intermediaries, spreading the idea of "six degrees of separation" throughout the world.[27] Whether this theory holds water or not is still under debate, but here in Israel, it certainly feels like a small village in which everyone is connected to everyone else. In professional niches like aging or tech, we're probably closer to zero degrees of separation than to six.

Fewer degrees of separation and a decent dose of chutzpah can go a long way toward enabling partnerships and cross-sector collaborations that perhaps would not have been possible in other places. It is quite miraculous, honestly. I invite anyone reading these lines to visit and experience firsthand the wonder of Startup Nation's longevity hub.

Keren Etkin is a gerontologist and the author of *The AgeTech Revolution*, a book about the intersection of technology and aging. Etkin is the founder of *TheGerontechnologist.com*, a media platform that covers the global AgeTech ecosystem and offers online education through the AgeTech Academy. In 2021 she founded AgeLabIL at Shenkar College of Engineering, Design and Art in Israel with the purpose of providing AgeTech education to design and engineering students. Previously, Etkin was the first employee at Intuition Robotics, maker of ElliQ, a pioneering social robot designed with and for older adults, and cofounder & VP of Product at Sensi.ai, a startup that developed the first artificial intelligence solution for remote care monitoring. She holds an MA in gerontology and a BSc in life sciences from Ben-Gurion University.

## Notes

1. "Better Life Index," OECD, accessed January 20, 2023, https://stats.oecd.org/Index.aspx?DataSetCode=BLI. Life expectancy statistics reflect 2019 data.

2. "Fertility Rates," OECD, 2022, https://www.oecd.org/els/family/SF_2_1_Fertility_rates.pdf; "Population Growth (Annual %)—OECD Members," The World Bank,

2022, https://data.worldbank.org/indicator/SP.POP.GROW?locations=OE; "Popula-tion Density (People per sq. km of Land Area)—OECD Members," The World Bank, 2022, https://data.worldbank.org/indicator/EN.POP.DNST?locations=OE.

3. Alex Weinreb, "Why Is Israel's Life Expectancy So High?," *State of the Nation Report: Society, Economy and Policy in Israel* (2016): 437–472.

4. Ruth Sinai, "Together in Social Action: JDC-Israel and Its Major Partnerships," JDC-Eshel, 2012, https://www.thejoint.org.il/wp-content/uploads/2020/11/Major PartnershipsHeb.pdf.

5. "Optimal Aging in an Era of Living to 100," JDC Israel Eshel, 2022, https://www .thejoint.org.il/en/digital-library/jdc-eshel-programmatic-diamonds-document/.

6. "The Israeli Technological Eco-system: A Powerhouse of Innovation," Deloitte, accessed January 21, 2023, https://www2.deloitte.com/il/en/pages/innovation/article /the_israeli_technological_eco-system.html.

7. "The Israel Innovation Authority," The Israel Innovation Authority, accessed January 21, 2023, https://innovationisrael.org.il/en/contentpage/israel-innovation -authority.

8. "About," Myers JDC Brookdale, accessed January 21, 2023, https://brookdale.jdc .org.il/en/about/.

9. "Welcome," The Minerva Center on Intersectionality in Aging (MCIA) at the University of Haifa, accessed January 21, 2023, https://mcia.haifa.ac.il/.

10. "5-Year Strategic Plan for Optimal Aging in Israel (2021–2025)," JDC Israel Eshel, 2021, https://www.thejoint.org.il/en/digital-library/5-year-strategic-plan-for -optimal-aging-in-israel/.

11. "Assistive Technological Solutions for the Disabled—'Ezer-Tech,'" Israel Inno-vation, accessed July 9, 2023, https://innovationisrael.org.il/en/program/assistive -technologies-disabled.

12. "Open Calls," Innovation Israel, 2018, https://innovationisrael.org.il/en/open call/israel-cabhi-3rd-call-proposals.

13. "Essence SmartCare Sees Surge in International Growth with Over One Mil-lion Connected Digital Devices Deployed," Essense Smartcare, 2021, https://www .prnewswire.com/il/news-releases/essence-smartcare-sees-surge-in-international-growth -with-over-one-million-connected-digital-devices-deployed-301362526.html.

14. "Resources," GaitBetter, accessed January 21, 2023, https://www.gaitbetter.com /resources/.

15. Shelly Appleberg, "מייסד מובילאיי לאוניברסיטה העברית—ימים לפני עסקת המיליארדים עם אינטל התרגיל שעשה," The Marker, 2017, https://www.themarker.com/markets/2017-09-06 /ty-article/0000017f-edaa-d4cd-af7f-edfaaacb0000.

16. "Older Drivers," NSC Injury Facts, accessed January 21, 2023, https://injuryfacts .nsc.org/motor-vehicle/road-users/older-drivers/.

17. "Japan: Yoshida Taxi Company Lowers Collisions Rates by 85% with Mobileye Technology," Mobileye, 2019, https://ims.mobileye.com/fleets/au/case-study/japan -yoshida-taxi-company-lowers-collisions-rates-by-85-with-mobileye-technology/.

18. Ariel Zilber, "Elderly New Yorkers to Get Robots to Help Relieve Loneliness," New York Post, 2022, https://nypost.com/2022/05/25/elderly-new-yorkers-to-get -robots-to-help-relieve-loneliness/.

19. Dor Skuler, "2022 ElliQ Impact Report," ElliQ, 2022, https://blog.elliq.com /2022-elliq-impact-report.

20. Jill Wyler, "Overview of Israel's Venture Capital Landscape," GINSUM, 2021, https://www.ginsum.eu/overview-of-israels-venture-capital-landscape/; "Is This the End of the Israeli 'Start-Up Nation' Era?," Israel Innovation Authority 2021 Report, 2021, https://innovationisrael.org.il/en/reportchapter/end-israeli-start-nation-era.

21. "Essence Group Wins Two Twice Picks Award for CES 2022," Essence Group, 2022, https://www.essence-grp.com/press-releases/essence-group-wins-two-twice-picks -award-for-ces-2022/.

22. "About Kalit," Kalit, 2022, https://www.clalit.co.il/he/info/Pages/about_us.aspx.

23. "TytoCare," TytoCare, accessed January 21, 2023, https://www.tytocare.com/.

24. "Statistics by Localities," National Insurance Institute, 2022, https://www.btl .gov.il/mediniyut/situation/statistics/btlstatistics.aspx?type=2&id=6.

25. "Statistics by Localities," National Insurance Institute.

26. Merav Arlozorov, "קשיש בישראל זוכה לטיפול מהיר יותר מבעולם המערבי, אך מצבו מידרדר מהר יותר מבעולם המערבי", The Marker, 2022, https://www.themarker.com/news/health/2022-01-25/ty-article /.highlight/0000017f-db0b-df9c-a17f-ff1b9b1f0000.

27. Stanley Milgram, "The Small World Problem," Psychology Today 2, no. 1 (1967): 60–67.

# 19
# Thailand EEC

Pongsak Hoontrakul and Thanasak Hoontrakul

## Introduction

Thailand is in a demographic predicament. It's trapped at an intermediate income level while facing demographic challenges typical
of high-income nations: increasing average longevity combined
with an ongoing baby bust, leading to population aging.[1] These circumstances hold major ramifications for the Thai economy, politics, and society—already disturbed by the COVID-19 pandemic,
war in Ukraine, and ensuing supply-chain and inflationary effects.

This predicament also holds opportunities for Thailand, however.
Its middle-income status allows it to offer foreign investors and older
consumers—especially expatriate retirees and health tourists—a relatively low-cost geography that is equipped with modern physical,
medical, and legal infrastructures. With the help of strategic government involvement, this influx of invaluable entrepreneurial energy
and investment is being channeled into a mature biomedical cluster,
centered around cutting-edge research and product development.
Initial efforts to meet foreign expatriate demand for services in this
cluster may ultimately benefit the aging local population, whose
healthcare, eldercare, and housing needs continually grow.

This trajectory has precedent, mirroring Thailand's experience with the automotive sector starting in the 1960s. Once a manufacturing hub for Japanese automakers due to its resources and low business costs, Thailand transformed over time and with significant government investment, becoming a high-skill, knowledge-intensive production center for technologically sophisticated products. A similar process is unfolding today, in which local investment, originally aimed in part at yielding income from foreign expatriates seeking a low-cost retirement environment with high-value services, is creating the conditions necessary for a self-sustaining, mature ecosystem aimed at the well-being of both expats and older Thais. The extent to which this process will scale to the national level, however, and benefit the broader, older, poorer Thai population, especially in rural areas, remains to be seen.

## Demographic Challenges

Thailand is an aging society with 17.5 percent of its population aged 60 and above. As of 2022, its mortality rate has exceeded its birth rate—which, at less than 1.5 children per woman, is among the world's lowest. The trends responsible have resulted in a shrinking workforce, suppressing the country's economic growth for two consecutive years.[2] Fewer babies today mean fewer workers, consumers, savers, investors, and taxpayers tomorrow. Adding to the aging trend, Thai life expectancy has increased steadily in the last few decades, rising from about 65 years in the 1980s to 78.7 years as of 2021 (74.5 for men, 83 for women).[3] By 2035, people aged 60 and up are projected to account for more than 30 percent of Thailand's population.[4]

Traditionally, Thailand's government has treated population aging as a fiscal liability. As of 2020, a vast majority of elderly Thais are of low to moderate income, and receive some form of public support, totaling of over 350 billion THB ($9.26 billion USD).[5] The graying population trend will exacerbate these needs and impact Thailand in other ways as well. The old-age dependency ratio will increase from 18 percent as of 2020 to 30 percent in 2030.[6] As a result, annual GDP growth is projected to drop from 3.3–3.5 percent as of 2021 to 2.6–2.8 percent in 2030.[7] The government could mitigate some of these effects by adding support for voluntary savings via the national Retirement Mutual Fund, raising the retirement age from 60 to 65 years, and expanding tax collection and the tax base. However, some of these measures come with severe side effects and may prove insufficient to counter future demographic challenges.[8]

## Retirement: Thailand's First Longevity Export

Despite these concerns and drawbacks, population aging is a growing source of income for Thailand, which is fast becoming one of the world's most popular retirement destinations. Nevertheless, its retirement housing industry is still in its nascent stage. As of 2022, there are only approximately 40,000 senior living units operated by the state, nonprofit organizations, or the private sector, the last of which accounts for less than half of all units.[9] Industry growth paused from 2019 to 2022 due to lockdowns, but as restrictions relax, planning and construction has begun. In the senior housing industry, the prospect of aging as a megatrend, and the opportunities afforded by the longevity economy, have become common knowledge. Nevertheless, no single operator has yet constructed a commercial project on a scale as large as can be seen in the United States. Perhaps this hasn't happened because longevity business models are new and still being tested; perhaps it's because the health and eldercare infrastructure necessary to support such a project is still being built.

For generations, Chiangmai has been one of Thailand's retirement hubs. Thai people often choose to retire in this northern,

rural region, which offers a temperate climate, rich natural environs, relatively low living costs, and indigenous culture. Foreign
expatriates, too, have long found this region appealing. In 1907,
the American missionary Dr. James W. McKean founded a leper asylum in Chiangmai on an island in the Ping River, which evolved
over the following century into a planned community, intended
especially for American and international retirees with chronic and
critical illnesses.[10] When the Vietnam War ended, more American
expat retirees, many veterans, flocked to this region.

The period from 1990 to 2010 ushered in unprecedented economic growth, with Europeans rediscovering Thailand as a tourist
destination. Foreign spending led to an explosion among culinary,
hospitality, and service providers. Europeans, meanwhile, mainly
from the UK, Germany, France, and Scandinavia, began to vacation,
and then retire, in southern beach resort areas, such as Phuket, Krabi,
and Hua Hin. As tourists gave way to retirees, entrepreneurs began to
see the potential to create niche, longevity-economy markets cater-
ing to the needs of expat retirees, especially regarding housing.

The first waves of dedicated retirement and senior housing destinations were created by private-sector entrepreneurs: usually
foreigners who targeted expats from their respective home countries. Dok Kaew Gardens, a retirement home at McKean Hospital,
caters mainly to international residents, particularly Americans.
Care Resort Chiang Mai, set up by a British entrepreneur, targets UK
expats and Europeans with a luxury, adult care retirement facility.
Vivobene and the Baan Kamlangchay center were set up in 2004 by
Swiss groups to accommodate mainly Swiss and German patients
with Alzheimer's. Many of these destinations started as hotels or
resorts before offering retirement housing products.

By 2020, the US expatriate retirement community, joined by Japanese and European expatriates, had largely coalesced around Chiangmai. That year, *US News and World Report* ranked it the world's
fourth best affordable overseas retirement destination.[11]

Retirement housing developments aren't limited to Thailand's northern regions, however. Starting in the 1960s, Japan made major capital investments in Greater Bangkok and the Eastern Seaboard, creating clusters of Japanese industrial conglomerates (e.g., Toyota and Honda in the automobile sector; Mitsubishi and Sharp in electronics). Local hot spots developed where Japanese culture, food, and language predominated. Many managers and engineers from Japan decided to retire or have their second home in these familiar, southern environs, especially in the Sri Racha region of Chonburi province (knowns as "Little Osaka"), as well as Bangkok's Thong Lor area ("Little Tokyo").

In Thailand's southern region, the retirement housing industry is also booming, propelled by the demand of European expatriates who became familiar with Thailand through tourism. Today, Thai companies, some working with foreign companies, build and operate many southern retirement communities. For example, Phuket's Kamala Senior Living, a prime beachfront and hill-country resort and mixed-use residential development, was developed in 2017 as a joint project by four Thai real estate developers: Nye Estate, Chewathai, LPN Development, and CH Karnchang. It is managed and operated by Otium Living, a global senior living specialist firm, alongside Audley Group: the UK's top developer and operator of luxury retirement villages. In another case, Hua Hin, 200 kilometers south of Bangkok, has been a favorite beach resort for the Thai Royal Family and aristocrats for over a century. Quite a few golf courses in this small town now offer senior housing, many collaborating with local Thais and expats to build and operate large senior living villages, such as Sansara at the Black Mountain Golf Course.

Retirement communities cannot exist in a vacuum, however. To meet retirees' ever-increasing needs, they must be interlinked with modern infrastructure, especially health and eldercare infrastructure, and biomedical research. In certain regions of Thailand, this linkage has begun. For instance, Chiangmai University (CMU), founded in 1964 as a leading public research university, launched its CMU Senior Wellness Centre in May 2022.[12] Similarly, the Thai government has made a significant longevity-economy investment in the form of the CMU's Hariphunchai Medical Centre, in Lamphun: a 200-bed general hospital with a total budget of about 300 million THB ($90 million USD).[13] Apart from boosting local medical tourism, it serves elderly patients from Thailand's 17 northern provinces and the Greater Mekong subregion, including Cambodia, China's Yunnan province, Laos, Myanmar, and Vietnam.

This process—supporting both a foreign expat aging population as well as local aging adults through government investment in advanced medicine and research—is still happening at a relatively small scale. A new, multi-sector effort to erect a business and innovation hub in Thailand's Southeast, however, hints at the possibility of far greater impact.

## Thailand's Government Responses to an Aging Society

The Thai government has recognized the importance of the silver economy and has taken a proactive approach toward increasing participation in it.

Part of this effort involves investing in Thailand as an international healthcare provider. Already, Thailand is home to the world's fifth largest medical tourism market. In 2019, it hosted over 3.5 million medical tourists who spent over $600 million USD on health care. In 2021, Thailand was ranked first in Asia and fifth worldwide in the Global Health Security Index.[14]

In 2019, Thailand's Board of Investment (BOI) began to promote investment in the growing expat and domestic longevity market, offering incentives to companies in medical and wellness tourism, senior housing, elder care, and health care.[15] A corporate income tax (CIT) exemption is available, for instance, for certain manufacturing businesses (e.g., medical and scientific devices, active pharmaceutical ingredients, and other medical products), as well as valuable healthcare-related services (e.g., medical embedded software and specialty medical centers). Non-tax incentives include a liberalized approach to long-term visas and working permits, as well as official sanction of 100-percent-foreign-owned companies and land.[16] As of 2022, the government has augmented these measures with grants and other forms of support awarded on a case-by-case basis for research and development, IP licensing, advanced technology training, development of local suppliers, and improved packaging and product design. Finally, to simplify these offerings and other regulatory concerns, the BOI offers a "One-Stop Service Center."

With these incentives in place, large hospital and real estate operators are increasingly seeking to take part in Thailand's longevity economy. For example, Bangkok Dusit Medical Service PCL (BDMS), Thailand's largest private healthcare operator, has prioritized opening elderly care centers in its hospital chain,[17] while both Bumrungrad and Thonburee Hospitals have expanded into nursing and retirement homes. BDMS also acquired the luxury resort Swissotel Nai Lert Park, Bangkok, and invested 14.2 billon THB ($400 million USD) to transform it into a holistic services medical center.[18]

The government has gotten directly involved in senior housing and aging care, too, via state-built housing facilities for older adults constructed in 1996 at Sawangkanives, Samut Prakarn.

Thailand's ongoing development of aging-related industry, its strategic use of state investment, incentive policies, foreign capital, physical and digital connectivity, and its population's growing demand is reminiscent of its approach to the 1990s' automotive industry. In the years ahead, as with the auto industry, a disproportionate amount of this energy will be focused on Thailand's southeastern seaboard.

## EEC and EECmd

Thailand began its Eastern Seaboard Development Program (ESB) in the 1980s to build and decentralize heavy industry around two of its major ports while setting up infrastructure necessary for ongoing growth. The region—and country—is now entering a new phase of development. In Thailand's 13th National Economic Development Plan (2023–2027), the country plans to pursue goals—including achievements in research and development, investments in human resources, and provisioning Thais with equal economic prospects—that will help it transition to a high-value-added, knowledge-based economy.[19] In this transformation, southeastern communities will play a critical role, thanks to a new, regional development initiative called the Eastern Economic Corridor (EEC).

The EEC's purview is broad. Under the new initiative, three provinces—Chonburi, Rayong, and Chachoengsao—are designated Special Economic Zones (SEZ) with their own laws, governed by the EEC's main committee and chaired by the prime minister. Like the BOI, the EEC offers businesses One-Stop Service, and can legally approve, permit, and grant a suite of rights and concessions to industry actors.[20] Its broad sectoral mandate includes several facets of the longevity economy, targeted by several of the EEC's designated geographic hubs. One of these, EECg, is a genomic research hub centered on Burapha University's Bangsaen campus, which plans to develop a Thai genome library, with potential downstream products including precision medicine and regenerative therapeutics, digital health services, and personalized medicine. EECi, situated in Wangchan, focuses on innovation; its purview includes medical devices, plus retirement-adjacent products like smart and green housing.

Perhaps most relevant to the longevity economy, EECmd is a medical hub whose ambition is becoming "the Pillar of the Modern Medicine of ASEAN."[21] There, a general hospital with budget approval of over 900 million THB ($25.2 million USD) is under construction. EECmd's final goal is to create a smart medical city that will nurture digital innovations, modern medicine, and med tech development for the healthcare and wellness sector.

EECmd is an epicenter of Thai private and public investment in the longevity economy. To further explore this hub, we interviewed Dr. Kammal Kumar Pawa, an associate professor and Vice Rector at Thammasat University, who directly manages TU's Pattaya Campus and EECmd. This interview has been condensed and edited.

## Interview: Dr. Kammal Kumar Pawa on EECmd

**Q:** Please describe EECmd's geographical extent, sectoral involvement, and implicit and explicit goals.

**A:** The Eastern Economic Corridor Medical Hub, or EECmd, is based at Thammasat University (TU) Pattaya campus with an area of 220 acres. We envision this campus to be a high-end medical and longevity valley with three components: healthcare services (70 percent of the area), health technology (20 percent), and academic research (10 percent).

**Q:** Describe how EECmd will work: its formation, innovation priorities, and potential sources of collaboration.

**A:** The first area of focus will be healthcare services, including hospitals, nursing homes, rehabilitation centers. This plays to the strength of Thailand as a leading hospitality and healthcare destination. The academic hospital, operated by the university, is already under construction and will be completed by 2024. Another 100 acres will be leased out to private commercial sectors to build complementary services. For example, we have a real estate developer building a health resort with a focus on Japanese clients, while another developer is focusing on addiction rehabilitation. The focus will be on mid- to high-end customers, both locally as well as internationally.

The next area of focus will be healthcare technology. We have allocated more than 22,000 square meters of space for the private sector: especially startups focusing on digital health, genomics, and wellness. Nearly all the facilities in EECmd, from security guards to laundry, from i-clouds to utilities, will be commonly available and charged on a pay-per-use basis, like the sharing economy. This will help keep startup fixed costs low.

**Q:** What are the hub's likely major economic contributors and key success factors?

**A:** This hub is a public-private partnership (PPP). Total expected investment is approximately $200 million USD. The government will play the facilitator role, investing approximately one out of five dollars. The hospital is the key investment of the government. This will be the main draw that supports the rest of the private facilities. To attract private companies, the government is giving 15 years of corporate income tax exemption and granting special visas to bring international experts and their families to the area.[22] The key is to create medical needs-related traffic to the area for the hospital, nursing home, and wellness center. Consequently, health-tech companies and academic research will follow.

**Q:** How can your planned digital hospital and research and development agenda set you apart from regional and global competitors?

**A:** Thailand is already one of the biggest medical tourism destinations in the world, but it doesn't have an academic medical center. Thammasat University can attract existing high-end customers, who will be the first customer base of the EECmd. With further investments from the private sector, this hub would be set apart from the rest of the world as an affordable, service-oriented, and high-quality healthcare destination.

**Q:** What, if any, are the hub's feedback processes between consumers (especially elderly patients) and producers as they create new products and services?

**A:** This process would be within the purview of the profit-seeking companies. Our role is to provide infrastructure and facilities for private companies to innovate.

**Q:** What is the hub's future best-case scenario?

**A:** As for the hospital, in 10 years, our 300-bed hospital will be at full capacity, receiving 1,000 outpatient visits per day. Half of the patients would be foreigners. In addition, all the 100 acres set aside for the private sector would be fully leased out to private companies, who have thriving businesses. Business needs to prosper for this hub to be a success.

**Q:** What potential problems keep you up at night? Are you worried about attracting human resources to the area?

**A:** I am anxious about politics, both at the university level and the government level. Will the government continue to invest in EECmd if there is a change in administration? At the university level, will there be a change in leadership in two years? Will the new leadership reallocate resources out of the EECmd? The project requires long-term focus and investment to be successful.

## Selected Policy Discussions and Conclusions

In the longevity economy, government has found an opportunity to address twin economic issues: creating an economic growth engine and caring for an aging population.[23] Private-sector longevity economy companies, particularly in the retirement industry, have proven that serving older people can lead to economic growth. However, because this progress has been slow and fragmented, the

Thai state has begun aggressively pursuing foreign direct investment via a variety of incentives and state resources.

This approach has drawbacks. Unlike Thailand's past industrialization period, where major social benefits were achieved thanks to a private investment boom, this top-down approach will, at least initially, help only a small portion the country's poor, elderly population.

Instead of focusing only on the income-generating aspect of the longevity economy, the Thai government must also think in term of streamlining its public healthcare system with higher quality services. These measures could include deepening the digital transformation (particularly telemedicine) and amending relevant laws to support longevity economy products and services aimed at lower-income and rural populations. New online medical applications, such as Good Doctor, Mordee, and Clicknic, have been accepted by regulators at the National Health Security Office.[24] These tools are useful, but not sufficient to reach poor older adults who aren't tech-savvy or without ready internet access. A more community-based approach, particularly in rural towns, may help resolve these deficits. A strong state push for inter-organization resource sharing and interoperability in medical and technical resources (e.g., MRI access, lab work, digital medical records, doctors, and nurses) are urgently needed to form clusters of excellence nationwide, reducing redundancy and idle capacity in the big cities while bridging the scarcity gap in remote areas.

In addition to replicating past successes, Thailand's demographic predicament calls for forward-looking vision and outside-of-the-box thinking. EECmd may prove a successful bioscience and healthcare innovation cluster, but it may also serve as a protype for nationwide public medical clusters. Its high-value-added services can be more than mere profit engines if utilized to provide the local, impoverished elderly and the public with cutting-edge medical care. However, the government needs to overcome the failure in public coordination between different agencies—Ministry of Health, Ministry of Digital Economy and Society, and Board of Investment—to effectively implement these policies. Thailand's twin economic issues stemming from longevity can be addressed simultaneously with an integrated plan to improve overall social welfare.

Dr. Pongsak Hoontrakul is Chairman of Hoontrakul Corporation Ltd, his family-owned asset management and holding company focusing on financial investment, real estate development and startup firms in "age care value chain related businesses." Formerly, he has acted as an advisor to Chairman of Thai Airways Plc.; a member of the International Advisory Board of International Association of Deposit Insurance, Basel, Switzerland; a member of the International Advisory Council of the Schulich School of Business, York University, Toronto, Canada; a non-executive director and member of the nomination committee of UOL Group Ltd, Singapore; and an independent director and Chairman of the Audit Committee of UOB (Thailand) Bank Pcl. In the public sector, Dr. Hoontrakul was appointed as an advisor to the Deputy Prime Minister in Charge of Economic Affairs; the Senate Committee for Fiscal, Banking and Financial Institutions; Parliamentary Committee of Economic Affairs; and Parliamentary Committee for Justice and Human Rights in Thailand. Until 2013, he held the Senior Research Fellow position at the Sasin School of Management at Chulalongkorn University, Thailand, and in this capacity, he extensively engaged with the World Economic Forum in numerous roles for over twenty years. He has written over 50 articles, papers and books. His latest book, *Economic Transformation and Business Opportunities in Asia*, was published by New York McMillan Palgrave in 2018. Dr. Hoontrakul holds a doctoral degree in Business Administration in Finance from Thammasat University, a Master of Business Administration degree from the Sasin School at Chulalongkorn University, and a bachelor's degree in Industrial and System Engineering at San Jose State

University, USA. He was the recipient of the Best Research Paper Award for ASEAN Scholars at the annual Asia Pacific Finance Association in 2001.

Thanasak Hoontrakul is the Founder and CEO of TH Healthcare Properties, a healthcare real estate company based in Thailand. He graduated from Tsinghua MBA-MIT Master of Management Dual Degree Program, during which he wrote two master's theses relating to the longevity economy. Prior to his graduate program, he cofounded FairDee Insurtech Co., Ltd., a tech startup in the insurance industry, and successfully exited the business. Thanasak holds a Bachelor of Engineering degree from National University of Singapore. He was a recipient of Singapore ASEAN Scholarship and Tsinghua Future Leader Award Scholarship.

## Notes

1. Pongsak Hoontrakul, "Asia's Longevity Economy," in *Economic Transformation and Business Opportunities in Asia*, ed. Pongsak Hoontrakul (New York: Springer International, 2018), 93–142, https://doi.org/10.1007/978-3-319-58928-2_4.

2. Duangjai Lorthanavanich, "Population Ageing in Thailand," Economic Research Institute for ASEAN, 2021.

3. "Life Expectancy at Birth, Total (Years)—Thailand," World Bank, updated 2020, https://data.worldbank.org/indicator/SP.DYN.LE00.IN?locations=TH.

4. Nawarat Pongpaiboon, "Situation of the Thai Older Persons," Institute for Population and Social Research Mahidol University, 2020, https://www.dop.go.th/download/knowledge/th1635826412-975_0.pdf.

5. Vipan Prachuabmob, "Aging in Thailand," Chulalongkorn University, 2019, https://www.un.org/development/desa/pd/sites/www.un.org.development.desa.pd/files/unpd_egm_201902_s3_vipanprachuabmoh.pdf.

6. "Thailand—Ratio of Population Aged 65+ per 100 Population 15–64 Years," Knoema, 2020, https://knoema.com/atlas/Thailand/topics/Demographics/Dependency-Ratios/Old-age-dependency-ratio-65-per-15-64.

7. Nacha Anantachotekul, "How Can Thailand Grow Its Business When over 40% of Thai People Reach Retirement Age?" KKP Research, 2020.

8. "Country Diagnostic Study on Long-Term Care in Thailand," December 2020, Asian Development Bank.

9. Thanasak Hoontrakul, "Review of US Business Models in Longevity Economy and Strategy Recommendation for the Thai Market" (Master's thesis, MIT Sloan, 2022).

10. Attrawut Sangboonruang, "McKean: From Leper Asylum to Rehabilitation Centre," Chiangmai City Life, 2016, https://www.chiangmaicitylife.com/clg/places/mckean-from-leper-asylum-to-rehabilitation-centre/.

11. Kathleen Peddicord, "The Best Affordable Places to Retire Overseas in 2022," U.S. News and World Report, 2022, https://money.usnews.com/money/retirement/baby-boomers/slideshows/the-best-affordable-places-to-retire-overseas?slide=6.

12. "รองอธิการบดีมหาวิทยาลัยเชียงใหม่ กล่าวต้อนรับและกล่าวถึงความเป็นมาของการโครงการศูนย์ส่งเสริมพฤฒพลังผู้สูงอายุ มหาวิทยาลัยเชียงใหม่," Chiang Mai University, 2022, https://www.swc.cmu.ac.th/news/2.

13. "มช. นำความพร้อมด้านการแพทย์ รองรับการขยายเขตเมืองสร้างศูนย์บริการทางการแพทย์หริภุญไชย จังหวัดลำพูน," Thailand Plus, 2021, https://www.thailandplus.tv/archives/444554.

14. Jennifer B. Bell and Jessica Nuzzo, "2021 GHS Index Country Profile for Thailand," GHS Index, 2021, https://www.ghsindex.org/country/thailand/.

15. Bonggot Anuroj, "Thailand 4.0—A New Value-Based Economy," BOI, 2019.

16. "TIR: Silver Economy—Opportunities with Thailand's Growing Senior Population," BOI, 2019.

17. Pongsak Hoontrakul, "Asia's Longevity Economy," in *Economic Transformation and Business Opportunities in Asia*, ed. Pongsak Hoontrakul (Springer International Publishing, 2018), 93–142.

18. Narongrid Galaputh, "Market Opportunities and Hospital Networks in Thailand," Thailand Board of Investment (Paris Office), 2022.

19. "Thailand's Measures to Drive Its National Agenda of Old Age: 6 Sustainable, 4 Change," Ministry of Social Development & Human Security, Royal Thai Government, 2019.

20. "Eastern Economic Corridor," EECO, 2021.

21. "Pushing TU to Be 'The Pillar of the Modern Medicine of ASEAN,'" QS GEN, November 2, 2021, https://qs-gen.com/pushing-tu-to-be-the-pillar-of-the-modern-medicine-of-asean/.

22. "Long-Term Resident (LTR) Visa," Bangkok Post, July 27, 2022, www.bangkok post.com/business/2355499/long-term-resident-ltr-visa.

23. "Thailand's Measures to Drive Its National Agenda of Old Age: 6 Sustainable, 4 Change," Ministry of Social Development & Human Security.

24. "Telemedicine Apps Take Off," August 18, 2022, https://www.bangkokpost.com /thailand/general/2370936/telemedicine-apps-take-off.

# 20
# Aging2.0

**Stephen Johnston**

Aging2.0 is a global ecosystem for aging innovation: in effect, a longevity hub for the world. It's a network of networks, comprising more than a hundred local city chapters, each with its own network of people devoted to serving the wants and needs of the growing older population. It's based on the simple premise that there are plenty of good ideas for innovation in aging, but not nearly enough information sharing and collaboration.

Over the decade since it was launched, Aging2.0 has accelerated the emergence of "agetech" as a new opportunity area, while helping individual startups launch internationally, land pilots and customers, and receive investment.

The Aging2.0 ecosystem consists of a distributed, diverse network of stakeholders: startups, corporates, investors, researchers, policymakers, and older adults themselves; organized in local chapters, coordinated by a small, centralized HQ team. HQ weaves the network together by setting and validating each chapter's missions, hosting events, and publishing reports and newsletters.

In the course of its development, Aging2.0 has encountered a variety of challenges inherent in building a bootstrapped global network: in particular, lack of business models, insufficient capital, and an insatiable need for research. The recent, 2022 acquisition of Aging2.0 by Louisville Healthcare CEO Council (CEO$^C$) may address some of these issues, however. (For more on this acquisition, see chapter 13.)

Looking forward, Aging2.0 (or a network like it) has the potential to evolve significantly, leveraging the new technologies involved in the decentralized vision of computing commonly known as "Web 3.0." Aging2.0 has already proven the principal that a network distributed both online and within specific geographic locations can promote vital cross-pollination across sectors and industries. Now, new technologies designed expressly for the distributed sharing of knowledge and intellectual property offer an exciting opportunity to use some of these emerging network principles to connect and empower the good—but still too often siloed—work done by longevity hubs around the world.

## Origin Story: Nokia2.0 Meets Venture Philanthropy

At one time in the mid-2000s, Nokia, the world's leading mobile phone company, was developing five podcasting apps. The trouble was, none of them knew about each other. I know because I was developing one of them. I was based in the headquarters, just outside Helsinki, where I knew many of the innovation teams, yet had somehow missed the other efforts, similar to my own.

At the time, Nokia didn't have a clear internet strategy, and so, inspired by attending early "Web2.0" conferences in San Francisco, I created "Nokia2.0": a "learning-and-doing" community within the company. It brought together otherwise-siloed departments through events, hackathons, and discussions: "connecting people," as per the Nokia tagline, across their cubicles and countries.

A significant amount of knowledge sharing and innovations emerged from Nokia2.0, including one of the first podcasting apps.

However, this bottom-up innovation wasn't universally embraced by the company's leadership. By the end of the aughts, Nokia's share price and innovative output were both on the decline, and the company was sold to Microsoft. Nokia Inc.'s demise had many silver linings; in fact, the resulting exodus of talent helped create Finland's world-renowned gaming and tech startup community. In my case, the open learning and action-first ethos we'd experimented with in Nokia2.0 stuck with me. It was the first of two experiences that formed the seed of the idea that became Aging2.0.

The second defining experience came while I was living in New York in 2010, having just left Nokia: helping a Texan billionaire's family discover and invent life-saving therapeutics for his aggressive dementia. Whereas Nokia2.0 was a "bottom-up," emergent community, the Tau Consortium, as this dementia-fighting effort was called, was a tightly orchestrated, "top-down" group of expert researchers that has gone on to direct over $100 million in cutting-edge research funding.

I remember one conversation with one of the family members clearly. She was searching all over the world for products to help with frequent wandering, an all-too-common result of dementia. She was staggered that nobody seemed to be focused on this market. I agreed, and not long thereafter, a mission-driven, global innovation community in aging was born. After some events in New York to test the concept, I teamed up with a fellow passionate innovator, PhD gerontologist Katy Fike, and moved to the San Francisco Bay Area to build Aging2.0 in earnest.

## Global Aging: A Collective Intelligence Problem?

Around the world, populations that were once shaped like pyramids, bottom-heavy with children, are turning into pillars as older people start to outnumber the young. Headlines focus on the growing burden of disease, the caregiver crisis, ageism, and stretched healthcare systems, often leading to calls for massive investment. However, today's systems—from the built environment to health systems to financial services—weren't designed for aging societies. Our health systems, in particular, were designed more for reactively addressing individual maladies than for proactively dealing with ongoing and systemic issues of aging.

The path-dependency and inertia created by outmoded systems never built for aging populations presents one critical obstacle for anyone hoping to make a difference in global aging. The other obstacle is a lack of insight into what is happening globally. There are fantastic innovations happening around the world for older adults, but most people don't know about them. Innovations in health care, social care, housing, cities, transport, financial services, food, and entertainment are all connected, but tend to be dealt with in silos.

Aging2.0 was launched in 2012 with a vision to correct these fundamental problems: to build a global "collective intelligence" network for aging innovation. From the start, this vision was as ambitious as it was sparsely resourced: built by just a handful of enthusiastic, mission-driven people with minimal capital or organizational support.

The blueprint for Aging2.0, then as now, consisted of four elements: Why, What, How, and Who.

### Why? To Increase the Quality of Life of Older Adults Globally

Aging2.0's mission is to increase the quality of life of older adults. As a bootstrapped, independent organization, we could champion solutions that worked for older adults, not just those that worked for a particular payor or vested interest.

### What? Addressing the "Grand Challenges" of Aging

The sheer size of the "longevity economy"—up to 34 percent of the overall economy, according to AARP[1]—meant we needed to focus:

finding leverage points of maximum impact for effort expended. The result was our "Grand Challenges." These eight topics emerged from discussions with innovators, researchers, and older adults themselves about what matters most: brain health, care coordination, caregiving, end-of-life, engagement and purpose, financial wellness, daily living and lifestyle, and mobility and movement.

## How? Through a Global Network Designed for Systems Change

We aimed to transform aging into an opportunity by building a global innovation community to change fundamental assumptions and norms concerning aging. The goal is to create a paradigm shift spanning sectors and mindsets leading to real changes in individual behaviors, community norms, novel innovations, and benefits for the wider economy.

## Who? Championing Startups and Older Adults

While many industry associations in aging existed at the time of Aging2.0's founding, none focused on the intersection of startups and older adults. Aging2.0 set out to do so. The mission of aligning and aiding these two groups became one of the organization's guiding lights.

---

**Case Study Spotlight: Dr. June Fisher, Chief Elder Officer, Aging2.0**

Dr. June Fisher is a San Francisco–based, retired physician and advisor to Stanford in her eighties, who got involved with Aging2.0 in 2013. She noticed an article about the launch of the organization in her local newspaper, and offered to help translate her experiences and insights. For example, she often struggled bringing back groceries from the farmers' market. Her experience formed the basis for "City Cart," a walker/cart hybrid that won the 2017 Stanford Center on Longevity Design Challenge. June has since become a fixture in the Aging2.0 ecosystem, and constantly exhorts the innovators in the network to "design with us, not for us."

---

## The Growth of a Global Ecosystem

Over its first decade, Aging2.0 built up a global ecosystem of interconnected city chapters. This section explores what was built, and how.

### Chapters: 100-Plus Cities and 1,000-Plus Local Events

Aging2.0's volunteer "ambassadors," who spend many hours a week cultivating and curating their local chapters, have proved the linchpin to the organization's growth. They have generally discovered Aging2.0 via word of mouth—the organization has no advertising budget—and were attracted by the idea of hosting a local innovation network. They usually would submit a detailed application, including a video; then, once onboarded, they would build a team and a plan. As of 2022, Aging2.0 has over 100 ambassador-run chapters in nearly 30 countries, who have collectively hosted over a thousand events in the past decade.

Often, chapter events served to showcase local startups and innovators. Occasionally, these would feature storytelling sessions by older adults imparting their experiences, or lectures by researchers. The "pitch event"—a tried-and-tested format borrowed from startup events outside the aging space—was standard; it provided a sense of excitement and dynamism that was often missing from dry, academic presentations that had been the norm in aging research.

### CoverAGE: A Newsletter with 30,000 Subscribers

Starting in its early days, Aging2.0 put out a regular newsletter, CoverAGE, which acted as a roundup of recent innovations, event recaps and industry trends. The newsletter became a key communication platform within the network.

### Academy: The First Agetech Accelerator

In 2013, Aging2.0 launched its first startup accelerator program, the Academy. Housed in the offices of the Institute on Aging in

San Francisco (itself a well-established innovator in the space), this effort brought in startups for a focused program of learning, mentorship, and support, in return for a slice of equity. Several of the startups that went through the program went on to significant commercial success, including SWORD Health (valued at over two billion dollars as of 2022), Care Linx (acquired), True Link and Care Coach (strong and growing businesses worth millions of dollars), among others.

**OPTIMIZE and HQ Events**

Aging2.0's first Global Summit was held in 2014 at the University of California, San Francisco. In 2016, the organization renamed its annual event "OPTIMIZE." These recurring events brought together people we'd worked with remotely all year, as well as members from disparate global chapters.

In addition to these events, Aging2.0 explored multiple formats to foster connections within our global network. In 2015, we joined forces with Scott Peifer and his AgeTech West initiative to introduce a series of "Pitch for Pilot" events, where startups would pitch a roomful of providers, and then walk away from the one-hour event with up to five offers to run "pilots": a high return on their time. In 2017 we hosted European and Asian Summits in Belgium and Taiwan respectively. And in 2018 we hosted innovation for a on caregiving (in San Francisco) and dementia (in Toronto), which allowed us to connect global subject-specific experts. We also had a number of Coffee and Clicks events, where we hosted a group of older adults and startups, who then spent a few hours discussing issues and sharing ideas. These allowed the startups to get a rare sense of the product experience in the field.

**Alliance: A Range of Corporate Sponsors and Partners**

As its network and events grew, Aging2.0 became a valuable connection point between startups and corporates. The organization formalized this connective tissue in the form of the "Alliance": a membership community for corporate stakeholders who received priority access to the network's startups and other corporate members, as well as knowledge-sharing opportunities.

## Impact

We measured Aging2.0's impact across two dimensions: the growth and activity of the ecosystem itself, and the measurable impacts that individual stakeholders in the network experienced.

Perhaps the biggest impact of Aging2.0 has been its contribution to a general mindset and paradigm shift around the opportunities for innovation in aging. We have built on the work of trailblazers in the space such as Mary Furlong, Joe Coughlin, Ken Dychtwald, Lori Orlov, and innovative leaders in AARP (who funded the original descriptive research into the longevity economy), the Milken Institute, World Economic Forum, and Leading Age, among others. However, Aging2.0 was the first organization focused on startups with a cross-sectoral, global, mission-driven mandate. Before Aging2.0 there were very few tech startups dedicated to the aging market, and certainly no place where they could go to feel at home. Witnessing the birth of agetech as a new multibillion-dollar economic opportunity has been a point of significant satisfaction for those involved.

The following quotations from figures in the aging startup world illustrate Aging2.0's positive influence.

Virgilio Bento, the CEO of the Portuguese startup SWORD Health, emphasized the value of Aging2.0 in terms of finding strategic partners, as well as accelerating his company's market entry to the United States:

> In 2014 we knew that to successfully enter in the US healthcare market we needed the guidance from domestic players. That is why,

last November, we were in a selection process to enter either Aging 2.0 or [prestigious startup accelerator] Y Combinator. In spite of all the hype around Y Combinator, we knew that Aging 2.0 was the program that would help us to get to product/market fit faster. Because in the end, it all comes down to knowledge of the aging and healthcare market, a network of major stakeholders in this area and a culture of innovation. This is where Aging2.0 is really good, combining these three things.

Throughout the academy program, the value proposition of SWORD increased almost exponentially because of all the feedback retrieved from the Aging 2.0 team and pivotal partners such as Genesis Rehab Services. We started Aging 2.0 with the objective of specifying SWORD toward the US market but we ended up creating a global product.

Sherwin Sheik founded CareLinx, which went on to be acquired in 2021. He says:

We presented at one of the first Aging2.0 Chapter events in San Francisco, and we met a number of people and organizations who went on to become key strategic partners and investors in CareLinx. CareLinx participated in the Academy program and got valuable market feedback directly from the key customers to refine our go-to market strategy, and we were introduced to strategic investors like Generator Ventures who ultimately became a value-add investor in CareLinx.

CareCoach's Victor Wang, another of the Academy startup founders, shared this perspective:

Thanks to the Aging2.0 team for everything you've done to accelerate our field and our collective mission. The ripples of your impact are far-reaching and enduring, and I'm sure at a global level unfathomable to even someone as myself who has personally benefited so much from the mentorship, peer support, and powerful network that is Aging2.0.

Cubigo's Geert Houben benefited from Aging2.0's partnership with Google, which hosted him on a learning tour and also accelerated his company's growth into the US. He says:

I've known Aging2.0 from their early days and I have seen them growing into the strongest global network for aging innovation in the world. As an entrepreneur it's extremely helpful to tap into such an extensive network of innovators. The team of Aging2.0 had a great mix of talents and experiences and operated with an impressive "can do" mentality. Their conferences were unique in the industry with a clear focus on innovation and pushing things forward. Because of the partnership with Aging2.0, Cubigo had a tremendous kick-start in the US market.

## Barriers to Growth

Throughout its existence, Aging2.0 struggled against a set of obstacles structural to the aging space, with some variation by country. These repeatedly cropped up in the form of issues with finding sustainable business models, capital, and funding for research.

One of the key challenges of healthy aging—always one of the central goals of Aging2.0—is that it lacks a clear business model. As a result, many of the startups we worked with struggled for funding, which made it hard to charge them much for participating in the program. On the provider side, most healthcare providers in the US are still effectively operating on a fee-for-service basis. As a result, an "ideal" customer, ironically, is the opposite of healthy. Multiple, chronic morbidities are expensive to society but good business for today's health system.

Raising capital posed another challenge. Aging2.0 was bootstrapped until a small investment came in from the mission-aligned investor Arnie Whitman. This helped with day-to-day operations, but wasn't at the level of breakthrough funding that could have funded bold new experiments, pay for a large team, or create a differentiating tech platform. We were grateful to receive foundation support from the Robert Wood Johnson Foundation, too, but in general we found grant funding hard to come by, given our for-profit status.

Research, so often necessary to innovation, posed its own problems. Our mission-driven approach was new and didn't fit in standard industry silos, so we had to invent definitions, taxonomies and market maps. A collaboration with a research institute might have helped (and it might still), as well as more structured integration of insights from older adults, such as in the popular "living lab" model.

## A Strategic Partnership Gives Aging2.0 Stability and New Options

I imagine there's an aphorism somewhere that says after ten years, every innovation program needs to innovate itself. And that's what we've now done, through Aging2.0's acquisition by Louisville Healthcare CEO Council (CEO$^C$) in 2022. In acquiring Aging2.0, CEOc addresses a number of the barriers to growth. It's a well-funded, nonprofit organization supported by large corporate providers, such as Humana, Kindred, and Atria. They have access to capital via a new 50 million-dollar-plus fund,[2] as well as the corporate venturing arms of their partners. And they have existing research programs and budget to do more in-depth research into emerging topics of interest.

## Looking to the Future: From Collective Intelligence to Collaborative Impact

In the decade since we started Aging2.0, the challenges associated with demographic shifts have only magnified. Meanwhile, government finances and attention have not kept pace, leaving a growing innovation gap.

Technology too, has shifted massively, as it is prone to do. Exponential technologies are making information and access ubiquitous, and Web3.0—a vision for a new, more decentralized internet—has changed how networks are being built and funded.

In the current version of the web—Web 2.0—companies, especially social media platforms like Facebook, WhatsApp, and YouTube, provide the platform, and allow consumers to spend considerable time creating data and content, which the tech companies both own and monetize with ads. In the still-developing Web3 world, however, individuals may bring their own infrastructure to bear: their own profiles and content, which they own and maintain themselves and share according to their own terms, not companies' terms of service and shareholder priorities.

With this shift to cryptographically maintained individual ownership and control of assets and contracts, we will see networks owned by builders and users, who are able to maintain ownership and control of their data, which is in turn valued more highly.

Web3 models may reward community members for their contributions in new ways. "It takes a village," as the saying goes, to age in place, but it also it takes a village for an aging-focused startup to succeed. Today it's generally just formal financial investors who benefit, whereas Web3 could distribute rewards to the community who helped a given company in its early days, for example via "tokens." These provide far more flexibility (though more regulatory uncertainty) than today's equity models. Such benefits could also potentially accrue to the older people and frontline staff who provide design and marketing insights.

As has been made clear by the stories in this volume about longevity hubs in Boston as well as other cities around the world, there's a tremendous amount of innovation happening around aging, taking place in tens—even hundreds—of cities and regions. Each of these hubs represents a unique local ecosystem that surfaces the needs and solutions in a specific market. However—and to return to the roots of Aging2.0—there's little transparency about what's happening *in* each of these hubs. This book is an important first step toward bringing them together into the same space.

Rather than any one organization "owning" global aging innovation, a new, distributed ownership model may emerge; one that allows ecosystems to share their data and insights, but also work collaboratively together on common problems. This shift from collective intelligence to collaborative impact would be enabled by Web3 systems that allow stakeholders to keep ownership of their data, and yet also share it and get rewarded for the impact it delivers.

Making this happen would be challenging; these models of distributed, collaborative impact are only just emerging. Given the enthusiasm and talent in the space, however, as well as the ever-growing level of need, maybe aging is where the shift from collective intelligence to collaborative impact will happen first.

Already, Aging2.0 has raised awareness of the growing need for innovation in the aging space and attracted a group of "digital natives" to work on this problem. It will be fascinating to see where and how this community evolves, and what impacts it has, in the years ahead.

Stephen Johnston is the founder of Fordcastle, an impact-focused innovation consultancy. Passionate about transforming aging and longevity, in 2012 he cofounded Aging2.0, a global network to accelerate innovation in the space. Together with a small team, he grew the community to more than 100 city chapters and 30,000 innovators, until its acquisition in 2021. He recently joined SOMPO Digital Lab as Fellow, Healthy Longevity and is curator of the LookingForward.life newsletter on healthy longevity. He is coauthor of *Growth Champions*, studied Economics at Cambridge University, and has an MBA from Harvard Business School, where he was a Fulbright Scholar. He currently lives in Melbourne with his wife and young family.

# Notes

1. "Global Longevity Economy Outlook," AARP, 2022, https://www.aarp.org/con
tent/dam/aarp/research/surveys_statistics/econ/2022/global-longevity-economy
-report.doi.10.26419-2Fint.00052.001.pdf.

2. Chris Larson, "LHCC Announces Acquisition, $50M Fund for Aging Care Inno-
vators," September 28, 2021, Louisville Business First, https://www.bizjournals.com
/louisville/news/2021/09/28/louisville-health-care-ceo-fund-acquisition.html.

# Conclusion

Joseph Coughlin and Luke Yoquinto

To the different schools of thought concerned with innovation clusters, Silicon Valley's birth story has something for almost everybody. It has all the classic agglomerative elements Alfred Marshall and his subscribers could ask for, including a professional culture and labor laws ideally suited to the sharing of knowledge. Other cluster-promoting factors that have worked in its favor include a great deal of local defense spending, a first-rate university in Stanford that has actively promoted tech research and ventures, an astonishingly clement climate, and a fertile and creative local culture.

In addition to these broad advantages, Silicon Valley has also benefited from the actions of certain key individuals. One of these, William Shockley, was part of the trio of researchers who invented the transistor: the typically silicon-based device that gave the Valley its name. The Shockley Semiconductor Laboratory, later known as the Shockley Transistor Corporation, was the first semiconductor company in the region. The firm itself was short-lived, but it served as a classic "seed" company (as Jon Metzler points out in this volume), giving rise to local spinoffs and spinoffs-of-spinoffs. These included Intel, Advanced Micro Devices, and Fairchild Semiconductor, whose own offspring were so numerous they became known colloquially as the "Fairchildren."

Why did Shockley decide to set up shop in the region? Several of the area's many advantages played a role—especially Stanford's efforts to set up a major industrial complex. But he had another good reason, too. His mother, May, whose health was declining, lived there.[1]

For the purposes of explicating what makes longevity hubs tick, May Shockley's quiet influence on industrial history suggests something important. Efforts to understand what makes a community successful—in business innovation or any other sense—stand to benefit from thinking holistically about the people who live there, and their interrelationships. Family, for instance, also influenced Bill Gates and Paul Allen in their decision to relocate the fledgling Microsoft from Albuquerque, New Mexico, to the Seattle area in 1978.[2] Any scope of inquiry capable of factoring in such ties must necessarily zoom out to take in more than just the activities of prime-age workers in the formal economy. It must include everyone in a community, including people at either extreme of the age spectrum.

The need to consider the full age span, including young children, applies even to longevity hubs, which cannot survive on the activities of older adults alone. Take, for instance, Karuizawa: a town whose population is old even by Japan's standards, as Metzler describes. In its efforts to draw in teleworkers and bolster local economic activity, it has found it necessary to invest in its local schools. In the US, too, the Florida retirement mecca The Villages decided to build schools in order to support the families of its local workforce, without whom it simply could not function.[3]

The reason aspiring longevity hubs must retain some degree of age diversity is also the reason it's important for them to have abundant housing, transportation infrastructure that works for residents, a nonprohibitive cost of living, and sources of critical services—including health care, child care, and elder care. Put simply: If you want a thriving longevity hub, it appears you'll need a thriving community, complete with healthy organs of economic and civic life.

This prerequisite can have a chicken-and-egg quality, since playing host to an innovation cluster, and the revenues it can bring, may be exactly what a municipality needs to build out services and infrastructure. And yet, success does not only breed success: it also breeds snarled highways and housing shortages.

Boston is worth examining in this light. On paper (literally: its hometown newspaper, where much of this volume was first published), Boston is a prime contender for the title of a world-leading longevity innovation hub. It is home to a remarkable amount of cutting-edge, aging-oriented activity across a variety of industries, supported by neutral nonprofit organizations, a growing venture funding apparatus, leading academic institutions, and key government actors. There's one glaring problem, however. On net, residents—including older adults—are voting with their feet and leaving the city and the state,[4] a trend in keeping with many other regions of the northeastern United States. This outmigration trend is a complex issue with a variety of potential causes, but a major contributor is likely the cost of housing in Boston and its surroundings.[5]

In other longevity hub candidates, meanwhile, different factors could drive older people away, such as high taxes relative to other states or provinces, a high cost of living beyond housing, or a lack of critical services.

What happens to aging innovation under such conditions? At first glance, it appears not to make much of a difference. The steady, southerly trickle of older Bostonians, for instance, will not prevent the city's entrepreneurs and product designers from accessing the detailed demand knowledge they'll need to succeed in the longevity economy. There are, after all, still plenty of older people remaining in the area—themselves entrepreneurs in many cases—as well as increasingly robust connective tissue capable of converting their knowledge into product and service innovation. (Meanwhile, Boston's institutions continue to act like an antenna, picking up on knowledge from a wide catchment area. T. J. Parker's idea for Pill-Pack may have begun with his father's pharmacy business in New Hampshire, but it was transformed into a company in Greater Boston, thanks to the draw of the city's educational institutions and startup infrastructure.)

However, product and service innovation are not the only means by which longevity hubs can be assessed. At a fundamental level, when we talk about longevity innovation, we are talking about a mechanism for providing a higher quality of life to older people. Hubs that manage to export quality-of-life improvements globally, via products and services, while simultaneously neglecting their own older population at home may, frankly, be a pattern we will see in the years ahead. So, however, may the inverse: regions that outperform in terms of local quality of life without necessarily selling things at scale to large older markets. Such regions may not compete fiercely to meet global demand, but they may nevertheless prove themselves to be islands of stability in a world coping unevenly with unprecedented changes, of which global aging is but one example.

In fact, the contributions in this volume suggest the existence of spectrums of longevity hubs, running along at least two axes that are not mutually exclusive: competence at creating scalable, exportable products and services; and local quality of life. Other variables include levels of top-down direction from governments and anchor firms versus a more grassroots form of organization, and levels of external funding and investment.

Only time and further investigation will tell which, if any, of these factors will determine regions' success against the backdrop of an aging world. Still, it may be tempting to conclude from the preceding pages that innovation in readily scalable sectors such as consumer technology (in "new-age" markets, per our terminology) is the most surefire route to explosive economic growth; while on the other hand, the more traditional, "old-growth" markets, especially concerning housing and the care professions, will not see comparable returns. (The character "cousin" Greg Hirsch stammered out this idea in a senior-housing-centric episode of the television show *Succession*: "I think it's hard to make houses seem like tech, 'cause we've had houses for a while now."[6])

The reality may not be so clear-cut. The long-standing and widespread barriers that have obstructed the creation of products genuinely appreciated by older people, combined with once-in-history demographic trends, equates to growth opportunities even for regions and industries devoted to difficult-to-scale product categories.

Meanwhile, even if this type of growth turns out to be merely geometric, not exponential, such an approach may still produce significant advantages for regions, by strengthening local friend and family ties to the area. Remember: Silicon Valley took root not only where defense spending could be tapped into, and where top engineers were attending college and graduate school. It also was the place where May Shockley happened to be living.

In the future, regions equipped to offer a high quality of life to locals of all ages may find themselves benefiting from family and friend network advantages, ultimately playing host to innovative activity simply because innovators choose to live there.

The idea that a region's relatively high quality of life might beget innovation comes close to begging the question, however. Isn't the nominal point of innovation, from a community's perspective, that it will make life better for the people who live there? If life is already good, then what's the point?

The answer is, for older people in particular, even if life is good in an area relative to its neighbors, it can always be better. Decades of underappreciation of the true concerns of older adults means the bar for meaningful problem-solving is low. We can and must do better for today's older population—and tomorrow's. And in the meantime, there's no reason to assume that inaction will be safe. The concept of regional or national competitive advantage isn't just about getting ahead: it's also about making sure you don't get left in the dust.

Regardless of how aging-market innovation develops, it can't happen without an accurate understanding of how to respond to demand. This knowledge may take different forms. Classically, the clusters literature has drawn a line between the sort of tacit, local knowledge that doesn't travel well, as opposed to codified knowledge that can be readily transferred via various forms of media or formal education. But reality is more complicated—as has been demonstrated by the academic subfield devoted to exploring "pipelines" created by businesses for the express purpose of making hard-to-transport information portable.[7]

It is too much to hope that this book, or any other, could serve as such a pipeline. The information in the previous pages is by definition knowledge of the portable variety: the kind that flows along trucking routes, shipping lanes, and fiber optic cables. We do hope, however, that this book will help inspire organizations and institutions to do their utmost to understand the aging market, leading to the sort of deep, localized knowledge that may pay dividends in the longevity economy. This is what the companies studying personal and government-mediated demand in Newcastle are up to, for instance, as well as those getting involved with Aging2.0. They have identified key information gaps, and are working to fill them.

Such deliberate strides toward better serving older people, whether undertaken by industry, policy, nonprofit, or academic actors, will prove important in the years ahead. Our older future may resemble a race, where regions vie to snap up market share of a burgeoning population that remains poorly understood. But it is more than that. Demographic change means communities must seek and deploy new strategies to help residents of all ages thrive. Every community is now part of a race to create a high quality of life—a race against time.

## Notes

1. William R. Kerr and Frederic Robert-Nicoud, "Tech Clusters," *Journal of Economic Perspectives* 34, no. 3 (2020): 50–76; "How Did Silicon Valley Become Silicon Valley?," Endeavor Insight, July 2014, https://endeavor.org.tr/wp-content/uploads /2016/01/How-SV-became-SV.pdf.

2. Kerr and Robert-Nicoud, "Tech Clusters"; Enrico Moretti, *The New Geography of Jobs* (Boston: Houghton Mifflin Harcourt, 2012).

3. Joseph F. Coughlin, *The Longevity Economy: Unlocking the World's Fastest-Growing, Most Misunderstood Market* (PublicAffairs, 2017), 149.

4. Robert L. Santos and Ron S. Jarmin, "Domestic Migration of Older Americans 2015–2019," U.S. Census Bureau, September 2022, https://www.census.gov/content /dam/Census/library/publications/2022/demo/p23-218.pdf; Travis Andersen and Ashley Soebroto, "Suffolk County Has Lost 30,000 Residents since Start of Pandemic, According to US Census," *Boston Globe*, March 30, 2023, https://www.bostonglobe .com/2023/03/30/metro/mass-population-declines-by-8000-residents-us-census -figures-show/.

5. "Can Massachusetts Overcome Its Cost and Demographic Headwinds to Compete for Talent?," Massachusetts Taxpayers Foundation, May 2023, https://www .masstaxpayers.org/sites/default/files/publications/2023-05/MTF%20Demographics %20-%20Spring%202023%20Chartbook.pdf.

6. "S04e06—Living+—Succession Transcripts—TvT," April 30, 2023, https://tvshow transcripts.ourboard.org/viewtopic.php?f=191&t=62519.

7. Jason Owen-Smith and Walter W. Powell, "Knowledge Networks as Channels and Conduits: The Effects of Spillovers in the Boston Biotechnology Community," *Organization Science* 15, no. 1 (February 2004): 5–21, https://doi.org/10.1287/orsc .1030.0054; "Clusters and Knowledge: Local Buzz, Global Pipelines and the Process of Knowledge Creation—Harald Bathelt, Anders Malmberg, Peter Maskell, 2004," accessed July 9, 2023, https://journals.sagepub.com/doi/10.1191/0309132504ph469oa.

# Acknowledgments

A vast, world-spanning, and increasingly interconnected community of people made this book possible.

First, we would like to thank the team at the *Boston Globe* Opinion section for running our original Longevity Hubs series in 2021 and 2022—especially Marjorie Pritchard, the series editor, who worked tirelessly not only in editing the pieces, but also brainstorming with us about contributors, and bringing them in.

We would also like to thank those *Globe* contributors: Marc Freedman, Anne Doyle, Tim Driver, Jody Shue, Alice Bonner, Doug Dickson, Ryan Chin, Katherine Freund, Jo Ann Jenkins, Kyle Rand, Danielle Duplin, Joseph Chung, Libby Brittain, Sheila Lirio Marcelo, Wayne Ysaguirre, Seth Sternberg, Nancy LeaMond, Lisa D'Ambrosio, Brooks Tingle, Jean Hynes, Lorna Sabbia, Deepak Ganesan, Niteesh Choudhry, Benjamin Marlin, Li-Huei Tsai, Amy Schectman, Elise Selinger, Gina Morrison, Susan McWhinney-Morse, Joseph Carella, Marisa Morán Jahn, Rafi Segal, Heather Cox, Michelle A. Williams, Jean Accius, and Elizabeth Dugan.

A very special note of appreciation goes to Renee Lohman, a tireless creator of innovative housing and services for older adults, who wrote in the *Globe* about a new approach to housing design. Lohman passed away in 2022. She and her commitment to building better lives for older people will be deeply missed.

As the *Globe* series concluded, the MIT Press welcomed the idea to turn the series into a larger, book-length project. We would like to express our appreciation to the MIT Press—Robert Prior, Anne-Marie Bono, and Judith Feldmann in particular—for investing in this effort, and for their hard work and expertise on this book.

The *Globe* pieces only account for the first half of this book, however; the second half arrived in the form of original chapters from contributors around the world. We would like to express our deep thanks to these authors: Alyaa AlMulla, Bruce Broussard, Jon Metzler, Emanuela Notari, Gregor Rae, Colin Williams, Layla Vallias, Keren Etkin, Pongsak Hoontrakul, Thanasak Hoontrakul, and Stephen Johnston.

Special thanks goes to Jon Metzler, for his valuable thoughts on our introduction; and to William Kerr of Harvard Business School, and Anders Malmberg of Sweden's Uppsala University, for sharing their thoughts with us on the longevity hub concept.

This book could not have existed without the support of colleagues and friends at MIT. These include the terrific team of researchers at the MIT AgeLab (including Nour Al Maalouf, who helped assemble the references for the pieces that originally ran in the *Globe*); as well as the AgeLab's parent organization, MIT's Center for Transportation and Logistics. CTL's leader, Yossi Sheffi, has our continued appreciation, and his book *Logistics Clusters* is a worthy read for anyone interested in learning more about the geography of business innovation and logistics.

We would also like to thank the MIT AgeLab's sponsors, who keep the lights on and the research flowing.

We would like to thank our families: Emily, Mary, and Catherine; Kelsey, Hope, and Griffin.

Our final note of appreciation is for Hope and Griffin's grandparents. The informal, unpaid labor of grandparents undergirds much of the world's economic productivity, and this book is no exception. Thank you, Eileen and Bill; Ray and Susan—or, as you're better known at home: Bee and Pop-Pop; and Mimi and Ba.

# Index

Page numbers in italics indicate figures.